Since 2010, World Central Kitchen (WCK), the global nonprofit founded by chef and humanitarian José Andrés, has cooked hundreds of millions of fresh, nourishing meals for people impacted by natural disasters and other crises. In the organization's first cookbook, WCK shares recipes inspired by the many places they've cooked and provided support, as well as captivating narratives from chefs, volunteers, and the incredible communities they've met and worked with along the way.

From an allspice-infused lamb and tomato-topped Lahmajoun Flatbread served after a devastating explosion rocked Beirut, to comforting beet- and paprika-rich Ukrainian Borsch offered to refugees fleeing war, to Chicken Chili Verde laden with tomatillos and fire-roasted green chiles that has become a WCK classic, these dishes nourish both body and soul during difficult times. Chefs from around the world, community activists, long-time WCK team members, and even a first lady and a duchess offer recipes and perspectives that celebrate the dignity, perseverance, and unending depth of the human spirit.

THE WORLD CENTRAL KITCHEN COOKBOOK

JOSÉ ANDRÉS
& World Central Kitchen, with Sam Chapple-Sokol

FOREWORD BY STEPHEN COLBERT

THE
WORLD
CENTRAL
KITCHEN
COOKBOOK

Feeding Humanity, Feeding Hope

RECIPE PHOTOGRAPHY BY KRISTIN TEIG

CLARKSON POTTER
New York

CONTENTS

FOREWORD

If you love José Andrés's cooking, you are not alone.

If you love how José Andrés talks about cooking, you are not alone.

If you love how José Andrés uses cooking as an expression of love, you are not alone.

José and World Central Kitchen have shown that in our darkest hour, often what we need most is *companionship*, which, to him, literally means "sharing bread." Even in the best of times, while the body may be nourished by bread, the spirit is nourished by love. That caring companionship opens a window of hope, especially in moments of great pain, because in suffering we find the opportunity to share in our common humanity, to serve each other, and, through that service, to make love visible.

Thankfully, José's love is not only visible, it is edible. From a patient paella to a quick olive oil–fried egg, he makes everything with infectious enthusiasm, artistic abandon, extraordinary flavor, and startling generosity. The first time we met, he approached me at a party and said, "I would like to cook for you and your family." While I (fool that I am) never took him up on that offer, I believed it. I believe he would like to cook for your family, too. Maybe he already has—so far WCK has provided hundreds of millions of meals, all across the world.

While I am always moved by José and WCK's mission, I am also, as a lifelong improvisor, inspired by the way that they do it. When disaster strikes, they go. And, like a good improvisor, they don't know how it will all happen. They pay attention to the needs on the ground, access the resources, and use their talents to address the urgency of the moment. In WCK's case, when possible, that means adopting local recipes to provide food and comfort through familiar flavors that can restore a shattered person's sense of home, even when their house is in ruins.

That acknowledgment of the individual's identity and needs, both physical and emotional, is, I think, the simple but powerful message that José Andrés and World Central Kitchen deliver with every meal.

You Are Not Alone.

—STEPHEN COLBERT

A NOTE FROM JOSÉ

Friends of World Central Kitchen! The book you are holding in your hands is filled with the heart and soul of the most amazing people you will ever meet. They are from every corner of the globe and from all walks of life. When they come together in the kitchen, united for one purpose, they do something truly amazing . . . they show how much they care. It may sound simple, but in our world, sometimes the simple act of caring is the most important thing we can do.

And as you will see, the people in this book are not *them*, they are *us*. You and me. Whoever you are, if you are reading this, you are now one of us, the proud people of World Central Kitchen.

You might think I'm joking. "Me, José?" you might say. "I'm just here for the recipes!" I will tell you right now . . . I'm not joking.

I believe that by picking up this book, you have entered into a world that is bigger than you, than me, than all of us. This is a place that is full of empathy and hope, a place where we are building longer tables, not higher walls. And what you have in your hands is a guide to enter that world, to understand what goes into the work that the WCK Relief Team does. You see, there's no one right way to feed people in the aftermath of a disaster. It's a way of listening and learning, of thinking, and of acting in the world that we are sharing in a million and one ways with this book.

I will tell you one thing as a cook who had spent many years working in kitchens before creating World Central Kitchen . . . I never could have expected a disaster relief nonprofit to have so many requests for recipes! Recipes are a big part of our work, yes, but I think even more important are the stories, histories, and moments of cultural understanding that are behind each recipe and meal we serve. Here we share these stories, whether it's the arroz con pollo that fueled our work in Puerto Rico after Hurricane María, or the Ukrainian Easter bread recipe that's been handed down from grandmother to mother to daughter for generations.

The great culinary philosopher Jean Anthelme Brillat-Savarin wrote that the discovery of a new dish does more for human happiness than the discovery of a new star. Together, the dishes in this book represent a skyful of beautiful constellations, as cooks and chefs around the world look up and see the endless possibilities for feeding their communities.

When I cook for family and friends at home, I want them to feel like they are being cared for, like they are the most important people in the world. You can ask my wife, Tichi, and she'll tell you that the times I am happiest, the way I show that I care, is when I am feeding you.

But it's not enough to me to be able to feed a small handful of people at home or at my restaurants . . . I am only one cook! Instead, we have put up this signal to the world so that we can be building bridges and friends wherever we go, wherever there's need. This is World Central Kitchen, an opportunity to show your friends and family, your neighbors, your community, and complete strangers how much you care—not just when times are good, but even more when they're hard.

So I am here to encourage you to get motivated by this book, however it inspires you. Whether it means you are cooking a meal for a neighbor in need, volunteering at your local food pantry, joining our Relief Team as we respond to a disaster somewhere in the world—or simply making dinner for your family and learning about where that dish came from.

Here is your invitation to become one of us, to fill yourself with the spirit of World Central Kitchen. We will together be feeding humanity, feeding hope, one plate at a time. Building longer tables, together. You and me, the people of World Central Kitchen.

Wherever there's a fight so that hungry people may eat . . . we'll be there.

—JOSÉ ANDRÉS

INTRODUCTION

In September 2017, Hurricane María slammed into Puerto Rico, the most powerful storm to hit the island in nearly a century. The devastation was widespread and deadly; the storm killed thousands of Puerto Ricans and left millions more without water or power for months.

But in the wake of that catastrophe emerged hope. A group of chefs, cooks, delivery drivers, community leaders, and relief coordinators—loosely led by Chef José Andrés and his nonprofit organization World Central Kitchen—banded together to cook thousands, then tens of thousands, then hundreds of thousands of meals a day to feed the island. They called themselves Chefs For Puerto Rico.

Fast-forward five years to 2022, nearly to the day, and it was raining in Puerto Rico. Hurricane Fiona had spun over the island as a Category 1 storm, but gained strength frighteningly fast and dumped more than thirty inches of rain on parts of the island. Power and water were gone. Again.

And the chefs were back.

It wasn't the circumstance that they would have wanted to mark the anniversary of their original heroics, but there they were, stationed around huge pans of arroz con pollo. The legion, spread across San Juan in the north and Ponce in the south, was larger now and worked with an efficiency born of the experience of having done it before. Many of the faces were familiar—Yamil López, Yareli and Xoimar Manning, Roberto Espina, Christian Carbonell, Manolo Martínez—and many were new. They quickly generated enough energy to meet the urgency.

Those chefs weren't the only familiar faces.

In 2017, Ricardo Omar Colón Torres (pictured with José on page 15), whom the team took to calling Ricardito, showed up every day for weeks to help support the team's operations. Ricardito was twenty-two and has a rare genetic developmental condition, and he volunteered to do every job he was given. He put WCK stickers on meal lids, he built boxes to transport those meals, and he handed out bottles of water to people waiting in line. If there was a job to do, Ricardito did it to perfection with an eye for detail that kept everything moving at peak efficiency. His mom, Iris, volunteered, too, helping distribute meals to their community on the outskirts of San Juan.

And in 2022, Ricardito and Iris were back, once again helping out with the operation.

It's a devastating reality that Fiona replicated the pain and loss caused five years earlier by María, wiping out infrastructure for extended periods. It was the worst kind of déjà vu. But with the bad there was also hope, a silver lining to the storm's dark clouds. An immediate start, with the team making sandwiches before the storm even passed, meant people were getting fed faster. And a reunion of the team with volunteers like Ricardito and chefs like Yareli and Roberto was the fuel needed to power through. So, sure, history repeats itself, but the happy parts repeat along with the difficult ones.

The span from when Hurricane María hit Puerto Rico in 2017 until Hurricane Fiona hit in 2022 provides a microcosm of the work World Central Kitchen does around the world, offering people the healing power of food and goodwill in a moment of crisis. It also provides a timeline of sorts for this book, which is a collection of recipes and stories about people we have encountered and worked with over those five years, in locations from Puerto Rico to Port-au-Prince, Caracas to Kyiv, and virtually every corner of the world. These recipes and stories contribute to what we know as a universal truth, that food has the power to change the world, one plate at a time.

But let's not get too far ahead of ourselves . . . the story of World Central Kitchen starts well before Hurricane María.

ORIGINS

The year was 2010, and José was near the top of his game. He had ten popular restaurants around the US. He'd been named Best Chef in the Mid-Atlantic by the James Beard Foundation and was well on his way toward an Outstanding Chef nod a year later. The year prior, he was named *GQ*'s Chef of the Year. Yet the most important award that José had received to date was the Vilcek Prize.

The Vilcek Foundation's mission is to celebrate the lives and work of immigrants in America and it awards two prizes annually: one to a biomedical scientist and the other to someone in the sphere of arts and humanities. José is one of only two people to be honored for the culinary arts; chef Marcus Samuelsson, a longtime friend and Frontline Advisor of World Central Kitchen, is the other.

The prize included a $50,000 check, no strings attached. José's career was on the rise, but he was far from wealthy. He and his wife, Patricia (Tichi), had three young daughters, and the rapid growth of the restaurants had left him stretched thin. But he and Tichi didn't even have to discuss what to do with the money; they decided to put the entire prize toward funding a new nonprofit with the goal of changing the world through the power of food.

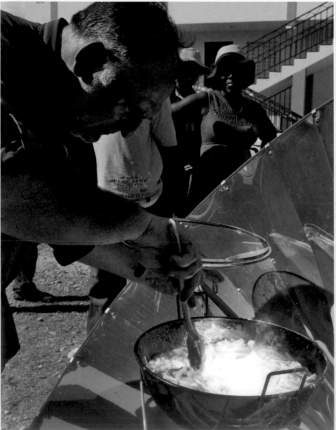

José had just visited Haiti in the aftermath of one of the deadliest earthquakes in history. He traveled with CESAL, a Spanish nonprofit organization that advocates for cooperation and social action, and they brought solar cookstoves to cook meals without electricity. It was also a chance to learn about the realities on the ground after a disaster of such immense magnitude. He quickly realized that he—and his entire profession of cooks—could be doing more. Having spent years volunteering in and around Washington, DC, notably at Robert Egger's DC Central Kitchen, José decided he wanted to get involved in Haiti's rebuilding by applying his skills to develop new ways to feed the world. His initial idea, based on the early work he had done with CESAL, was to introduce solar cookstove technology to Haiti.

José started talking to his longtime business partner Rob Wilder about launching a new organization to fulfill that dream. Rob and José had worked together for years: Rob had originally hired José in 1993 to work in a newly developed Spanish restaurant, Jaleo, which introduced tapas to downtown Washington, DC. Over the years, Rob, José, and their original partner, Roberto Alvarez, built a handful of concepts in DC and beyond: Café Atlántico, minibar, Zaytinya, and Oyamel, to name a few. These restaurants, and José's burgeoning identity as a culinary prodigy, led to the accolades of the 2000s.

HE QUICKLY REALIZED THAT HE—AND HIS ENTIRE PROFESSION OF COOKS—COULD BE DOING MORE.

Rob Wilder and his wife, Robin, matched José and Tichi's donation, so the project—which they named World Central Kitchen, inspired by the hometown heroes—had $100,000 to get the work started. (According to Tichi, José walked around with the actual Vilcek Prize check for $50,000 in his wallet for months before cashing it!)

José and Rob brought on Javier Garcia, a lawyer and food importer whom José knew from DC's Spanish community. Javier had recently started his own nonprofit and was familiar with the process—vital for navigating the legal challenges of creating a new NGO.

The three of them brought on Fredes Montes (pictured left), a World Bank financial specialist, as executive director, and put together a passionate board of directors, including Robert Egger, and an advisory board full of experts in multiple disciplines: disaster relief, technology, agricultural development, economics, solar energy, and more. With the seed money, a solid structure, and the motivation to create positive change in Haiti, the small team got to work.

LONGER TABLES

The first project that José and Fredes ran was simple but profound. In the first year of operating, they traveled to Haiti regularly to listen and learn, determined to understand the need before asserting what their role would be. On one visit with CESAL, they went to Cité Soleil—Site Solèy in Kreyòl (Haitian Creole) or Sun City in English—a neighborhood of a few hundred thousand people in the capital city of Port-au-Prince that's one of the most impoverished communities in the Western Hemisphere. They visited a nutrition center for mothers and their babies; the center's mission was to both feed the mothers and teach them about healthy eating for their families. José and Fredes noticed that the women were scattered around the room, holding their kids while trying to eat. It seemed awkward for the women, difficult to focus on the lessons while juggling the kids and food. It wasn't the educational moment the organizers had planned.

There was something elemental missing from the event's venue: a table. The women had to hold their babies as they balanced their plates of food, a juggling act that made it difficult to pay attention. By introducing a place for the women and their children to sit and eat, the organizers created a comfortable environment that facilitated learning. The women got a moment to relax and eat a meal with their babies as well as pay attention to the program. It took off from there, with more and more women from the community joining the conversations each week.

It was a minor victory, but it was also a catalyst: It set the path for the organization, both strategically and metaphorically. It was proof that very simple solutions can have profound impacts, which has always been a motivating driver for José and now a tenet of World Central Kitchen. People are hungry? Feed them. They're thirsty? Give them water. Farmers need a boost after a disaster destroys their equipment? Give them money to rebuild.

José was laying the groundwork for the next ten years. One of his mantras eventually became "Longer tables, not higher walls." While this was a rallying cry in the second half of the decade, José was living the idea before he ever said it by setting a table and inviting people from all walks to sit around it, treating everyone with dignity and respect.

After returning from his first trip to Haiti, José wrote a series of op-eds for the Spanish newspaper *El Mundo* in which he more or less laid out his argument for what would become WCK—though he hadn't come up with the catchy name yet.

It's all right there. So many of José's motivating principles for WCK: the importance of chefs, feeding the many, disaster relief, supporting local economies. It's a road map for the future of the organization, the structure of which José started to develop with Tichi, Rob, Javier, and Fredes.

"COCINEROS SIN FRONTERAS EN HAITÍ."
El Mundo, April 17, 2010 , José Andrés
(EXCERPT)

Tengo una gran necesidad de que mi profesión, no solo sea una profesión para la élite y alguno más. No solo servir al 0.1 por ciento de la población, también quiero tener el mejor restaurante. Pero no uno sin lo otro. Pienso que algún día, nosotros, los cocineros, formaremos parte de esa "mesa" donde se deciden las grandes acciones mundiales.

Algún día no muy lejano pienso que tendremos que crear un "Cocineros sin fronteras". Donde una flota con cientos de camiones cocina se podrán enviar a las zonas con hambre crónica o en emergencias puntuales. Camiones cocina que podrán producir cientos de miles de comida. Comida caliente con cocineros voluntarios que acudirán a la llamada ante una urgencia.

Con estos Camiones cocina podremos utilizar los productos locales, ayudando rápidamente a la economía local. Cuando llegan alimentos de afuera los productores locales no venden su producto. Los precios se desploman. Nadie compra. Y en momentos de desgracia es importante que el comercio interior continúe. Soy un soñador.

I have a strong need for my work to be something more than serving the elites. I do want to have the best restaurant, but I also want to reach beyond the top 0.1 percent. These two goals are not mutually exclusive. I think that one day, we cooks will form a part of this "table" where we help decide initiatives on a global scale.

Someday, not too long from now, I think we'll have to create a "Cooks without Borders." Where a fleet of hundreds of trucks equipped with kitchens will be sent to areas with chronic hunger or other emergencies. Trucks with kitchens that will be able to produce hundreds of thousands of meals. Hot food with volunteer chefs that answer the call in an emergency.

With these food trucks, we will be able to utilize local products, quickly helping the local economy. When food and other goods come from abroad, the local producers can't sell their product. The prices plummet. Nobody buys anything. And in these moments of misfortune, it's important that the local economy continues. I'm a dreamer.

The original articles of incorporation for the organization, codified in August 2010, stated that WCK's purpose was "to provide food for vulnerable people, to support local agriculture, and to promote environmentally sustainable cooking fuels and technologies." As you read through this book, you'll see that those three pillars shaped our mission.

COOKS WITHOUT BORDERS

Tichi remembers José's early passion for creating an organization centered around cooks and chefs: "Food is José's world—not just food in terms of high-end cuisine, but the fact that he loves to entertain, to cook for people; he loves to see people enjoying food. His way of showing that he cares for you, to show love, is to feed you." As a cook, José wanted to share that love more broadly—not just for him to feed his family and friends but for cooks everywhere to feed their own communities.

In 2014, the organization first launched our Chef Network, a group of notable chefs who were committed to supporting the cause when José and WCK called on them. Anthony Bourdain, Carla Hall, Andrew Zimmern, Victor Albisu, Aarón Sánchez, and others made up "José's Front Line," with dozens of other chefs representing the "Committed Crew." A handful of chefs traveled with WCK to do culinary trainings abroad. Award-winning pastry chef Pichet Ong traveled to Zambia to teach baking classes, while Victor Albisu went to Nicaragua to teach knife skills and food safety.

The idea, now known as the Chef Corps, was revitalized in 2019 and then expanded over the following years. Our network has always been vast, but as we've cooked in more cities, states, and countries, we get to know more and more chefs around the world who are driven to care for their neighbors because they believe hospitality expands beyond the walls of their restaurants.

Now, WCK's Chef Corps has hundreds of representatives in dozens of countries who are standing by, ready to run to the frontlines when disaster strikes. In this cookbook you'll find a handful of recipes from Chefs Corps members, including Eric Adjepong (page 235), Reem Assil (page 141), Sofia Deleon (page 266), Guy Fieri (page 219), Tyler Florence (page 220), Sanjeev Kapoor (page 223), Emeril Lagasse (page 215), Marcus Samuelsson (page 91), Brooke Williamson (page 209), and Brian Yazzie (page 56).

ROOTED IN RELIEF

Before Hurricane María, no one thought of WCK as a disaster relief organization. There were a few moments of foreshadowing, though, like in 2016 when Hurricane Matthew hit Haiti's southern Tiburon Peninsula head-on, destroying hundreds of thousands of homes and affecting more than a million people. Longtime WCK board member Jean Marc DeMatteis, a friend of José's who helped establish many of our early projects in Haiti, worked with José and David Destinoble—a prominent Haitian chef and cofounder of the Haitian Culinary Alliance—to set up a field kitchen outside the city of Les Cayes. The 15,000 meals they cooked by the end of the operation were the first emergency food relief WCK produced, paving the way for hundreds of millions more.

Less than a year later, María devastated Puerto Rico, and the organization learned what we could contribute under the worst circumstances. It's where José met Ricardito and thousands of other volunteers who showed up every day to support the mission. It's where Nate Mook, a friend of José's and a documentary filmmaker, first made his mark on the organization, becoming CEO for the next half decade. It's where the Chefs For Puerto Rico team, the first food fighters, came together to cook hundreds of thousands of meals, motivated by the fact that they were the only ones taking responsibility for feeding their communities.

María was just the beginning. Since then, WCK has worked in dozens of countries on six continents and served hundreds of millions of meals. In the following pages, we'll share the stories of many of those operations, the people responsible for cooking those meals, the communities who receive them, the friends and partners we've made along the way, the farmers and fishers who help supply our kitchens, and, of course, the recipes for many of the dishes we've served to nourish, empower, uplift, and give hope to the people we serve.

SO . . . HOW DOES WCK DO WHAT WE DO?

Lunch and dinner for 20,000 hungry people is an operation most chefs aren't prepared for. Even chefs who work as caterers or in banquets rarely prepare meals for more than 1,000 or so—and almost never twice in a day. World Central Kitchen's Relief Team regularly cooks thousands of lunches and then starts all over again for dinner—seven days a week over the course of an operation.

The Relief Team has a skill set well beyond cooking—we need to have expertise in supply chains, transportation logistics, diplomacy, communications, nutritional analysis, and more. Our teams receive on-the-ground training throughout each emergency response and develop other skills when we're not in the field, such as food safety, first aid, anti-racism, and crisis response management. And beyond the operational logistics of feeding people in the aftermath of disaster, there is an emotional component to every response—the WCK team will give a hug, lend an ear, or share a cry with people who have lost friends and family, pets, homes, businesses, belongings. We must be emotionally prepared to enter into some of the most intense situations facing humanity—and be equipped with an endless supply of empathy.

Each operation is different, but they share many similar challenges. Each prepares WCK for the next, and leaves our team better equipped, better able to handle whatever is thrown our way.

WHEREVER THERE'S A FIGHT

Art serves as an inspiration for so much of life, and the work of World Central Kitchen is no exception. A simple quote José borrowed (and slightly paraphrased) from one of his favorite authors, John Steinbeck, has become our tagline. In the 1939 novel *The Grapes of Wrath*, the main character, Tom Joad, is processing the death of the preacher Jim Casy—and Joad makes a commitment to be a better man in the future, to be more like Casy.

I'll be aroun' in the dark. I'll be everywhere—wherever you look. Whenever they's a fight so hungry people can eat, I'll be there. Whenever they's a cop beatin' up a guy, I'll be there . . . I'll be in the way guys yell when they're mad an'—I'll be in the way kids laugh when they're hungry an' they know supper's ready. An' when our folks eat the stuff they raise an' live in the houses they build—why, I'll be there.

José latched on to one line, "Whenever they's a fight so hungry people can eat, I'll be there." He adapted it to highlight collective effort:

Wherever there's a fight so hungry people may eat, we'll be there.

If you ask anyone on the Relief Team what their driving mantra is, they'll cite John Steinbeck—whether they know it or not. This at-all-costs attitude underlies every moment of every mission. The team will always throw a few extra sandwiches and bottles of water into the car as we make deliveries, just in case we find someone who hasn't had lunch yet.

Really! If you're hungry and see a vehicle with the WCK logo on it, flag it down. There's a pretty good chance there's a brown bag with a ham-and-cheese sandwich in there with your name on it.

HOW TO USE THIS BOOK

This book is set up a bit differently from most other cookbooks—how often do you pick up a cookbook from a disaster relief organization? The chapters are laid out not by season, meal course, or protein but by WCK's values, which are intrinsic to who we are as an organization. So it made sense that they would drive the structure of this book.

And for us it's an opportunity to share not just recipes but the stories behind them, and the people and places that make each dish special. If it weren't for them, we wouldn't be able to do the work we do.

Many of these recipes come from WCK kitchens around the world, developed either by our staff or the volunteers and partners who work with us. Most of the recipes were developed for large batches, but they've been scaled down to serve four to six without sacrificing the soul of the dish. On page 35 you'll find tips for scaling the recipes up for larger serving sizes, should you find yourself cooking for a crowd.

Many of the dishes were adapted. Where ingredients are difficult to find, we've tried to include reasonable, culturally appropriate substitutions. But if you cook one of these dishes and it doesn't taste exactly like you've had it in Indonesia or Ukraine or Haiti, it might be because the recipe was adjusted to make it accessible to the widest possible audience. That said, sometimes we chose to stick with tradition—like in the Rondón (page 251), which just wouldn't be the same without the conch and the pig tail.

A CHAPTER OVERVIEW

The chapters follow the core values and inspirations of WCK as an organization: empathy, urgency, adaptation, hope, community, resilience, and joy. Here's what to expect in each.

EMPATHY (PAGE 44)

The ability to put yourself in someone else's shoes and understand how they're feeling is instrumental to the work WCK does. The team will cry and laugh with people, give a comforting hug, and spend time listening and learning about their lives. The recipes in this chapter embody warmth and love; these are recipes that take time. They need to cook for hours (like long-braised meats), or spices need to be toasted and ground by hand, or ingredients need to be marinated overnight to lend a profound flavor to a dish. These are the dishes that will warm your kitchen and invite everyone in the neighborhood by smell alone.

URGENCY (PAGE 77)

Much of WCK's work is on the road. Refugees and migrants need something to fortify them on their journeys. Firefighters, first responders, and medical professionals may only be able to snack throughout their shifts; a nourishing, hot meal is a welcome sight. The food here is for people on the move. Sandwiches, arepas, tacos, tamales, and other handheld foods have been developed over centuries to nourish travelers and workers, and kids, too (many of these recipes would be a perfect addition to a lunch box).

ADAPTATION (PAGE 114)

In a 2006 essay, the late Anthony Bourdain, a close friend of José's, wrote about the concept of System D. It's a bit of kitchen slang for an ability to work your way out of any situation. The *D* stands for the French *débrouille* (or alternatively *démerde*), meaning to figure something out (or to get out of the shit, depending on what kind of kitchen you're working in).

In a disaster context, pretty much everything needs to be figured out—System D is everything. Adaptation is all about dishes that can be adapted for real-time challenges, using sheet pans, paella pans, and baking dishes to quickly and easily feed the many. You may even develop a knack for System D in your own kitchen: It's Tuesday night and your fridge is empty . . . quick! Adapt!

HOPE (PAGE 153)

The feeling of hope after a disaster can seem so far away. But as José likes to say, we must always be looking over the horizon, finding a place that still has light and love. The dishes here are ones we make to bring hope after a crisis, soups and stews to nourish and warm you . . . sancocho for the soul. Make some extra for your freezer—you never know when you might need a little hope.

COMMUNITY (PAGE 192)

At the center of World Central Kitchen's work, everywhere we go, is community. Neighbors helping neighbors, families volunteering together, people stepping up to help each other get through tough times. It's the beating heart of WCK; without the community, the organization wouldn't exist. These are recipes that are perfect for a communal dinner. They're mostly vegetarian, mostly side dishes, all delicious, and easy to scale up—whether you're feeding your family or hosting a dinner for fifty, they're flexible.

AS JOSÉ LIKES TO SAY, WE MUST ALWAYS BE LOOKING OVER THE HORIZON, FINDING A PLACE THAT STILL HAS LIGHT AND LOVE.

RESILIENCE (PAGE 225)

One of WCK's longtime goals has been not only to feed people in the direct after-math of crises but to help rebuild food systems to withstand future shocks. This work became the Resilience program, which was a major part of the organiza-tion for years. The recipes in this chapter come from the places where we've sup-ported rebuilding efforts—Haiti, Puerto Rico, Guatemala, and The Bahamas—as well as others in which WCK worked with farmers during relief operations to keep the local economy running. Use these dishes as an opportunity to seek out a new ingredient—you'll be well rewarded for your quest.

JOY (PAGE 254)

To round things out, we have sweets (and a couple of cocktails!). Joy, like hope, might not be the first emotion you think of during a crisis, but it's vital to not lose sight of it. Kids are among the most vulnerable to the impacts of disaster, and so WCK gives them extra attention to bring them a little delight and happiness. Sweets—like the breads, cakes, and bars in this chapter—are a great way to bring a smile to a child's face, even in the most difficult situation. And for the adults, we have a couple of drinks—to enjoy alongside a sweet treat or not.

A NOTE ON BAKING RECIPES

Throughout the book, whenever a recipe has a baked element (or a dough), you'll find both volume (cups) and weight (grams). The goal of providing the gram weights is precision; in the kitchen whenever the WCK team bakes, we rely on weighing the ingredients to ensure everything is consistent from batch to batch.

For dishes without any kind of dough or batter, that level of precision isn't as key, so no gram weights are included. However, in a recipe like Chicken Pot Pie (page 123), which includes both a dough (for the biscuits) and a stew, the measure-ment for the biscuits needs to be more precise than it does for the stew, which is why you'll find gram weights in one part of the recipe but not in the other.

If you don't have a scale, you can stick to the volume measurements—though the single easiest way to improve your skills as a baker is to buy an inexpensive digital kitchen scale!

THE WORLD CENTRAL KITCHEN PANTRY

Because WCK cooks all around the world, we have the opportunity to experience new ingredients all the time, from rare chiles in Puerto Rico to cured hams in

Kentucky. Wherever we are, we go to the markets, talk to farmers and chefs, and try to taste as many local dishes as possible to understand the culinary context. Here are a few of the ingredients that you may not know about and others that might need some extra clarification.

ACHIOTE

Called achiote in Mexico and annatto in parts of the Caribbean and South America, this tropical American spice is usually used to add a vibrant red color to rices, stews, and marinades for meat and fish (like the Sierra en Escabeche, page 70). Achiote is sold at Latin markets as dried seeds, powder, cakes, or paste; the recipes usually call for the powder. Besides coloring your food, achiote will also stain your hands, clothing, and bowls, so be careful when handling.

ASAFOETIDA

Known as hing in Hindi, asafoetida is the dried resin of the root of an herb in the celery family. It's notable for its pungent smell and its ability to amp up the other flavors in a dish. Food writer Priya Krishna writes that "it makes Indian food taste more Indian." It's an important addition to Sanjeev Kapoor's Dal Tadka (page 223), but if you can't find it, you'll still end up with a tasty dish. Look for asafoetida at any Indian grocery store or online at Kalustyan's.

CHEESE

Cotija Cotija is an aged cow's milk cheese whose salty crumbles are great for sprinkling on top of dishes. Originally from the town of Cotija in Michoacán, Mexico, it's easy to find at Latin grocery stores or well-stocked general grocery stores. If you have trouble, you can substitute shredded parmesan or crumbled feta.

Queso fresco Milder and less salty than Cotija, *queso fresco* (literally "fresh cheese") is slightly tangy and unaged. It can be swapped out for Cotija in dishes like Baleadas (page 99) and Chilaquiles (page 130).

Queso llanero *Queso llanero*, or "herder's cheese," is the queso of choice for Venezuelan Arepas (page 109) for its smooth and melty qualities. Stringy, mild cheeses like Mexican queso Oaxaca or mozzarella work as a substitute.

CHILES

Ancho Ancho chiles are dried poblanos, commonly used in Mexican and American southwestern cuisines. Sweet and mild, anchos are great for adding smoky flavor to marinades, sauces, and soups.

Guajillo Guajillos are dried chiles with a fruity, mild to medium heat, most commonly used in salsas and other sauces in Mexican dishes like Chilaquiles (page 130). Look for guajillos that have smooth, shiny skin.

Habanero Originating from the Amazon region of Peru, this small pepper is about seventy-five times hotter than the average jalapeño. Habaneros are beloved for their complex flavor that offers notes of citrus, fruit, and smoke.

Hatch Hatch chiles are grown exclusively in the Hatch Valley region of New Mexico. They have a brief, highly anticipated season each August and September and are usually roasted to bring out their vegetal, smoky, and earthy flavors. If you can't find fresh or frozen Hatch chiles for Robert's Green Chile Posole (page 189), canned green chiles will do.

Lombok These peppers from the Indonesian island of Lombok are key for the Sambal (page 289). They have medium heat and sweet flavor. If you can't find them at your local Asian market, substitute a combination of Thai bird's eye chiles and cayenne chiles for more heat, or red serranos for less.

Pasilla Sweet, earthy, and mild, pasillas, the dried version of the chilaca pepper, are used in moles and other sauces, often along with ancho and guajillo (as in the Tamales, page 83). The Spanish word *pasilla* means "little raisin."

Scotch bonnet Named for its hat-like shape, these extra-hot chiles are piquant like habaneros with a tropical, sweet flavor. Also called Jamaican hot, Bahamian, or Martinique chiles, they're the most widely used hot pepper in the Caribbean.

COCONUT MILK

Coconut milk is made by grating mature coconuts and straining the liquid; it adds creaminess and fat to both sweet and savory dishes and drinks. Unless otherwise specified, "coconut milk" throughout the book refers to canned unsweetened full-fat coconut milk—the only times you'll find sweetened coconut milk is in the cocktail recipes for Kremas (page 277) and Coquito (page 278). Avoid "light" coconut milk, which doesn't have the creamy fat that gives a dish richness and flavor.

CORN

Corn flour and cornmeal Both corn flour and cornmeal are made by grinding uncooked dried corn. Corn flour is fine textured, and cornmeal has a coarse, gritty texture. The size of the cornmeal grind can range from fine to medium to coarse; the larger the grind, the longer it will take to cook.

Grits Grits are made from coarsely ground cornmeal or hominy and are usually served as a thick porridge. A staple in the American South after being introduced by Indigenous Americans in the sixteenth century, variations of grits are consumed throughout the world, like xima in Mozambique (see Eric's Piri-Piri Shrimp over Coconut Grits, page 235).

Hominy Hominy is corn kernels that have been nixtamalized, a process developed in Mesoamerica thousands of years ago (the word is Nahuatl/Aztec in origin). The corn kernels are soaked in an alkaline solution, which changes their structure and makes their nutrients more available. The kernels can then be used in their whole form—like the hominy in Robert's Green Chile Posole (page 189)—or ground into masa harina, a corn flour used to make tortillas, Tamales (page 83), and more. Rancho Gordo sells a superior hominy.

Masarepa Unlike corn flour, masarepa, which is used predominantly for Arepas (page 109), is corn that has been precooked before being milled into flour. While many families grind their own corn to make masarepa, we recommend getting it at the grocery store (we like the brand P.A.N.)—yellow or white will both work.

CULANTRO

This pungent, citrusy herb is known by many names: culantro or recao in Puerto Rico and the Dominican Republic, ngo gai in Vietnam, coulante in Haiti, and shado beni or chadon beni in English-speaking parts of the Caribbean. Often confused with cilantro, culantro can be differentiated by its look and flavor: Culantro has long, serrated leaves and a much stronger, more bitter flavor. If you can't find culantro, substitute cilantro or a 50/50 blend of cilantro and parsley.

FARRO

Farro, a grain old enough to have fed Roman soldiers, is a type of wheat that's cooked until soft, with a little more chewiness than barley. It can stand in for rice, thicken soups, or add texture to salads (see Brooke's Carrot-Farro Salad, page 209). Just make sure not to get quick-cooking or pearled farro, which doesn't keep its texture as well.

FREEKEH

Freekeh, which gets its name from the Arabic word for "to rub," is young wheat that's harvested before it's fully ripe, then burned and rubbed to remove the chaff. The technique, which has been done in the Middle East for hundreds of years, imbues a smoky, nutty flavor. (See Kamal's Freekeh with Caramelized Onions, page 246.)

GALANGAL

Similar to its cousin ginger in appearance, galangal is stronger and more astringent, with piney, spicy, citrusy notes and a dry, fibrous texture. Peel it before slicing or grating, or bruise the whole root, as is done in the Beef Rendang (page 51). While dried galangal can be easier to find, fresh galangal is more flavorful, so look for it at Southeast Asian grocery stores.

JACKFRUIT

Jackfruit, the star of Indonesia's Sayur Gori (page 204), is a large tropical fruit grown in South and Southeast Asia. A distant relative of figs, the fruit has flesh that is sweet and tropical when ripe, but when it's young and unripe, the texture is its main selling point: It's meaty and toothsome, perfect for meat-free curries and stews. Boil your own jackfruit or just buy it in a can—Trader Joe's green jackfruit in brine is a good choice.

MAKRUT LIME LEAVES

An important ingredient in Thai cooking, makrut lime leaves are intensely aromatic and citrusy. The leaves are commonly used whole or thinly sliced in fried rice, soups, and curries like Lamb Massaman Curry (page 182). They can be found fresh, frozen, or dried at Asian markets; just know that the farther the leaf is from the tree, the less fragrant it will be. If using whole leaves, be sure to remove them before serving, as you would bay leaves.

ÑAME

This large tuber from the yam family is a staple in Caribbean cuisine. Brought to the Americas from Africa through the slave trade, ñame has a hairy, bark-like skin and a dry, pale-yellow flesh with a mild, nutty flavor. It's versatile like a potato: It can be served boiled, fried, or added to stews like Rondón (page 251). Look for ñame at Latin, Caribbean, or West African grocery stores.

PIGEON PEAS

Pigeon peas are grown and eaten throughout the tropical world, from the Indian subcontinent to the Caribbean. Split pigeon peas, known in Hindi as toor dal, are used in Sanjeev Kapoor's Dal Tadka (page 223). Find toor dal at Indian grocery stores or online spice shops, like Kalustyan's.

PLANTAINS

Relatives of bananas, plantains are grown and used throughout the tropical world. Unripe, green plantains are usually eaten fried, as in Bannann Peze (page 288) or in soups and stews, such as Rondón (page 251) and Sancocho (page 181). Riper yellow-black plantains, known as maduros or amarillos, are used in both savory and sweet preparations.

RICE

Rice is one of the most common staples in the world; it's eaten daily by billions of people, and throughout the book we call for a handful of different types, such as the long-grain rices basmati and jasmine, and medium-grain rice (look for the brand Arroz Rico or a Calrose rice, such as Botan) used in Arroz con Pollo a la Manolo (page 147). If you prefer, though, you can use brown rice; just be mindful that cooking times and water-to-rice ratios may differ.

RUM

Distilled from sugarcane juice or molasses, rum is made throughout the Caribbean and beyond. Clear rum, like the Don Q Cristal rum used in the Rum Sour (page 281), isn't aged, while brown rums, like the Rhum Barbancourt used in the Kremas (page 277), are aged for years in oak barrels. A linguistic note: Rum made from pure sugarcane juice is called rhum agricole; other rums are made from molasses (the dark, sticky by-product of sugar production).

SALT

The majority of savory dishes in this book call for kosher salt, but be aware that there is a difference in how much salt is in a measured amount depending on the brand (some brands are coarser and fluffier). But if you're tasting your dish as you go, you'll be able to adjust for your own palate. Some savory recipes, especially ones from islands, may call for sea salt instead of kosher salt. For most of the baking recipes in this book, we prefer fine sea salt or table salt; the finer crystals dissolve more easily, meaning you won't have overly salty bits here and there.

SEAFOOD

Catfish Found in the coastal waters of nearly every continent, this white-fleshed fish has a sweet, mild flavor and firm, dense texture that stands up well to pan-frying. It's incredibly versatile and can be dressed up with sauces, marinades, or rubs, as in Marcus Samuelsson's Spiced Catfish Sandwiches (page 92). If you can't find catfish, try tilapia.

Conch One of The Bahamas' favorite native ingredients, conch is a sea snail with a firm, chewy white flesh similar to calamari. Throughout the Caribbean, conch is served in a variety of ways, from fresh salads to fritters to stews (like Rondón, page 251). It's difficult to find fresh conch outside of the Caribbean, so look for canned conch, often labeled with its Italian name, scungilli.

Salt cod Salt cod, known as bacalao in Spanish, is a centuries-old preparation for preserving fish. It needs to soak for 24 hours to rehydrate before using in dishes, such as Bacalao al Club Ranero (page 73), so plan accordingly. Look for bacalao with its skin still on.

Snapper Red snapper can be found throughout the Caribbean and along the mid-Atlantic coast. Its delicate and mild flavor makes it a very popular white fish—try it in José's Red Snapper Suquet (page 157). If you have difficulty finding snapper, monkfish (which is called for in many Catalan suquet recipes) makes a good substitute.

TARO
Taro, also known as eddo or dasheen, is a staple root vegetable in many African, Caribbean, Pacific Island (see Soupe Joumou, page 163), and Southeast Asian cuisines. While it's poisonous raw because of its high levels of calcium oxalate, it's perfectly safe (and delicious) when cooked—it has a sweet, nutty flavor and a kaleidoscope of purple freckles. It's a good idea to use gloves when handling raw taro to avoid skin irritation.

YUCA
Yuca (or cassava) is a staple root used regularly in many Caribbean, South American, and African dishes, such as fritters, chips, mashes, and stews (like Sancocho, page 181). Yuca, like taro, is poisonous when raw, so you always need to cook it.

HOW TO SCALE A RECIPE

There's both art and science to scaling recipes up from the family-size dishes in this book to large batches to feed the many. Learn how to properly scale and you're ready to take any dish in this book and cook it for your community.

KNOW YOUR RECIPE INSIDE AND OUT
Answer these questions before you get started: What are the ingredients and how do they each need to be prepped? What are the most important flavors and how can I express them in the final bite? How am I building flavor throughout the cooking

process? How about the textures: How should each of the individual components, as well as the final dish as a whole, feel?

If you're planning to cook a recipe for 1,000 people, you'll want to do a trial run and cook it a few times for four. What do you notice about the final version that you like, or did something not work out? Were there any inconsistencies in batches, and can you isolate what you did differently?

Knowing the answers to these questions will help guide your process as you scale up.

DO THE MATH

You may know you want to cook X ounces of protein, Y ounces of vegetables, and Z ounces of grains, but you may not realize that raw ingredients don't weigh the same as their cooked counterparts due to water loss or gain. If our chefs learn that it's culturally appropriate for each person in a community to receive 4 ounces of protein per meal and we're cooking for 1,000 people, then we need to end up with 4,000 ounces (250 pounds) of *cooked* protein. But we need to figure out how much raw product that requires. Let's say we're cooking brisket: The USDA tells us cooked brisket weighs about 70% of what it weighed raw, so we'll want to start with about 5,750 ounces (360 pounds) of raw brisket.

The USDA gives guidelines for vegetables, too: Cooked, sliced carrots yield about 76% of the original raw weight, while bell peppers yield about 73%. With vegetables, it's generally less vital to get the precise final weight, since we usually serve a blend of vegetables, but know you'll lose 20% to 30% of the vegetables' weight in water loss during cooking.

With grains, it tends to work the opposite way: Rice, barley, and other grains expand when cooked, so 1 pound of raw material will give you 2 to 4 pounds of cooked, depending on what you're working with. With rice, plan on cooking ½ cup of raw rice per person you're feeding—it's a large portion, but you'll be in good shape to make sure everyone gets enough. A little math here goes a long way. Do your calculations before you go shopping and you'll get the right yields to feed as many as you need to.

PLAN AHEAD

When you're cooking for four, you may be able to prep as you go, but if you're cooking for a hundred or more, you need to have your recipe prepped before you start. Bowls are your friends: If your onions and garlic cook together, chop them and put them in a bowl together. Use separate bowls for spices, other vegetables, meats. That way, when you're working through the recipe, you'll be organized and ready for each step as it comes.

Give yourself more time to cook a large batch than you would a smaller one; not only does the prep take more time, it also usually takes longer to cook down more ingredients in a larger cooking vessel. Only you know your pace when chopping, cleaning, and prepping, so plan accordingly. And build in more cooking time than you would need for a smaller batch, just in case each step runs longer than anticipated.

USE THE RIGHT EQUIPMENT

If you're planning to cook for hundreds or thousands, you'll need much, much larger vessels to cook in; one of our standard pieces of equipment is a 16-gallon tilt skillet (an industrial cooking tool that lets us tip the pan forward to pour cooked food into serving containers). If you think you'll be cooking for a hundred people, start with a 50-quart (12½-gallon) stockpot.

Paella pans are another common tool for WCK; they're incredibly versatile and transportable, and we can set them up without any infrastructure in a field kitchen on a cooking ring with a fuel tank. Our paella pans range from 3 to 4 feet in diameter. For your own purposes, here's a rough guide—knowing that not just the circumference but also the depth of a pan can change serving numbers: A filled 15-inch paella pan serves 10 to 12; a 22-inch pan serves about 25 to 30; a 38-inch pan serves 200 to 250; a 52-inch pan will serve about 500.

And don't forget that you'll need longer stirring tools for these massive pots and pans. We tend to use paddles or spoons that are up to 4 feet long.

Everything else may need to be scaled up as well. If you need a mixer, blender, or immersion blender, consider finding a commercial size.

BUILD FLAVOR

When you are scaling a recipe, think about what you need to do to build flavor. What is necessary to get it to shine at the end? Do the proteins need to be marinated overnight instead of a few hours? Do you need more spice paste or to deeply toast your spices? Do you need to dedicate extra time for searing meat because the volume is so much greater? When you're cooking for hundreds or thousands at a time, it's easy to lose flavor and make something that tastes "institutional." But when you take the basics of building flavor and turn them up to 11, your final dish will taste exactly how you intended.

TASTE, TASTE, TASTE

Taste the dish at *every* step of the process. Taste it so often that by the time you serve it, you're not hungry. This is how chefs learn. Chefs taste all sorts of dishes tens, hundreds, thousands of times so that when they go into the kitchen to start cooking, they can imagine what they want to make and even what it will taste like. Let your taste buds guide you!

BEWARE RESIDUAL HEAT

When cooking in large batches, the internal residual heat of the dish is greater than when cooking a family-size amount. We use this to our advantage: It's great for keeping food hot when we transport it. But sometimes it can be destructive to the dish. Rice, vegetables, and pasta can quickly get mushy; and meats can go from tender to tough if you're not careful.

When it comes to pasta, we stop cooking it before al dente, calculating that it will keep cooking to the right texture. With chicken and meat, though, we won't stop until it's properly and safely cooked—we use thermometers to make sure we are at a safe temperature, and then take it off the heat so it doesn't overcook. Different cuts of meat also behave differently with residual heat, and some are more forgiving than others. If you're making a big batch and are worried about overcooking, choose pork shoulder over loin, chicken thighs over breasts, and beef roasts over steaks, for example. It's a dance and sometimes the only way to get it right is to mess it up the first time as you refine your technique.

BACK ENGINEER

Ultimately, you don't just have to know your recipe forward—you also have to know it *backward*. Once you've thought through all of these steps, you'll have a great handle on what the dish looks, feels, smells, and tastes like throughout the process. The final product is the goal; how do you get there? Certain ingredients may break down entirely in a bigger batch size with longer cooking times. Diced bell pepper, for example, will pretty much disappear over the course of cooking a large portion. So if you want the texture and color of the pepper in the dish when you serve it, you could either add it later in the cooking process, or add it in two batches: first to build flavor in the beginning and then more later to remain in the final dish.

———

Like all things WCK does, scaling is not an exact science. You can't plug in a formula and—*voilà!*—end up with a perfectly scaled dish. It's the nuance, the tasting, the collaboration, and the intention that guide our chefs to success. If you want to practice on a simple, forgiving dish, start with the Firefighter Chili (page 42). So good luck, get a big pot and lots of tasting spoons, and go cook for the many!

FIREFIGHTER CHILI

This is chili at its most basic and delicious, the platonic ideal of beef chili. We usually make it in California during wildfire season, since chili is firefighters' comfort food. The tablespoon of cornmeal in the small batch might feel like an insignificant amount, but it in fact serves a double purpose: It both thickens the chili and adds a slight sweet corniness in the background, subtly suggesting a slice of corn bread alongside the bowl. This is a great basic recipe to practice scaling up. Make it for your family to get to know the flavors, the spicing, the timing, and the process, and then try your hand at the 100-person version (note: you're going to need a bigger pot!). If you have even more mouths to feed, start at the 100-person version and work up from there using the tips for scaling a recipe on page 35.

1. (Directions for cooking for 100 are in parentheses.) In a large pot (or a 50-quart pot or very large paella pan), heat the oil over medium-high heat. Add the onion and garlic and cook until translucent, 3 to 5 minutes (10 to 12 minutes). Add the ground beef and cook, breaking it up as you mix it with the onions, until the meat has started to release some liquid, 2 to 4 minutes (8 to 10 minutes).

2. Stir in the tomato paste, chili powder, cumin, oregano, mustard powder, paprika, salt, and pepper. Continue to cook and stir until the spices become aromatic, about 1 minute (about 5 minutes). Add the beef stock, crushed tomatoes, chiles, kidney beans, black beans, and cornmeal and bring to a boil. Reduce the heat to low and simmer, uncovered, until the chili is slightly thickened and coats the back of a spoon, about 1 hour.

3. Taste the chili and adjust the seasoning with salt and pepper. Serve in bowls and top with scallions and shredded cheese.

SERVES 4 TO 6	SERVES 100	INGREDIENT
1 tablespoon	1¼ cups	**extra-virgin olive oil**
1	7½ pounds	**medium yellow onion(s), diced**
4	1 pound	**garlic cloves, minced**
1 pound	20 pounds	**lean ground beef**
2 tablespoons	2½ cups	**tomato paste**
1½ tablespoons	1¾ cups	**chili powder**
2 teaspoons	¾ cup	**ground cumin**
1 teaspoon	½ cup	**dried oregano**
1 teaspoon	½ cup	**mustard powder**
½ teaspoon	¼ cup	**sweet paprika**
1 tablespoon	1 cup	**kosher salt (see Note)**
½ teaspoon	¼ cup	**freshly ground black pepper**
3 cups	4 gallons	**beef stock**
1 (28-ounce) can	5 (#10) cans	**crushed tomatoes**
1 (4-ounce) can	10 (7-ounce) cans	**diced green chiles, such as Ortega or Hatch**
1 (15.5-ounce) can	3 (#10) cans	**kidney beans, drained and rinsed**
1 (15.5-ounce) can	3 (#10) cans	**black beans, drained and rinsed**
1 tablespoon	1½ cups	**cornmeal**
1 bunch	5 pounds	**scallions, finely chopped**
½ cup	2 pounds	**shredded cheddar cheese, Monterey Jack cheese, or a mix**

Note: With this volume of salt, variations between brands become very noticeable. This recipe uses Diamond Crystal; if you are using Morton's, you'll probably need less salt. But you should always be tasting, tasting, tasting!

EMPATHY

BRAISES AND OTHER LONG COOKS

I believe that each of us has a deep reserve of empathy, something that we can all tap into if we just look. Everywhere I've been, I've seen neighbors helping neighbors and communities supporting themselves through crisis. When things look the darkest, the best of humanity really shines through.

Without empathy, nothing works.

—JOSÉ ANDRÉS

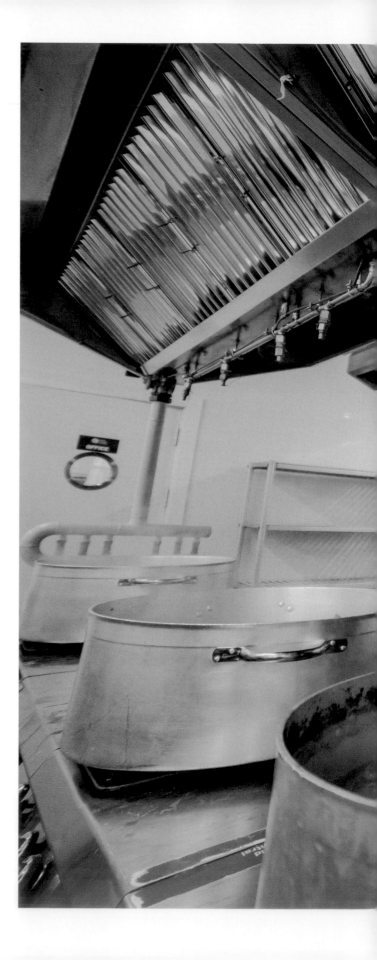

CLOSE YOUR EYES. Imagine living through a wildfire that destroyed your neighborhood: Your belongings are charred ashes, you don't know where your pet is, you have no cell service, and you haven't heard from your family across town. Or maybe it wasn't a fire—maybe it was a hurricane or a tornado or a flash flood that swept through your community, upending trees and lives in its path. Can you imagine the despair?

Putting yourself in the shoes of people affected by disaster is the best way to access the deep reserves of empathy we all need in times of crisis. Among WCK's fundamental beliefs is that the best way to show empathy and humanity is through food—homey, comforting dishes that cook slowly and build flavor over time. Ideally, they'll taste as if they were made in a warm kitchen for Sunday dinner with family and friends. There is discernible love in the flavor of a slow-cooked dish as the spices bloom, the meat falls apart from constant low heat, and the sauce thickens and gets richer as it simmers for hours.

> PUTTING YOURSELF IN THE SHOES OF PEOPLE AFFECTED BY DISASTER IS THE BEST WAY TO ACCESS THE DEEP RESERVES OF EMPATHY WE ALL NEED IN TIMES OF CRISIS.

During many of our operations, we'll have a long braise in the weekly rotation, the recipe often coming from a local chef who knows what home tastes like to the people we're serving. Sometimes we need to get food out as fast as we can (see the Urgency chapter on page 77), and sometimes we can take all day to make a dish that reaches something deeper.

The recipes in this chapter aim to give you that feeling. Sure, they take some work, but the hours you spend in the kitchen searing, simmering, and slowly building flavor show the people you're feeding that you care with a depth that's nearly impossible to express in any other way. Yes, the Stew Chicken (page 63) from Saint Vincent needs an overnight bath in a bright green herbal marinade before it becomes its true self; Puerto Rican Sierra en Escabeche (page 70) soaks in its tangy, spicy mixture of garlic and whole black peppercorns for days; and Haitian Griot

(page 52) cooks not once but twice, resulting in beautifully burnished, tender cubes of pork.

Besides recipes, we'll meet two chefs who help others create warmth in the kitchen through a deep dive into their cultures and traditions. Chef Mi-Sol Chevallier (pictured to the right with École des Chefs culinary students in 2018), was one of WCK's first team members and ran our culinary school in Port-au-Prince, Haiti, from 2015 to 2022. She has served as a protective matriarch on a never-ending quest to raise the level of cooking and hospitality in the country by sharing her vision with hundreds of students over the years. Brian Yazzie (pictured above) is a Diné (Navajo) chef bringing traditional ingredients and techniques to Indigenous communities in the Minneapolis area, where he and his team cooked hundreds of thousands of meals for the city's elders with WCK throughout the Covid pandemic.

To us, this is what good cooking is. It's not just the salt, the spice, the texture—it's the time and intention devoted to making a recipe. When you can see the world through someone else's eyes and listen as they tell you about their experience and current reality, that's empathy—an intangible ingredient that will make your cooking unforgettable.

Note:
Rendang doesn't suffer from freezing; in fact, many expat Indonesians request that family visiting from the islands bring them frozen rendang to get an extra-comforting taste of home.

BEEF RENDANG

Rendang—a long, slow braise in coconut milk and spices—is known as one of Indonesia's national dishes, originating in West Sumatra. The cooking process, in which the beef absorbs the richness and liquid of the coconut milk, preserves it for days or weeks, making it a smart dish to turn to when delivering meals to rural areas, as WCK has done in the aftermath of typhoons, earthquakes, and a volcanic eruption. After braising, the beef becomes incredibly tender, and the thick, rich sauce keeps it hot for hours. It can be a celebratory dish, eaten at weddings or holidays, so it brings joy even in difficult moments.

SERVES 4 TO 6

SPICE PASTE

4 dried **árbol** or **Sichuan chiles**, stemmed
2 large **fresh cayenne chiles** or other medium-hot fresh red chiles, chopped (seeded for less heat)
1 large **shallot**, roughly chopped
6 **garlic cloves**, roughly chopped
2-inch piece **fresh turmeric**, peeled, or 2 teaspoons ground turmeric
¼ cup **macadamia nuts**
¼ teaspoon **kosher salt**

STEW

2 tablespoons **neutral oil**
2 tablespoons **dark brown sugar**, plus more to taste
2 **lemongrass stalks**, bruised and tied in a knot (see Note, page 204)
2- to 3-inch piece **galangal**, bruised
4 **makrut lime leaves**
2 **bay leaves**
2 **cinnamon sticks**
2 teaspoons **kosher salt**, plus more to taste
1 teaspoon **ground coriander**
2 pounds **brisket** or **stew beef**, cut into 1½- to 2-inch cubes
1 (13.5-ounce) can **full-fat coconut milk**
Steamed **long-grain white rice**, for serving
Sambal (optional; page 289), for serving

1. MAKE THE SPICE PASTE: Bring a small saucepan of water to a boil. Add the dried chiles and boil until plump and soft, 2 to 3 minutes. Drain and add to a mortar (or blender/small food processor). Add the fresh chiles, shallot, garlic, turmeric, macadamias, and salt. Use a pestle to grind and mash (or process in the blender) until you have a thick orange paste.

2. MAKE THE STEW: In a wok or large deep skillet, heat the oil over medium-high heat. Add the spice paste and sauté, stirring frequently, until fragrant, 4 to 5 minutes. Add the brown sugar, lemongrass, galangal, lime leaves, bay leaves, cinnamon, salt, and coriander and mix well.

3. Add the beef, stirring to coat the meat with the spice paste. Cook over medium-high heat, stirring occasionally, until the chunks have browned a bit, about 5 minutes. Add 2 cups water and bring to a boil. Add the coconut milk, reduce to a simmer, stir well, cover, and simmer the meat for 1 hour, stirring every 15 to 20 minutes.

4. After 1 hour, uncover and cook until the sauce is beautifully thick and the meat is starting to fall apart, another 45 minutes. Taste it a few times throughout and adjust the flavor by adding salt or brown sugar as needed.

5. Once the sauce is thick, increase the heat to medium-high and cook, stirring constantly, until the meat has absorbed almost all the sauce and the oil starts to separate out, which will vary based on your pan size but will likely be after 10 to 20 minutes. At this point, the beef will begin to caramelize and get an even deeper golden brown as it "fries" in the oil—this is a good thing. Once you're at this step, let it caramelize for 10 to 15 minutes, continuing to stir until the meat can easily be shredded with a fork.

6. Remove the lemongrass, galangal, lime leaves, bay leaves, and cinnamon sticks and serve warm with a side of rice. Accompany with sambal, if desired.

HAITIAN GRIOT

Griot is party food in Haiti. The name comes from West Africa, where griots and griottes are high-status storytellers and community leaders. The dish—cubes of pork braised in an allium-rich, lime-spiked marinade before being roasted or fried—was once expensive to make and reserved for important people and special occasions. Now, because inexpensive imported pork is available (the local indigenous breed was exterminated through an infamous international campaign in the 1980s), it's become a mainstay at parties. You can eat it party-style with toothpicks or make it a meal and serve it with Pikliz (page 290), a quick-pickled spicy cabbage slaw, and Bannann Peze (page 288), twice-fried plantains. The acid and heat from the pikliz cut through the griot's unctuousness, while the crispy fried plantains provide a textural foil to the pork. If you plan to make other Haitian dishes, like Soupe Joumou (page 163), double the garlicky Épis (page 290) so you have plenty on hand.

SERVES 4 TO 6

2 tablespoons **extra-virgin olive oil**

2 pounds **boneless pork shoulder** or **butt**, trimmed of skin and excess fat, and cut into 1½- to 2-inch cubes

¼ cup **Épis** (page 290)

8 **whole cloves**

1 medium **yellow onion**, peeled but left whole

8 to 10 **fresh parsley sprigs**

5 to 6 **fresh thyme sprigs**

4 medium **garlic cloves**, peeled

1 **Scotch bonnet pepper** or other hot chile

1½ teaspoons **coarse sea salt**, plus more to taste

Juice of 2 **limes**

Pikliz (page 290), for serving

Bannann Peze (page 288), for serving

1. The day before you plan to serve the griot, in a heavy-bottomed soup pot or Dutch oven, heat the olive oil over medium-high heat until shimmering and aromatic. Add the cubed pork (in batches if necessary so you don't crowd the pan) and cook until browned on all sides—it doesn't have to be perfect, but get some nice golden color on most of the surfaces. Remove from the heat and add the épis, stirring to coat the meat. Cover the pot and let it cool at room temperature for 20 to 30 minutes, then transfer it to the fridge. Marinate for at least 6 hours or overnight.

2. The next day, start by making an *oignon clouté* (literally "studded onion," a traditional French flavor booster) by inserting the pointy end of the cloves into the surface of the onion until it's studded all over. Remove the pot with the pork from the refrigerator, uncover, and add the clove-studded onion and enough water to just cover the meat. Use kitchen twine to tie the stems of the parsley and thyme together and add to the pot along with the garlic, Scotch bonnet, and sea salt. Bring to a boil, then reduce the heat to medium and simmer, uncovered, until the meat is tender but not falling apart, about 2 hours, using a spoon to occasionally skim any foam from the surface.

3. About 30 minutes before the meat is done, preheat the oven to 400°F.

4. Once the meat is tender, use a slotted spoon to transfer the meat to a large roasting pan. Strain the cooking liquid from the pot and measure out 1 cup (save the rest of the cooking liquid to use in other dishes, like Refried Beans, page 296). Add the lime juice to the 1 cup cooking liquid to make a marinade. Taste the marinade and adjust as needed: It should be well seasoned and have a nice, bright tang. Pour it over the meat.

5. Roast the meat until it's golden brown and most of the liquid has evaporated, about 45 minutes, carefully turning the meat over once or twice during roasting so all sides can brown.

6. Serve with pikliz and bannann peze.

BRINGING HAITIAN CULINARY TRADITIONS INTO THE FUTURE

If you look up a dozen recipes for griot, or any other Haitian meat or chicken dish for that matter, chances are that many will instruct you to start by washing the meat with lime or bitter orange juice, then rinsing it, then boiling it—or maybe pouring scalding water over the meat, a technique known as shodé. Chef Mi-Sol Chevallier, a French-trained former restaurateur and the one-time director of École des Chefs, a culinary school in Port-au-Prince that became Atelier des Chefs in 2022, wants to end this habit. Mi-Sol joined WCK in 2014 after José Andrés visited her Port-au-Prince restaurant and invited her to run the school. Over her tenure with WCK, she taught fifteen classes of students, preparing a new generation of the country's hospitality industry for the future.

Back to griot and shodé. Washing meat with citrus juice and then boiling it was a two-step technique once used as a way to clean bacteria from the surface of the meat. During colonial times and prior to mass refrigeration, meat was salt preserved to keep it bacteria-free, and boiling helped remove the salt used in preservation. The process was all part of keeping the food safe, but modern refrigeration and freshly butchered meat make those steps unnecessary.

Instead, Mi-Sol encourages her students to start by browning the meat without rubbing it with lime. "The effect of adding acid in the beginning is that with meat, and even more with fish, the moisture is drawn out and the protein dries up," she instructs. Mi-Sol adds lime or bitter orange juice near the end of cooking to lend bright, fresh flavor to the dish.

Mi-Sol has more updates for the griot process: Traditionally, after the meat was boiled with aromatics, it was deep-fried until glistening and bronzed. Sure, it tasted good, but it added unnecessary oil to an already rich dish. Instead, in Mi-Sol's griot (see page 52), she first sears and then poaches the meat to cook it and then braises it in a marinade spiked with lime juice, letting the griot infuse with savory goodness while also becoming meltingly tender. It's not a lean dish, but the braising cuts some fat without sacrificing flavor or texture. "History is a good guide, but we can always be learning and looking to the future. The techniques of the past made sense then, but today we don't need to be doing the same things we did in 1804."

YAZZIE'S SAGE AND AGAVE BRAISED BISON

American bison, called tatanka in the Lakota language of the Upper Great Plains, was hunted nearly to extinction by American colonists as part of a program of cultural genocide of the continent's Indigenous people. Now, though, Indigenous chefs like Brian Yazzie (Diné/Navajo), a member of WCK's Chef Corps, compare bison's resilience to that of tribal communities (see Feeding the Elders, page 59)—the population of bison throughout the US has rebounded from just over five hundred in the late nineteenth century to five hundred thousand today. Yazzie's recipe for bison, which uses other indigenous ingredients like fresh sage and dried juniper berries, is beautifully sweet and savory with a faint herbal earthiness. There are farms that specialize in bison meat throughout the country—a little online research pays off; plus you'll be supporting small farmers and the future of an animal that's been around for more than ten thousand years.

SERVES 6

¼ cup **kosher salt**, plus more to taste

¼ cup **onion powder**

¼ cup **garlic powder**

¼ cup **sweet paprika**

8 **fresh sage leaves**, minced

1 cup **sunflower oil**

4- to 5-pound **bison chuck roast**

2 medium **red** or **white onions**, peeled and quartered

5 medium **garlic cloves**, peeled

6 **juniper berries**

½ cup **agave syrup**

4 to 6 cups **vegetable stock**

1. In a medium bowl, combine the salt, onion powder, garlic powder, paprika, and sage. Rub 2 tablespoons of the oil over the bison roast and carefully massage the seasoning mix over it, making sure to get it in the nooks and crannies. You may not need all the seasoning mix to get a nice even layer all over the meat. (If you have any left over, add yogurt or sour cream and some buttermilk for a respectable ranch dressing!) Wrap the bison tightly in plastic wrap, put it in a large bowl or baking pan, and place in the fridge at least 8 hours or up to overnight.

2. In a large Dutch oven, heat ¼ cup of the oil over medium-high heat. Add the onion quarters and sauté until they start to soften, stirring regularly, 8 to 10 minutes. Add the garlic and juniper berries and sauté just until fragrant, about 30 seconds. Transfer it all to a bowl, mix in the agave, and set aside.

3. Preheat the oven to 200°F.

4. Remove the bison roast from the fridge and unwrap. Add the remaining 10 tablespoons oil to the Dutch oven and heat over medium-high heat until shimmering. Sear the meat for 1 to 2 minutes on each side—if it ever starts to char or burn, turn it until seared and golden brown on all sides.

5. Add the onion-agave mixture and enough stock to reach halfway up the bison roast, cover the pot with a sheet of foil, and place the lid on tightly.

6. Place the roast in the oven and braise until when you stick a fork into the thickest part, the meat is tender enough to be shredded, 7 to 9 hours, depending on the size of your roast. Begin checking for tenderness after the first 6 hours or so. If it isn't tender at that point, re-cover with the foil and lid and braise up to 3 hours longer, checking the tenderness every 30 minutes.

7. Using tongs and a big spoon, carefully transfer the roast to a big bowl. Shred the meat and taste it, adding salt if needed. If you like, turn the stock into a pan sauce to serve with the bison. Simply strain the stock, skim off any fat (there will be a lot of excess oil), and boil the skimmed stock for another 45 minutes, until it's about three-quarters its original volume.

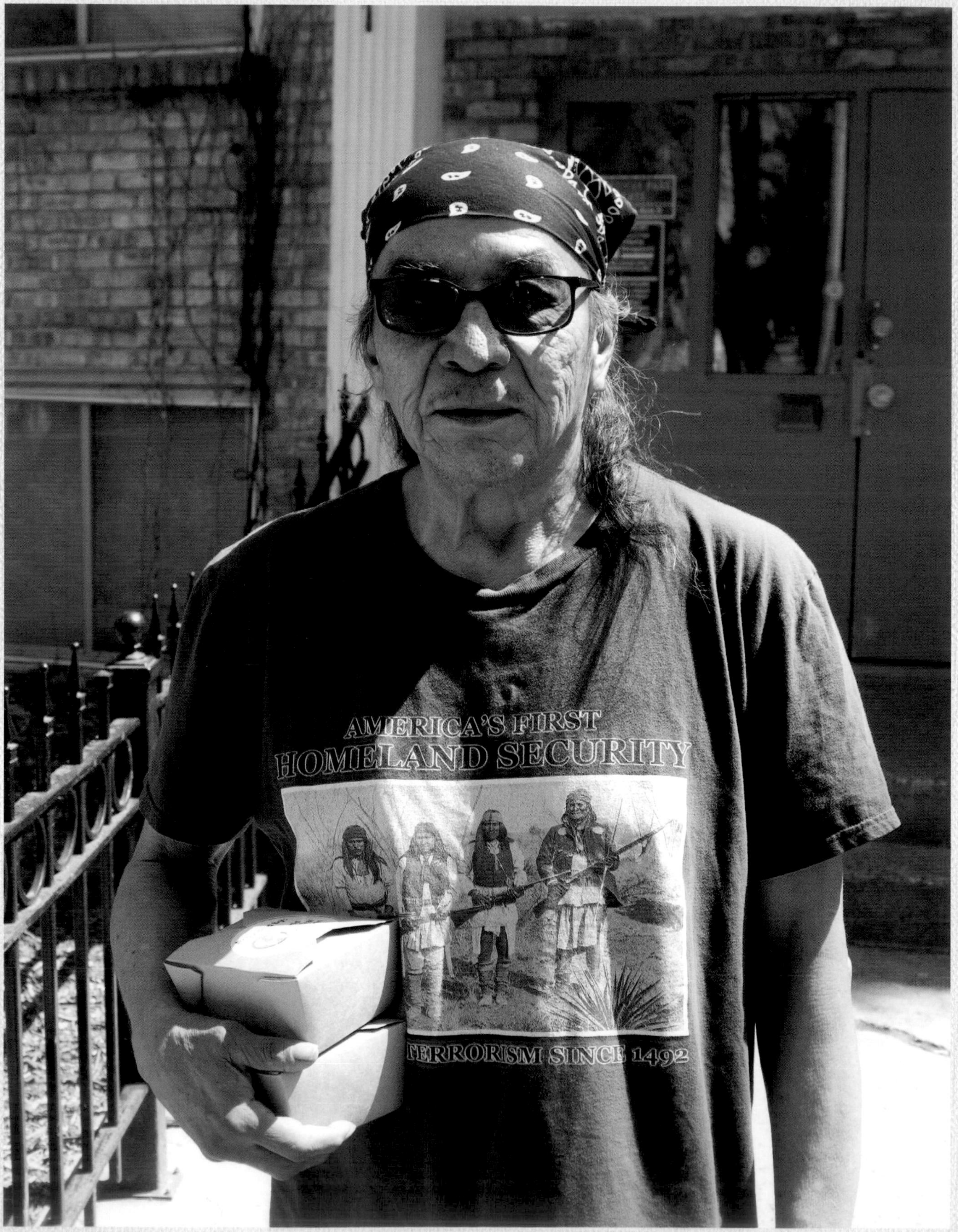
AMERICA'S FIRST
HOMELAND SECURITY
TERRORISM SINCE 1492

FEEDING THE ELDERS

The Minneapolis American Indian Center, which was founded in 1975, serves one of the largest populations of Indigenous Americans in the country. Many Indigenous people—more than 35,000—came to the Minneapolis-Saint Paul area after the 1956 Indian Relocation Act, a move by the US government to relocate Indigenous people to urban areas and disconnect them from their familial homes. The center works to resist assimilation by celebrating and preserving cultural traditions through art and language, as well as workforce training and nutrition programs.

At the heart of the center is Gatherings Cafe, which applies the group's mission to its menu, decolonizing the diet of the local community to improve health and wellness. During the pandemic, the cafe brought on chef Brian Yazzie (Diné/Navajo), who grew up on the Navajo Nation in Dennehotso, Arizona, before going to culinary school in Saint Paul. For Yazzie, serving and celebrating indigenous food—like Three Sisters, a traditional combination that showcases the symbiotic relationship between corn, beans, and squash—are crucial for reintroducing disconnected urban communities to their cultural identity. He's an educator who's traveled the world and throughout America's pueblos and reservations to understand the state of indigenous food and nutrition—he has come to find that many Indigenous Americans of all ages don't know a lot about their own cultural history.

Over the course of the pandemic, Yazzie and his team at Gatherings Cafe delivered meals to the community's elders as a part of WCK's Chefs For America program. The team served 300 meals a day, helping reintroduce indigenous ingredients like wild rice, walleye, and tepary beans to elders. By delivering meals focusing on indigenous and healthy ingredients, Yazzie addressed both cultural and nutritional education. That was particularly important during the pandemic, as many elders faced higher risk due to compromised immune systems. His menus used more than 50 percent indigenous ingredients, featuring Red Lake Nation walleye, Oneida hominy, and maple syrup from the Odawa community of northern Michigan.

Yazzie is especially devoted to serving bison, a lean, heart-healthy protein, sourced from the Cheyenne River community of South Dakota, as part of his menu for the elders: "When a bison's life is taken for food and living materials, it is done with ceremony, and all parts of the animal are utilized." During the pandemic, he served bison tongue nachos, bison short ribs, bison meatballs, and Sage and Agave Braised Bison (page 56). "I believe that food is medicine—and that bison is one of the best proteins out there. To me, the return of the bison helps us reconnect our tribal communities to our land."

BRAISED PORK AL PASTOR

Pork cooked al pastor is a uniquely Mexican preparation, but its roots come from halfway around the globe. It originated as a take on vertical spit-roasted shawarma, which was brought to Mexico by Lebanese immigrants. The meat was sliced off the rotating spit and piled on a pita-like flatbread that became known in Puebla as tacos árabes. The traditional meat for shawarma was lamb, but local taste and availability led to a switch to pork. Even the onion that topped the shawarma spit was swapped out in favor of pineapple, which helped season and tenderize the meat. This version is another step down the evolutionary tree: an improvisation that gets you the flavor and texture of a true al pastor, with a method better suited for serving the masses. We served this to families displaced by powerful earthquakes in Southern California in 2019. You can serve it with white rice and black beans, or wrap it up in a warm tortilla topped with fresh pineapple chunks and raw onion.

SERVES 6

3 tablespoons **sweet paprika**

2 tablespoons **kosher salt**

1 tablespoon **freshly ground black pepper**

1 tablespoon **ground cumin**

1 tablespoon **ground coriander**

2 teaspoons **dried oregano**

1 teaspoon **garlic powder**

1 teaspoon **chili powder**

¼ teaspoon **ground cloves**

¼ teaspoon **ground cinnamon**

4 pounds **boneless pork shoulder** or **butt**

1 (20-ounce) can juice-packed **pineapple chunks**, juice reserved, or 1 cup ¾-inch chunks **fresh pineapple** (make sure the pineapple is very ripe and sweet) plus 1 cup pineapple juice

5 medium **garlic cloves**, minced

1 medium **yellow onion**, diced

½ cup **apple cider vinegar**

½ cup **fresh cilantro**, minced

Chopped **onion** (optional), for serving

Diced **fresh pineapple** (optional), for serving

1. In a bowl, combine the paprika, salt, pepper, cumin, coriander, oregano, garlic powder, chili powder, cloves, and cinnamon. With a paper towel, pat the pork dry and put it in a baking dish or Dutch oven. Using a knife with a sharp point, make 1-inch incisions all over the meat and insert chunks of the pineapple into the holes you're making—do this 12 to 15 times (there's no need to be precise). Massage the spice blend onto the pork, making sure to cover all surfaces and folds, including the pineapple-filled slits. Rub the minced garlic and diced onion over the meat—don't worry if some of it falls off into the baking dish. Put the dish in the refrigerator uncovered and marinate it for at least 4 hours or up to overnight.

2. Preheat the oven to 450°F.

3. While the oven is heating, remove the dish from the refrigerator and add the vinegar, pineapple juice (and any remaining chunks), and 1 cup water. Cover the entire pan with foil and seal as tightly as possible. Place the pork in the oven and reduce the heat to 300°F. Cook until the meat becomes very tender and starts to shred when prodded with a fork, about 3 hours, removing the pan from the oven, uncovering, and basting the pork every 30 to 45 minutes.

4. Remove the foil from the pan and increase the oven temperature to 450°F. Roast until the pork is golden brown on top, another 15 to 25 minutes.

5. Remove it from the oven and let it rest for 30 minutes. Remove the pork from the baking dish and place it in a large bowl. Use two forks to pull and shred the pork, then pour the juices and any pineapple bits from the pan over the shredded meat. Garnish with fresh cilantro and serve with chopped onion (if using). If you'd like an extra burst of sweetness, add some chopped fresh pineapple.

STEW CHICKEN

There are two tricks to this recipe, which we learned on the Caribbean island of Saint Vincent (see Vincy Stew Chicken and the Art of Listening, page 64): marination and caramelization. Marination you've done before; just make sure to give yourself enough time for the bright, punchy green seasoning to work its way into the chicken. Caramelization might be a new one: It's a unique way to add bittersweetness to the dish. For balance, it's important to cook the sugar until it's a deep, dark brown, but keep a close eye on it so it doesn't burn—you want it just on the edge. And be careful when adding the chicken—it'll spit and hiss as the fat hits the caramel, so make sure to use tongs and oven mitts. Serve with white rice or a Vincentian favorite, steamed ground provisions—a combination of roots including sweet potatoes, yams, cassava (yuca), and dasheen (taro)—on the side.

(see Vincy Stew Chicken and the Art of Listening, page 64)

SERVES 4 TO 6

¾ cup **Green Sauce** (recipe follows)
3 pounds **bone-in, skin-on chicken thighs** and/or **drumsticks**
1 teaspoon **canola oil**
2½ tablespoons **dark brown sugar**
1 medium **yellow onion**, slivered
1 teaspoon **ground cinnamon**
2 **whole cloves**
2 cups **chicken stock** or **water**

1. The day before you are planning to serve the stew, make the green sauce. Place the chicken in a bowl and add the green sauce. Using your hands, generously rub the paste into the chicken. Cover the bowl with plastic wrap and refrigerate overnight or up to 24 hours.

2. The next day, in a large pot, heat the oil over medium heat until shimmering. Carefully add the brown sugar, stirring occasionally. The sugar will liquefy, start bubbling, and turn deeper brown—

keep stirring. Put oven mitts on and once the sugar looks and smells like it is just about to burn, remove it from the heat and, using tongs, quickly add the chicken pieces, skin-side down. As the fat and liquid from the chicken touch the caramel, they may start to boil and pop, so move quickly and carefully. You can layer the pieces in the pot if it isn't wide enough to fit them all in a single layer; just make sure each piece has been coated in the sugar mixture.

3. Once all the chicken is added, return the pot to the heat. Add the onion, cinnamon, cloves, and chicken stock. Cover and cook until you can start to smell the spices, about 15 minutes. Gently turn the chicken pieces so all sides are coated by the sauce. Reduce the heat to low, uncover the pot, and simmer until the chicken is tender and the gravy is dark and rich, about 45 minutes.

Green Sauce

This sauce can be refrigerated in an airtight container for up to 2 weeks.

MAKES 1½ CUPS

1 bunch **scallions**, roughly chopped
20 **fresh thyme sprigs**, leaves picked off the stems
½ bunch **fresh cilantro**
½ bunch **fresh flat-leaf parsley**
6 medium **garlic cloves**, peeled but whole
½ **red** or **green bell pepper**, diced
1 **celery stalk**, chopped
1 **Scotch bonnet pepper** or other hot chile, stemmed
¼ cup **fresh lime juice** (2 to 3 limes)
¼ cup **distilled white vinegar**
1 tablespoon **kosher salt**
1 teaspoon **freshly ground black pepper**
1 tablespoon **canola oil**

In a blender, combine all the ingredients and puree until it's smooth and bright green. Refrigerate until you're ready to use it.

VINCY STEW CHICKEN
AND THE ART OF LISTENING

The Hospitality and Maritime Institute, on the windward side of the Caribbean island of Saint Vincent, is a beautiful place with state-of-the-art kitchen equipment; plenty of classroom space for lectures on cooking, pastry, butchery, and more; and an airy courtyard populated by a handful of tranquil goats who double as an environmentally friendly compost system.

When the WCK team arrived, though, the school had been shut down for months, closed by the Covid pandemic. It wasn't Covid that brought WCK to the island and to the kitchen's reopening but another disaster: a massive volcanic eruption of La Soufrière that rocked the north side of the island in April 2021. It hadn't erupted since 1979, and over the course of one day, slopes that were once lush and green were buried under inches—or feet—of ash.

The explosion forced farmers and their families to flee south. Many moved in with extended family, while others moved to government-run shelters. The destruction of the farms came with compounding consequences: Animals had been buried alive and crops were destroyed, disrupting the local food system. What had been Saint Vincent's breadbasket almost instantly became barren. With the mass relocation of the northerners, some family homes ballooned from four to fourteen overnight. And everyone needed to be fed. The WCK team met a father and daughter who were sheltering *forty evacuees* in their home and attached bar—a huge number of additional mouths to feed.

The team quickly got into the kitchen at the Hospitality Institute, which would serve as the base for feeding as many people as we could. After months of being dormant, it took a few days to get the gas and water systems up and running, but before long, things were ready. Some of the instructors who had been furloughed from the school joined the brigade of students and chefs—some from the island, some not—who would feed the community.

As the Hospitality Institute was getting operational, we also began partnering with local restaurants to provide immediate meals for displaced families and essential-care workers. The French Verandah, a restaurant owned by Keisha Browne, was one of WCK's first partners and served us some of the meals they were already cooking for the community. One dish in particular stood out to our chef Elyssa Kaplan: stew chicken. Deeply flavorful, sweet from caramelized sugar, savory, and gently spiced with cloves and cinnamon, it was like a comforting hug.

As we planned our first menu—meals that fit culturally, could give comfort to evacuated families, and could be produced in large quantities—we brought up the stew chicken we'd tasted at Keisha's. It's a dish with a counterpart on most of the Caribbean islands: Jamaican brown stew chicken is probably the most famous, but there are versions in Trinidad and Tobago, Antigua and Barbuda, Barbados, and beyond. It's made by infusing chicken with an herby, bright green thirteen-ingredient marinade for hours before cooking in caramel (yes, molten sugar!) and then braising it until it's fall-off-the-bone tender and bursting with flavor. Each island has a general blueprint for the marinade, and then each household tweaks it to make it their own. The green seasoning is particularly thyme-intensive—both small leaf (the more common version in the US) and broadleaf (also known as Spanish thyme or Cuban oregano). It also includes garlic, scallion, and a Scotch bonnet pepper for heat.

Vincentians are particular about food: Everything needs to be made fresh, with just-picked herbs, freshly peeled garlic, and proteins broken down just before cooking. It's a lot of work—you can't just go to the grocery store and pick up a jar of minced garlic or a bag of chopped onions—but the attention to detail shines in the final dish. Even if you're making it for 1,000 people, it still needs to taste homemade.

We worked with our chef-student-instructor brigade to create a version of stew chicken that would make everyone happy while being feasible to prepare on a massive scale. We landed on a green seasoning that was an amalgam of the instructors' versions, fine-tuned to get the thyme packed in and enough spice to please the island's Indo-Vincentians, who like extra heat. Our process ended up taking even longer than a home-cooked version. Usually, after the marinade, the chicken is cooked in its caramel sauce for an hour or so, until tender and moist. To get the timing right for our lunch service—we usually start deliveries at 11 a.m., which doesn't give a whole lot of time in the morning for long preparations—we had to flip the process. Marination would start the morning before we planned to serve it, then at night we would make the caramel, sauté the chicken, and let it stew until the next day.

The hours in the marinade, plus the overnight cook, infused the meat with its herbal, allium-rich essence, and a subtle spicing came from a dose of cinnamon and clove, all flavors common to the islands thanks to spices grown on Saint Vincent and its neighbor to the south, Grenada.

The version coming out of the Hospitality Institute didn't taste *exactly* like someone's grandma made it, but it had the DNA of the dish, something deep and real we never would have achieved if we had taken shortcuts. The reviews from around the island were nearly all positive. Sure, some people wanted a bit more chile, others a bit less, but people knew and appreciated that it was cooked by Vincentians. "Once we found all the right ingredients," one of the culinary instructors said, "it tasted just like I expected it to."

When we first set foot into the Hospitality Institute, it was quiet, idle, and a bit ashy. Once the first long-marinated chicken hit the smoky caramel, though, you could close your eyes, breathe in, and feel right at home.

PEPIÁN DE POLLO

This ancient dish gets its name from the pepitas (pumpkin seeds) that thicken it. It dates to pre-Hispanic Mesoamerica and has become so identified with Guatemalan cuisine that it's been declared part of the nation's cultural heritage. Pepián originated in Chimaltenango in the nation's south, one of the regions affected by the devastating eruption of Volcán de Fuego in 2018. Our team, led by chef Fatima Castillo, served displaced families and first responders. We included pepián de pollo in our weekly rotation, either making the sauce ourselves or purchasing it from a local family and building the rest of the dish in our kitchens. The sauce itself is time intensive, as it requires toasting and blending to build flavor, but the result is worth it: aromatic, richly spiced, and deeply comforting.

SERVES 4 TO 6

CHICKEN
3 pounds **bone-in, skinless chicken thighs**
½ medium **yellow onion**, peeled
1 **plum tomato**, halved
1 tablespoon **kosher salt**
1 teaspoon **freshly ground black pepper**

SAUCE
2 tablespoons hulled **pumpkin seeds**
2 tablespoons **sesame seeds**
1-inch piece **cinnamon stick**
1 **whole clove**
1 **allspice berry**
1 **dried guajillo chile**, stemmed and seeded
1 **ancho chile**, stemmed and seeded
1 (6-inch) **corn tortilla**
1 pound **plum tomatoes**
½ medium **yellow onion**, peeled and quartered
2 medium **garlic cloves**, peeled
½ bunch **cilantro**, with stems
1½ teaspoons **kosher salt**

STEW
8 ounces **green beans**, ends trimmed, halved crosswise
1 pound **Yukon Gold potatoes**, unpeeled and cut into 1-inch chunks
2 medium **carrots**, peeled and cut crosswise into slices ¼-inch thick
2 tablespoons roughly chopped **fresh cilantro**, for garnish
Lime wedges (optional), for serving
Steamed **white rice**, for serving

1. COOK THE CHICKEN: In a medium pot, combine the chicken, onion, tomato, salt, pepper, and enough water just to cover. Bring to a boil over medium heat, then reduce the heat to medium-low and simmer until the chicken is fully cooked and reads 165°F at the center, about 45 minutes.

2. MEANWHILE, START THE SAUCE: In a medium skillet (cast iron is ideal), combine the pumpkin seeds, sesame seeds, cinnamon, clove, and allspice. Set over medium heat and toast until browned and fragrant, 1 to 2 minutes, shaking the pan every 30 seconds to ensure even toasting. Once toasted, transfer to a medium bowl and set aside. Add the dried chiles to the pan and toast over medium heat until they are fragrant and begin to brown, about 30 seconds on each side. Add to the bowl with the spices. Add the tortilla to the pan and toast until dark brown spots have formed on both sides and it has hardened, 1 to 2 minutes. Transfer to the bowl with the chiles and spices. Add the whole plum tomatoes, onion quarters, garlic, and half of the cilantro to the pan, cooking until everything is blackened on all sides. Add to the bowl with the other toasted ingredients and add the salt.

3. ASSEMBLE THE STEW: Once the chicken is fully cooked, use a slotted spoon to transfer it to a bowl and set aside. Use the slotted spoon to remove the simmered tomato and onion from the pot of cooking water and add them to the bowl with the toasted sauce ingredients.

(recipe continues)

4. To the pot of cooking water, add the green beans, potatoes, and carrots and simmer over medium heat until the potatoes are fork-tender, about 25 minutes. Remove the vegetables with a slotted spoon and transfer to the bowl with the chicken.

5. In a high-powered blender, combine all of the sauce ingredients with the rest of the half bunch of cilantro. Blend until the sauce is completely smooth, 3 to 5 minutes—it may feel like a long time, but the extended blend is necessary to give the sauce its luscious, thick texture and brick-red color. You can add a tablespoon or two of the cooking water to the sauce to loosen it up.

6. Arrange the chicken and vegetables on a platter and pour the sauce over the top. Sprinkle with the chopped cilantro. Serve with a lime wedge if you'd like an extra dose of acid, and rice on the side.

SIERRA EN ESCABECHE

Escabeche is a preparation found throughout the Spanish-speaking world and the Caribbean. This version from Puerto Rico is true to the dish's origins: fish steaks preserved in a highly aromatic oil-and-vinegar marinade, designed to improve over the first few days after preparation. Sierra, or king mackerel, is the fish of choice in Puerto Rico, but you can substitute swordfish steaks. You could serve this the day you make it, but if you're patient, a few days in the escabeche will turn it into something really special. Just warm it before serving with some of the marinade.

SERVES 4

1 cup **extra-virgin olive oil**, plus more for cooking the fish

¾ cup **distilled white vinegar** or **apple cider vinegar**

1 medium **Spanish onion**, thinly sliced into rings

4 medium **garlic cloves**, smashed and peeled

¼ cup **pitted green olives**

2 jarred **roasted red peppers**, julienned (or roast your own, then peel, seed, and thinly slice)

2 teaspoons **black peppercorns**

5 **bay leaves**

4 **king mackerel** or **swordfish steaks** (6 to 8 ounces each), ½-inch thick

Juice of 1 large **lime**

Adobo boricua, homemade (page 294) or store-bought

Fine sea salt

1. Preheat the oven to 200°F.

2. In a large baking dish or ovenproof saucepan, combine 1 cup of the olive oil, the vinegar, onion, garlic, olives, roasted peppers, peppercorns, and bay leaves. Transfer the escabeche to the oven and gently cook for 3 hours, until it's aromatic and the onions are translucent.

3. Meanwhile, arrange the fish steaks in a baking dish or other wide container. In a liquid measuring cup, mix the lime juice with 1½ cups water and pour it over the fish. Add more water, if necessary, until the fish is barely covered. Refrigerate until the escabeche has about 20 minutes left in the oven.

4. Once the escabeche has about 20 minutes left to go in the oven, take the fish out of the water and pat it dry with paper towels. Season the fish on both sides with 1 to 2 teaspoons of the adobo (any more will burn off when you cook it) and a sprinkle of sea salt. In a large sauté pan, heat 2 tablespoons olive oil over medium-high heat. Add the fish to the pan (you may have to cook in batches to avoid overcrowding) and cook on both sides until golden brown and the fish reads 145°F in its thickest part, 3½ to 4 minutes per side for ½-inch-thick steaks (if your steaks are thinner or thicker, adjust accordingly). Add a little more oil to the pan between batches, if needed.

5. Refrigerate the fish until it's completely cooled—2 to 3 hours, or overnight. When the escabeche is done, remove it from the oven and let it sit at room temperature until the fish is cooled.

6. When the fish and escabeche have both cooled, place the fish in a single layer in a baking dish or other wide container with a lid. Pour the escabeche over the fish, cover, and place in the fridge to marinate for at least 24 hours and up to 5 days. The longer you marinate, the more flavor will be infused into the fish.

7. To serve, heat the fish and a few tablespoons of the escabeche in a pan over medium heat until just heated through. Serve the fish with the warmed escabeche and season with salt as needed.

BACALAO AL CLUB RANERO

The WCK team served this Basque stew (read more about it on page 75) from our Madrid kitchen during the height of the nation's Covid outbreak, when we were feeding doctors, nurses, and seniors impacted by the crisis. It's a combination of two classic Basque recipes: bacalao al pil pil—a hearty salt cod (bacalao) stew thickened with the fish's gelatinous skin—and pisto, a vegetable-rich ratatouille-like dish laced generously with Spanish olive oil. Here, it's fortified with a generous amount of garlic that's been gently cooked in olive oil. The skins from the salt cod fillets melt in the garlicky oil, cooking into a rich, umami-packed gelatin that's used as a sauce for the sautéed vegetables and baked cod. Though the method may be a bit intricate—the garlic needs to poach and dehydrate for many hours, and the salt cod is soaked in successions of cold water for a full 24 hours before using—once those preliminary steps are complete, the final dish takes less than 30 minutes to make, and the results are transporting.

SERVES 4

2 large heads **garlic**, cloves separated and peeled
1 cup plus 2 tablespoons **extra-virgin olive oil**
1 pound **salt cod**, preferably skin-on
2 tablespoons **dried parsley**
1 large **yellow onion**, diced
1 large **green bell pepper**, roughly diced
1 (14.5-ounce) can crushed **tomatoes**
1 tablespoon **pimiento choricero paste** (see Note) or finely chopped roasted red pepper
Kosher salt and **freshly ground black pepper**

1. The day before you plan to make the dish, in a small saucepan, combine the garlic cloves and 1 cup of the oil. Cook the garlic confit over low heat for 2 hours.

2. Near the end of the confit time, preheat the oven to 200°F. Line a baking sheet with parchment paper.

3. Reserving the oil, drain the confited garlic cloves. Arrange half of the garlic cloves on the baking sheet and transfer to the oven to dehydrate for about 8 hours, or overnight. Transfer the remaining cloves to a small food processor and puree. Transfer the garlic paste to an airtight jar and refrigerate overnight. Pour the garlic-infused oil into a separate airtight jar.

4. Meanwhile, begin rehydrating the salt cod by placing it in a deep dish or zip-top bag with enough cold water to cover it. Store the soaking fish in the refrigerator, changing the water three or four times over the next 24 hours.

5. When the whole garlic cloves are dehydrated, let them cool, then coarsely chop. Mix the garlic with the dried parsley and set aside.

6. In a medium skillet, heat the remaining 2 tablespoons olive oil over medium heat. Add the onions and cook until they start to soften, 3 to 5 minutes. Add the bell pepper and cook until softened, 3 to 5 minutes. Add the crushed tomatoes, reserved garlic paste, and pimiento choricero and cook, stirring regularly, until the sauce starts to thicken, 10 to 12 minutes. Taste and season with salt. This sauce is the pisto.

7. Drain and rinse the cod fillets a final time and cut them into 4 equal pieces. In a large cazuela (shallow terra-cotta cooking pot) or wide sauté pan, heat the reserved garlic oil over medium heat until shimmering. Add the fish, skin-side down, and cook until the fish firms up and turns a shade whiter, 3 to 4 minutes. Flip and cook until cooked through, another 3 minutes.

(recipe continues)

8. Remove from the heat and carefully remove the fillets from the oil and to a plate. Pour the garlic oil into a glass measuring cup and let it rest for a few minutes. The oil should separate, with white liquid—collagen from the fish—settling at the bottom. Being careful to leave the white liquid in the bottom of the measuring cup, slowly pour off about half of the garlic oil into another container and set it aside. Pour the contents remaining in the measuring cup back into the pan and set over low heat.

9. Now here's the tricky part—using the underside of a small sieve (this is traditional; you can also use a whisk), stir the oil slowly in a figure-eight pattern. The oil and collagen should begin to emulsify. As the sauce comes together, slowly add the reserved garlic oil to the pan and continue stirring. Monitor the temperature and don't let it rise above 175°F. Continue stirring for up to 12 minutes—as the sauce comes together, it will turn a light yellow and thicken. (Skin-on fillets will have more collagen and produce a thicker sauce.) Taste the sauce and season to taste with salt and pepper. This sauce is the pil pil.

10. To serve, put a piece of cod on each plate and top with a generous amount of the thick pil pil, a side of the pisto, and a heavy sprinkling of the crumbled dried garlic/parsley mixture. It took a while, but you can be proud of that sauce!

Note: Pimiento choricero is a specialty Spanish pepper from the Basque region that is usually used to season and color chorizo sausage. It's available online.

ANOTHER HANDFUL OF RICE

Bacalao al Club Ranero was created by Alejandro Caverivière, a French chef living in the Basque city of Bilbao in the early twentieth century. He was a member of one of the city's txokos—private culinary clubs whose members would come together to cook and share ideas and techniques. Legend says they'd often play a drinking game involving a frog statue and some metal coins. (*Club Ranero* roughly translates to "Frogging Club".) During one of these particularly well-attended occasions, Caverivière had to stretch the dish he had planned to cook to accommodate extra mouths. He had enough salt cod on hand to make bacalao al pil pil for the expected crowd, but as more people showed up, he was forced to think on his feet and extended it with vegetables he found in the kitchen: tomatoes, onions, and peppers. A new classic was created, born of necessity.

José shares a similar memory from his childhood: When he was a young boy in Spain, his parents hosted friends and family for big paella cookouts in the mountains outside Barcelona. His dad would plan for a certain number of people, but more would inevitably arrive. "Just throw another handful of rice in the pan," his dad would say. Is it frugality, creativity, generosity, or just tapping into a long history of Iberian hospitality? Probably all the above.

URGENCY

—

SANDWICHES, AREPAS, AND FOOD ON THE GO

The urgency of now is yesterday!

—JOSÉ ANDRÉS

SOME PEOPLE WEAR THEIR HEARTS ON THEIR SLEEVES, BUT JOSÉ WEARS HIS MANTRA ACROSS HIS CHEST. His T-shirts often carry sly messages and pointedly evocative expressions: "Immigrants Feed America," "Fight Like Ukrainians," "Dreamer."

But there's one he sometimes wears that carries less a message than a statement of fact: "My Slow Is Your Fast."

José is among the most effective pep talkers you will ever encounter. His presence instantly commands attention, and he needs very few words to motivate action. And when people are hungry and dealing with the fallout of a disaster, it's vital to get the team moving quickly.

The WCK Relief Team has a deeply ingrained understanding of the imperative that it's not good enough to get things done in a week, a day, or even an hour. The time things need to be done is NOW. José calls this the "urgency of now"— words and concept borrowed directly from Martin Luther King Jr. and his seminal speech at the 1963 March on Washington.

In the aftermath of Hurricane María in 2017, the situation in Puerto Rico was dire—hundreds of thousands of people had no food, electricity, or water. When José touched down, he saw hungry people everywhere. Grocery stores were closed, produce was hard to come by, cooking fuel was nearly impossible to find, and credit card systems were down so people couldn't buy food even if they could find it. Official government conversations were focused on getting emergency food resources to the island—in a month. *A month.* If you're hungry, you're not thinking about what you can eat in a month—you're thinking about right now, getting what you need to survive today. *The urgency of now is NOW,* José realized, or the island's residents wouldn't survive the week, let alone a month. That's when José and WCK's Chefs For Puerto Rico team started cooking.

Since then, WCK has been driven by this tenet, working to establish a kitchen and start cooking within hours of a disaster—or even before it hits, if possible. Team members are mobilized to drop whatever they're working on, get in a car, on a plane, on a motorcycle, on a boat, in a helicopter, whatever, and start making calls. Find a kitchen where they can set up shop, figure out where to buy food, enlist local kitchen and logistics support, find restaurants to partner with, and begin coordinating with emergency response organizations on the ground.

The reason José's T-shirt works as motivation is that everyone knows it's true. Whether you are chopping peppers, cooking pasta, scooping rice, or wrapping sandwiches, you want to do it one minute faster than you think you can, as you imagine José would. Then the next person does their job a minute faster, and you're two minutes ahead. Multiply that down the line, and suddenly you're done—NOW—and people are getting fed, which was everyone's goal in the first place.

In late August 2019, the team started tracking a tropical storm in the Atlantic. The storm grew into Hurricane Dorian, and forecast models predicted it could make landfall anywhere from Puerto Rico to The Bahamas, then from Florida to the Carolinas. With such wide potential for damage, the team spread out and started scoping potential rallying points in the Caribbean and up the southeastern coast of the US. When it became clear that Dorian—by then a Category 5 storm—would make landfall on the northern islands of The Bahamas, team members arrived in Nassau, just south of the eye of the storm, to be ready. Even as the Abaco Islands were lashed by the wind and rain, the Nassau kitchen, a hundred miles away, was already humming, planning its first helicopter deliveries of food to the islands as soon as the storm passed.

This chapter is full of recipes that are good for people on the move—they sometimes take a minute to prepare, but they can be eaten quickly, are portable, and are infinitely variable by nature. Aline Kamakian, a heroic chef and author from Beirut, Lebanon, shares her recipe for Armenian lahmajoun, a savory flatbread that easily rolls up for a quick handheld lunch. Tamales, one of the oldest portable meals, are a bit involved, a job made easier with a team effort. Venezuelan arepas, brilliant in their simplicity and flexibility, are a perfect and hearty meal for a lunch box or a picnic. Guatemalan/Honduran baleadas are tortillas stuffed with beans, eggs, chicken, steak . . . really, anything you want. There are also a couple of sandwich recipes, one from the WCK team and the other from chef Marcus Samuelsson, but also a spread (see How to Build a Sandwich, page 92) that illustrates the broad spectrum of options in this most ubiquitous offering. (It's much more than ham, cheese, and mayo . . . though we do proudly make quite a few of those.) And finally, WCK friend and former First Lady Michelle Obama offers a recipe for breakfast tacos, a Tuesday tradition around her house.

When you're making these dishes in your kitchen, you may not need to move as fast as José or a WCK team member in the field. But if you have hungry people waiting for you at the dinner table, you definitely understand the urgency of NOW.

TAMALES

If anything unites Latin America and connects modernity to ancient tradition, it's the tamal. Depending on where you are, they may be called by another name: hallacas in Venezuela, chuchitos in Guatemala, but they'll always be made from masa—ground nixtamalized corn—stuffed with vegetables, meats, nuts, or fruits and steamed in either a corn husk or a banana leaf. Because they are an easy-to-transport meal, WCK has served them in Mexico, Honduras, Guatemala, and beyond. They have a special place at the table around the holidays, when families spend hours together constructing hundreds of them to share. So, gather your friends and family, put on some music, and get wrapping. The first couple may be challenging, but patience pays off; watch a few videos of abuelas making tamales and you'll catch on quick.

MAKES 12 TO 18 TAMALES

30 to 40 fresh or frozen **banana leaves**, thawed if frozen
Kitchen twine

TAMAL SAUCE
1½ pounds **plum tomatoes**, cored
2 **red bell peppers**, halved
1 dried **guaque** or **guajillo chile**, halved and seeded
1 **pasilla chile**, stemmed and seeded
¼ cup hulled **pumpkin seeds**
2 tablespoons **sesame seeds**
1 small **cinnamon stick**
2 **whole cloves**
1 teaspoon **ground allspice**
2 tablespoons **lard** or **oil**
1½ tablespoons **kosher salt**
1 teaspoon **achiote paste**

MASA
2½ pounds **instant masa**, such as Maseca
2 tablespoons **kosher salt**
1½ cups **lard** or **vegetable shortening**

ASSEMBLY
1½ pounds **cooked chicken** (see Note, page 124), shredded
½ cup **raisins**
1 cup rinsed and drained canned **chickpeas**
1 large **red bell pepper**, cut into thin strips
Pickled hot peppers (optional), such as guindilla or banana peppers
½ cup blanched **almonds**
½ cup **pimiento-stuffed olives** (or any pitted green olives)

1. Before you start cooking, rinse the banana leaves in cold water. Place in a large bowl filled with warm water and soak for 30 minutes, until they soften. Depending on the size of the leaves, cut them into large rectangles, about 14 inches long and 8 to 10 inches wide. Gently pat dry with a kitchen towel before using.

2. MAKE THE TAMAL SAUCE: In a medium pot, combine the plum tomatoes, bell peppers, guaque chile, and pasilla chile and add just enough water to cover the vegetables. Set over medium heat and simmer until soft, about 20 minutes. Using a slotted spoon, transfer the tomatoes and peppers to a blender, reserving the cooking liquid.

3. Meanwhile, in a small pan, combine the pumpkin seeds, sesame seeds, cinnamon stick, cloves, and allspice and toast over low heat, shaking the pan often, until browned and fragrant, about 10 minutes.

(recipe continues)

4. Transfer the toasted spices and tomato/pepper mixture to a blender. Add the lard, salt, and achiote paste and blend until smooth. Add a few tablespoons of the vegetable cooking water if you need to loosen it up; the sauce is supposed to be thick, luscious, and a little salty. Transfer to a medium bowl and set aside.

5. MAKE THE MASA: In a large bowl, combine the instant masa, salt, and 6 cups warm water and mix well with your hands; don't worry if it has lumps. Using a handheld mixer, blend the dough on medium-low, slowly adding 2 more cups warm water as you blend, until completely smooth.

6. In a large soup pot, bring 8 cups water to a boil. Add the masa mixture and reduce the heat to medium-low. Mix well with a wooden spoon, then add the lard and continue cooking and mixing well until it thickens, 5 to 8 minutes. The masa will continue to thicken as it cools down and should be similar to the consistency of cooked oatmeal or grits; if it's doughlike, it's too thick. You can always add more water.

7. ASSEMBLE THE TAMALES: To the center of each banana leaf, add about 1 cup of masa. Spread it into a rectangle ½ inch deep in the center of the leaf and make a small well in the middle with your hands. Add a generous amount of sauce and chicken, about 2 tablespoons of each. Add 5 raisins, 5 chickpeas, 2 bell pepper strips, 1 pickled pepper (if using), 2 almonds, and 1 olive. It doesn't need to be perfect; just make sure everything is well spaced over the sauce and chicken.

8. Bring the two long edges of the banana leaf up to meet above the filling, then holding the edges together, carefully fold them down twice to make a seal in the center of the filling, almost like you're wrapping a present. Fold both sides of the leaf down under the bulk of the filling. Some people like to wrap the tamales twice in case one of the leaves rips; if you have the patience, wrap the tamal in another banana leaf and repeat the same process, then tie kitchen twine around the center of the tamal to make sure it stays closed.

9. The hard part is over! Once you are finished wrapping the tamales, place a few banana leaves (this is a great use for any ripped ones) in the bottom of a large soup pot and add 4 cups of water (it needs to be enough to come up to the first layer or two of tamales). Stack up the tamales on top of the leaves, then cover them with a few more banana leaves. Cover the pot with a lid. Set the pot over medium-low heat and steam until the tamales feel hard and the leaves have turned a dark green, 45 minutes to 1 hour, checking on them after 30 minutes or so. If the water evaporates, add a little more.

10. Remove the tamales from the pot with tongs. Serve them warm, making sure to open them carefully as steam escapes. You can refrigerate them for up to 3 days or freeze them for 3 months; just rewarm them in a steamer or microwave before serving.

ALINE'S LAHMAJOUN

Lahmajoun is a flatbread of Armenian origin that gets its name from the Arabic words for "meat with dough." It is popular throughout Türkiye and the Middle East. Aline Kamakian, a Lebanese restaurateur of Armenian descent, immediately started making lahmajoun with her team for volunteers cleaning up the streets of Beirut after a horrific blast shook the city in August 2020 (see Urgent Heroism in Beirut, page 88). It's the perfect handheld meal—just fold the dough in half and go. Aline likes to roast long, thin eggplants over an open flame until smoky, sprinkle them with a bit of sea salt, and then roll up the lahmajoun around them, but a simple squeeze of lemon juice also perfectly complements the savory meat and soft and crispy dough. Traditionally lahmajoun is made in a wood oven, but you can get a nice version with a hot pizza stone in a home oven or even on a standard baking sheet—just heat it in the oven before baking the lahmajoun.

MAKES TWELVE 8-INCH LAHMAJOUNS

DOUGH
4 cups (480 grams) **all-purpose flour**, sifted, plus more as needed
2 teaspoons **dried milk powder**
1½ teaspoons **active dry yeast**
¼ teaspoon **sea salt**

TOPPING (SEE NOTE)
8 ounces **lean ground beef**
8 ounces **ground lamb**
1 tablespoon **tomato paste**
1 tablespoon **ground allspice**
1 tablespoon **kosher salt**
1½ teaspoons **Armenian red pepper paste** or finely chopped **roasted red peppers**
1½ teaspoons **sweet paprika**
1 pound **plum tomatoes**, diced

1 medium **red onion**, chopped
1 small **red bell pepper**, chopped
½ cup chopped **fresh flat-leaf parsley**
1 medium **garlic clove**, minced
Lemon wedges (optional), for serving

1. MAKE THE DOUGH: In a large bowl, stir together the flour, milk powder, yeast, salt, and 1 cup room temperature water until it forms a shaggy dough. You may need to add more water to get the dough to come together into a rough ball—if so, add it 1 tablespoon at a time, mixing after each addition. Knead on a floured surface until it's smooth and springs back to the touch, 4 to 5 minutes. Let the dough rest, covered with a clean kitchen towel, in a warm place until doubled in size, 30 minutes or up to 1 hour. At this point you can proceed with the recipe or cover the bowl with plastic wrap and refrigerate for up to 2 days. Bring it back to room temperature before proceeding.

2. MAKE THE TOPPING: In a medium bowl, combine the beef, lamb, tomato paste, allspice, salt, red pepper paste, and paprika. Gently mix in the diced tomatoes, onion, bell pepper, parsley, and garlic until well distributed—avoid overmixing.

3. Preheat the oven to its highest temperature, preferably with a pizza stone or foil-lined sheet pan in it.

4. On a lightly floured surface, divide the dough into 12 pieces (to do this, cut the ball of dough in half, then in half again, then divide each quarter into 3). Roll each piece into a round about 8 inches in diameter and about ⅛ inch thick. Put 3 to 4 tablespoons of filling in the center of the round and use a spoon to spread it out nearly to the edge, leaving a ¼- to ½-inch border all around.

(recipe continues)

5. Depending on the size of your stone or baking sheet, bake the lahmajoun in batches until they start to brown but the dough is still soft enough to fold over—the meat layer will be completely cooked by the time the dough is done. There are no rules for the time and temperature: The hotter the oven and stone, the shorter the baking time—and the tastier the lahmajoun. In a home oven that can reach 500°F, it should take 6 to 8 minutes to bake.

6. Serve warm. Lahmajoun are served folded over, sometimes with a squeeze of lemon, a yogurt dip, or the traditional Armenian Ayran yogurt.

Note: For a vegetarian alternative, see Vegetarian Lahmajoun Topping (right).

Vegetarian Lahmajoun Topping

MAKES ENOUGH FOR TWELVE 8-INCH LAHMAJOUNS

2 medium **tomatoes**, cut into ¼-inch cubes
1 small **zucchini**, cut into ¼-inch cubes
1 small **eggplant**, cut into ¼-inch cubes
1 medium **waxy potato**, cut into ¼-inch cubes
1 small **yellow onion**, diced
1 small **green bell pepper**, cut into ¼-inch pieces
½ bunch **fresh flat-leaf parsley**, chopped
4 fresh **basil leaves**, chopped
4 fresh **mint leaves**, chopped
1 tablespoon **red pepper paste** or finely chopped **roasted red peppers**
1 tablespoon **extra-virgin olive oil**
1 tablespoon **pomegranate molasses**
1 teaspoon **kosher salt**
Pinch of **sumac**

In a large bowl, mix together the tomatoes, zucchini, eggplant, potato, onion, bell pepper, parsley, basil, mint, red pepper paste, olive oil, pomegranate molasses, salt, and sumac. Use this filling the same way you would use the meat filling. You can use it immediately, or keep it in an airtight container in the refrigerator for up to 24 hours before using.

URGENT HEROISM IN BEIRUT

On August 4, 2020, a massive explosion rocked the port of Beirut, Lebanon. Hundreds were killed, thousands injured, and hundreds of thousands displaced from their homes. The tragedy was unimaginable.

Aline Kamakian (pictured right), a writer and Lebanese Armenian culinary ambassador, was on the terrace of Mayrig, her fine-dining Armenian restaurant. She was meeting with her management team just five hundred meters—about the length of five soccer fields—from the warehouse where tons of ammonium nitrate detonated. The compression of the explosion threw Aline and her staff to the floor and she lost consciousness. The next thing she remembers, she was performing CPR on a colleague—an instinct, maybe, from her days as a Girl Scout. She and other members of the team who could walk carried those who couldn't downstairs to get them in cars headed for the hospital. She brought five of her team members to safety; twenty-five members of the team needed to be hospitalized. Eventually, she found that she had broken several ribs and lost hearing in one ear. Many members of her team lost their homes, and the restaurant was left in ruins.

Heroism flourished that day. The whole of the city was impacted by the explosion, and within hours, teams of volunteers started the painful and arduous task of cleaning up. The city was littered with broken glass from destroyed cars and buildings. Beirutis—including an army of young people—mobilized to take care of the mess.

The WCK team arrived in the city within thirty-six hours of the blast and quickly got in touch with another legend of Beirut's food scene, Kamal Mouzawak, one of the nation's leading advocates for local agriculture. Kamal founded Souk el Tayeb, Lebanon's first modern farmers' market, in 2004 and has been a vocal supporter of the country's farmers and food producers (try Kamal's freekeh on page 246). He also started a series of restaurants, Tawlet, run by women from around the country who serve dishes from their hometowns.

Kamal and the WCK team quickly established a community kitchen at one of the Tawlet locations, distributing meals to the city's volunteer cleanup crews, first responders, and displaced families. Within a week, Aline's team was back at work, cooking thousands of meals from her other restaurant, Batchig. The menu featured comforting dishes like molokhia, a traditional Sunday stew, plus sandwiches and easy-to-carry wraps, including falafel, shawarma, kafta, and Aline's Lahmajoun (page 85).

In the aftermath, Aline and two members of WCK's local team, Reem and Tiffany, launched a new project, Sawa Blessed—"together blessed"—to continue

the hard work of keeping displaced Beirutis fed. Kamal, too, kept his community kitchen running out of the one remaining Tawlet location, serving 2,000 meals a day alongside the farmers and food producers of Souk el Tayeb. The horror of the port explosion underscores the perpetual need to be ready, to be prepared to act with urgency. Leaders like Aline and Kamal—and thousands of people committed to helping—are the heroes that every community needs to overcome an unimaginable crisis.

MARCUS'S SPICED CATFISH SANDWICHES

Marcus Samuelsson, the chef behind Harlem's famous Red Rooster, is among the first to the frontlines whenever WCK calls. Throughout the pandemic, his restaurants in New York, Newark, and Miami served hundreds of thousands of meals. "When my team and I put together our weekly WCK menus," Marcus said, "we always made it a point to bring fresh and vibrant flavors to the forefront of the meals we offered." This Haitian-inspired catfish sandwich is a great example. It's a perfect combination of spicy, savory pan-fried fish, tangy pikliz, and a bright, verdant aioli made from culantro (see page 31), aka shado beni. The recipe is flexible, and Marcus encourages adaptation: Try a different bread, swap in red snapper for the catfish, and if you can't find culantro, you can approximate the flavor using a combination of parsley and cilantro.

MAKES 4 SANDWICHES

SHADO BENI AIOLI
1 cup **mayonnaise**
Juice of ½ **lime**
1 bunch (about 2 ounces) **shado beni** (culantro) or 50/50 **fresh parsley leaves** and **fresh cilantro leaves**
2 medium **garlic cloves**, peeled
1 tablespoon minced **fresh ginger**
½ **Scotch bonnet pepper**, seeded (leave the seeds in for a hotter aioli)
1 small **shallot**, peeled
Kosher salt and **freshly ground black pepper**

SPICED CATFISH
4 teaspoons **pimentón** (smoked paprika)
4 teaspoons **Wondra flour** (see Note)
2 teaspoons **chipotle chile powder**
2 teaspoons **ground cumin**
2 teaspoons **kosher salt**
4 skinless **catfish fillets** (6 to 8 ounces each)
2 tablespoons **canola oil**

ASSEMBLY
4 (6-inch) **Haitian bread rolls**, **ciabatta**, or **sub rolls**, split and toasted
Pikliz (page 290)

1. MAKE THE SHADO BENI AIOLI: In a food processor, combine the mayonnaise, lime juice, shado beni, garlic, ginger, Scotch bonnet, and shallot. Blend until smooth. Season with salt and black pepper to taste. Set aioli aside until ready to assemble the sandwiches, or refrigerate in an airtight container for up to 1 week.

2. MAKE THE SPICED CATFISH: In a small bowl, combine the pimentón, Wondra, chipotle chile powder, cumin, and salt. Rub the catfish fillets on both sides with the spice mixture and let sit at room temperature for 15 minutes.

3. Meanwhile, in a large cast-iron skillet, heat the oil over medium-high heat until shimmering.

4. Gently transfer the fillets to the skillet and cook undisturbed until the spice rub turns dark brown and the bottom half of each fillet turns opaque, about 4 minutes. Flip and cook until the other side is also dark brown and opaque, another 3 minutes. Transfer the fillets to a plate.

5. ASSEMBLE THE SANDWICHES: Spread some aioli on each side of the rolls. Place one piece of catfish on the bottom half of each roll, followed by about ½ cup pikliz and the top of the roll. Serve.

Note: Wondra flour is a brand of instant flour, meaning it's been precooked and dried. It's great for getting crispy surfaces when frying. It's generally available at American grocery stores, but if you can't find it, you can make a reasonable substitute by mixing 2 cups all-purpose flour with 1 teaspoon cornstarch, then sifting the mixture twice.

HOW TO BUILD A SANDWICH

BETWEEN 2 SLICES OF BREAD

Ham and cheese (the classic, our way): 3 slices deli ham, 2 slices cheese (usually American), and a generous spread of mayoketchup (see Spreads, right). If you can get local ham, use it. In western Kentucky we were lucky to serve Col. Newsom's Aged Kentucky Country Ham.

Turkey and cheese: Replace the ham with 3 slices deli turkey.

Tuna salad (the usual): Water-packed tuna, flaked and mixed with mayo, celery, a little mustard, salt, and pepper. Made better with pickles for crunch and a splash of hot sauce.

Salami, cheddar, cucumbers: Savory from the salami, crunchy and fresh from the thinly sliced cukes, with the sharp bite of cheddar. An immediate favorite from Poland.

Chicken salad: A regular in the rotation, mostly when we have leftover chicken. Raisins are great for some sweetness and keep better than the more classic grapes.

ON A ROLL

Fried tilapia: Created in Haiti for one of WCK's first projects at Pwason Beni, a fish restaurant attached to the nonprofit Partners in Health's orphanage, which also ran a bakery on site. Pan-fried tilapia, Pikliz (page 290), some mayo.

Fried eggs, basil aioli, roasted tomatoes: Cook those eggs on a sheet pan! See how in Basil Aioli Breakfast Sandos (page 96).

Pulled pork: A beloved option from our friends at Excaliburger, a longtime WCK partner in Arkansas. Try it with leftover Pork al Pastor (page 60).

Ham salad: Chef Mi-Sol Chevallier whipped this up in Port-au-Prince using leftover deli ham and a healthy dose of spicy Scotch bonnet oil.

WRAPPED AND STUFFED

Vegetable wraps: Julienned carrots, sprouts, sliced cukes, hummus, maybe some olives—can't go wrong.

Chicken burritos: Rice, beans, shredded chicken, and whatever other add-ins you want—from cheese to salsa to avocado. We delivered burritos in an amphibious vehicle to a flooded Louisiana community after Hurricane Barry.

Breakfast burritos: As above, but replace the chicken with scrambled egg. On Election Day 2020, we served them hot in Fairbanks, Alaska, to people waiting in the −22°F chill.

Baleadas: Large tortillas stuffed with refried beans y más, folded over taco-style; we've made thousands in Honduras and Guatemala, stuffing them with everything from refried beans to ham and cheese (see Baleadas Sencillas, page 99).

Arepas: A griddled, flat masa pocket stuffed with a variety of fillings—Venezuela's answer to the sandwich (page 109).

Sandwich djej: Roasted chicken with garlic toum (Lebanese garlic sauce) rolled up in a flat, pocketless pita, Beirut-style.

SPREADS

Mayo: The basic. José swears by it. In 2018, an article ran in the *New York Times* proclaiming "José Andrés Fights Starvation with Mayo."

Mayoketchup: A 50/50 ketchup/mayo upgrade courtesy of Puerto Rico (chopped garlic and cilantro are common additions; exact recipes are up for debate).

Advanced mayoketchup: Add some dried oregano for aroma.

Polish special sauce: Ketchup, mayo, mustard, and dill mixed into cream cheese—a novel take on special sauce.

Dijonnaise: Dijonnaise is as popular in Spain as mayoketchup is in Puerto Rico: Combine 1 part mayonnaise to 1 part Dijon mustard.

MÁS MAYO!

The sandwich line is the beating heart of any World Central Kitchen relief response. WCK-style sandwiches are not that complex: Take 2 slices of bread, add sliced ham or turkey, sliced cheese, and a healthy—and we do mean healthy—dollop of mayo-ketchup, a Puerto Rican-bred, José-endorsed blend of mayonnaise and ketchup that gets generously slathered on both sides of each bread slice. ("Más mayo!" we all hear echoing in our heads, long after the day is over.)

Constructing the sandwich is only part of the recipe, which also calls for long tables, many hands, a song or two, good conversation, and plenty of patience. A well-oiled sandwich line can produce 1,000 sandwiches an hour, 10,000 in a day—day in and day out. Each one will then be placed in a brown paper bag with a piece of fruit and sometimes a container of salad, closed with a WCK sticker, and sent out the door to hungry families, first responders, and, well, anyone who needs lunch on the go.

We've done sandwich lines on six continents and in dozens of countries. In Colombia, where we cooked alongside Venezuelan chefs who had fled their home country, we made arepas stuffed full of cheese and avocado for refugees on the long road to safety (see Refugees and Migration, page 100). In Beirut, Lebanon, our sandwich line churned out meaty kafta and hummus sandwiches with parsley and sumac for the volunteer cleanup crews after the deadly explosion in the city's port. In The Bahamas, we made spicy tuna sandwiches to serve a community on the Abaco Islands who don't eat ham for religious reasons. No matter where we are, we're quick to construct and distribute these compact, mobile meals within hours of hitting the ground—whether or not they're bound by mayo.

Maybe mayo is a metaphor for the oil that keeps the sandwich assembly machine running smoothly. On the sandwich line, collaboration is vital, as are problem-solving skills: Are you going to lay out all the bread on the table and make open-face sandwiches, then go back through and add the tops? Or do you lay the bread out back-to-front for quick construction, at the cost of vital table space? What feels like a strategic use of table space could cause you to lose time by taking two trips down the line. Should you spread mayoketchup with a spoon, or did someone find a squeeze bottle in the kitchen? (Trick question! Squeeze bottles are inefficient!) We've seen it all, and every decision counts. When that sandwich line is humming, it's a thing of beauty to watch and a near-religious experience to take part in. And it all starts with mayo.

BASIL AIOLI BREAKFAST SANDOS

When you need to fry a couple of eggs, you reach for a frying pan. But when you want to make beautifully sunny-side up eggs for thousands? Time for an easy trick: Bake the eggs on a sheet pan. We served this sandwich during Chefs For Feds, our response to the 2018 to 2019 US federal government shutdown. Federal employees went weeks without pay, so we set up a kitchen halfway between the White House and the Capitol, serving sandwiches and hot soups to bring comforting warmth on those cold winter days. We love this veggie version, with soft roasted tomato and a bright green basil aioli, but you can easily add bacon or ham if you like a meatier breakfast sandwich.

MAKES 4 SANDWICHES

OVEN-ROASTED TOMATOES
4 **plum tomatoes**, halved lengthwise
2 tablespoons **extra-virgin olive oil**
3 **garlic cloves**, peeled
5 **fresh thyme sprigs**
Kosher salt and **freshly ground black pepper**

BASIL AIOLI
1 tablespoon **pine nuts**
½ cup **fresh basil leaves**, torn
2 **garlic cloves**, peeled
1 teaspoon **fresh lemon juice**, plus more to taste
½ teaspoon **kosher salt**, plus more to taste
½ cup **mayonnaise**

SHEET PAN EGGS
4 large **eggs**
Cooking spray or **extra-virgin olive oil**
Kosher salt and **freshly ground black pepper**

ASSEMBLY
4 **kaiser rolls**, split, or 8 slices **sandwich bread**
Extra-virgin olive oil
8 slices **provolone** or **cheddar cheese**
2 cups **baby arugula** (about 2 ounces)

1. MAKE THE OVEN-ROASTED TOMATOES: Preheat the oven to 400°F. Line a sheet pan with foil.

2. In a medium bowl, combine the tomatoes, olive oil, garlic, and thyme sprigs. Season with salt and pepper and toss until fully coated. Arrange the tomatoes, cut-side up, in a single layer on the prepared pan. Roast until the tomatoes are soft and bubbling, 40 to 50 minutes.

3. MEANWHILE, MAKE THE BASIL AIOLI: On a small sheet pan or in an ovenproof skillet, toast the pine nuts in the oven until fragrant and golden brown, about 5 minutes, stirring once. Remove the pine nuts from the oven and let cool in the pan.

4. Once the pine nuts are cool, add them to a small food processor along with the basil, garlic, lemon juice, and salt. Pulse until roughly chopped. You may need to scrape down the sides several times. Add the mayonnaise and blend until fairly smooth. Adjust the flavor with more salt and/ or lemon juice as needed. Transfer to an airtight container and set aside.

5. MAKE THE SHEET PAN EGGS: Once the tomatoes are finished, remove from the oven, transfer the tomatoes to a plate and set aside to cool. Leave the oven on for the sheet pan eggs and increase the temperature to 425°F. Discard the foil from the sheet pan and re-line with parchment paper. Place it on the middle rack of the oven to preheat for 10 minutes.

6. Crack the eggs into a liquid measuring cup. Once the sheet pan is preheated, remove it from the oven and place it on a flat surface. Working quickly, mist cooking spray onto the center of the hot sheet pan, coating it generously to prevent sticking. Pour the eggs from the measuring cup onto the center of the sheet pan, then carefully return the pan to the oven. Bake until the egg whites are set but the yolks are still jiggly, about 5 minutes, or until desired doneness. Sprinkle the eggs with the salt and pepper.

7. ASSEMBLE THE SANDWICHES: While the oven is still hot, lay the rolls out on another sheet pan, cut-side up. Brush each half roll or slice of bread with olive oil and bake them until they are warm and toasted. (Or toast them in a toaster oven.)

8. Spread 1 tablespoon of the basil aioli on each of the roll halves or bread slices. Using a knife or cookie cutter, cut the sheet pan eggs into 4 equal pieces, making sure the yolk is close to the center. Place an egg on the bottom of each roll or on 4 of the bread slices. Top with 2 tomato halves, 2 slices of cheese, and some of the arugula. Close the sandwiches and serve.

Note: Use store-bought flour tortillas if you'd prefer. You'll need 6 tortillas measuring 10 to 12 inches across.

BALEADAS SENCILLAS

Baleadas can be as sencilla (Spanish for "simple") or complex as you want them to be. At their most basic, this Honduran-born, pan-Central American staple is flour tortillas stuffed with refried beans, crema, and crumbly cheese and then folded over. Decisions include: Do you want to make your own refried beans? Your own tortillas? Want to add scrambled eggs, grilled chicken, or grilled steak? If you're making the Guatemalan version, do you include guacamole, mayo, cabbage, and scallions (like the thousands we served there and in Honduras when back-to-back hurricanes Eta and Iota followed nearly the exact same path of destruction through Central America in 2020). If you're making hundreds at once, it's easy to set up a production line with all the ingredients at the ready; for home cooking, though, it's probably smart to choose just a few fillings. Follow the recipes for the basic baleada below, and choose your own adventure from there.

MAKES 6 BALEADAS

FLOUR TORTILLAS (OPTIONAL; SEE NOTE)
3 cups **all-purpose flour**, sifted, plus more for working the dough
1½ cups **vegetable shortening** or **lard**
2 tablespoons **dried milk powder**
1 tablespoon **kosher salt**
1 tablespoon **baking powder**
2 teaspoons **sugar**
1 cup **warm water**
Vegetable oil, for the rolling pin

FILLING
12 large **eggs**, in omelets (see page 113) or your favorite scrambled egg recipe
2 cups **Refried Beans** (page 296) or **canned refried beans**
1 cup **sour cream** or **crema**
1 cup crumbled **queso fresco**

1. TO MAKE HOMEMADE TORTILLAS: In a large bowl, combine the flour, shortening, milk powder, salt, baking powder, and sugar and mix together with a fork or your fingers until it resembles coarse meal. Add the warm water slowly and start mixing with a wooden spoon until the dough holds together. Dump it out onto a clean counter dusted with flour and knead the dough until it's smooth and no longer sticks to your hands, 10 to 15 minutes, re-flouring the surface as needed (if the dough is very sticky, add flour 1 tablespoon at a time). Lightly flour the bowl and set the dough in it. Cover with plastic wrap or a clean kitchen towel and set aside at room temperature for about 2 hours.

2. Divide the dough into 6 equal portions and use a cupped hand to shape them against your surface (don't use any flour) into balls. Place a ball of dough onto a silicone mat or very clean work surface and roll it, from the center out, using a lightly oiled rolling pin, until it's about 1/16-inch thick—you can make them slightly thinner or thicker, and it will just affect the pliability of the final tortilla.

3. Heat a griddle, nonstick pan, or cast-iron skillet over medium heat. Cook the tortillas (the rolled homemade ones or store-bought ones) for 1½ to 2 minutes per side (slightly less for store-bought), until they're soft and pliable and starting to get a nice toasty brown in spots. If the tortilla is too crispy, it won't fold easily. Heat all the tortillas and set them aside wrapped in a clean kitchen towel to stay warm while you get the fillings—scrambled eggs, refried beans, and anything else you want—ready.

4. To serve, spread a layer of refried beans on each tortilla, then add a few spoonfuls of the eggs on one side and top with some sour cream and queso fresco. Fold the whole thing in half and serve immediately.

REFUGEES AND MIGRATION

The origin story of WCK is built around our work in the wake of natural disasters, but feeding migrants and refugees escaping manmade crises became a key piece of our mission for many years. People fleeing economic insecurity, political persecution, violence, and hunger can find themselves vulnerable to a range of challenges on their journeys. Many families are forced to live without a system of support.

2018, Tijuana, Mexico: WCK started working in the El Barretal refugee shelter, which was established in response to an influx of families arriving at the US-Mexico border from Central America. We quickly set up a kitchen, and within days we were serving thousands of meals daily, mostly to women and children arriving at the shelter. That Christmas, we served a full turkey dinner—and Santa even made a surprise appearance.

In the years since then, there has been a steep increase in the number of people arriving at the border. They are not only fleeing poverty and violence, but climate change, too—many farmers whose crops have failed are forced from their homeland and want to seek asylum in the US, a process that may take years, if it happens at all. In the meantime, families are often stuck near the border waiting for their cases to be heard—for days, weeks, months . . . or even years.

Teresa "Tere" Picos, who started managing the WCK kitchen in Tijuana in late 2018, met thousands of refugees. She designed the menus with them in mind, making sure nothing got too repetitive (her recipe for chilaquiles, a Monday favorite at the shelter, is on page 130). WCK and Tere hired migrants to work with her in the kitchen, teaching them kitchen skills, and also learning about their culinary traditions. The dishes they created together became a beautiful combination of dishes from Mexico, Honduras, El Salvador, and beyond; a pan-Latin menu that made everyone feel at home.

2019, Colombia: After a particularly fraught few months in Venezuelan politics, we started to feed refugees fleeing the country in Cúcuta, Colombia, just over the border. We established a kitchen and quickly added more kitchens along the migrants' route. The paths they traverse, especially a 125-mile, 9,000-foot ascent from Cúcuta to Bucaramanga, are particularly dangerous. On this road, we met thousands of Venezuelans, many of whom suffered from serious health problems and malnutrition. They shared stories about hyperinflation in their country: how a pound of meat suddenly cost a month's salary and how impossible it was to buy milk for their children.

For many Venezuelans, walking that dangerous path was the only option, considering that the alternative was staying home and starving to death. Some people

In 2018, WCK began serving meals at El Barretal,
a shelter for refugees near the US-Mexico border.

we met said they were heading to Medellín, the second-largest city in Colombia, where they thought they could find work; others planned to travel farther afield, to Peru, Panama, or Mexico. Many left without a plan beyond knowing they just couldn't stay.

Early on, it was mostly men making the dangerous trip, but as conditions worsened, we started seeing entire families. Along the route, there are Refugios de Paso—shelters of passage—where Venezuelans can rest, bathe, eat a healthy meal, and receive free medical services and clothing. We served millions of meals at these outposts, and one day we heard a shout: "We are eating meat! Fruit! Chicken! We haven't been able to eat like this for a long time."

2021, a global response: In August, quickly following a rapid offensive by the Taliban and subsequent withdrawal of American troops, many Afghan citizens felt they had no choice but to flee home and restart their lives thousands of miles away. The sudden exodus led to families being stuck traveling by plane for days at a time, with only the bags they had hastily packed and nothing to eat but airline snacks.

Some of these families had never before left Afghanistan. WCK welcomed them with a hot meal as they landed in the United States, Spain, and Qatar. In the DC area, we worked with local Afghan restaurants to provide familiar dishes for the new arrivals, serving fresh meals just as they waited to clear customs at Dulles Airport. Some restaurants we partnered with were run by Afghan refugees who themselves fled during earlier conflicts. "I was a refugee in the 1980s, so to give them a meal from the heart after they've been traveling for days, it tells them there's someone here who understands them," one restaurant owner, Khaleeq Ahmad, shared with our team.

In Madrid, Spain, we worked with Nadia Ghulam, a chef and writer who grew up in Afghanistan. (Her recipe for qorma-e-nakhod, a chickpea stew with a creamy goat cheese sauce, is on page 190.) Her own childhood was ravaged by war in the 1980s—her house was bombed, knocking eight-year-old Nadia into a six-month coma. Healing took years. At the age of eleven, she realized the only way she would survive in Afghanistan was to dress as a boy—which she did for ten years before moving to Spain for medical treatment. "I was really happy to be able to give something to my people," Nadia said about her work feeding Afghan refugees. "I am so glad I can do something for my country, even if it's far away. I'm glad they are not feeling alone, they can feel like there's someone who loves them."

2022, Ukraine: Early in the year, we found ourselves amid another refugee crisis, this time due to the Russian invasion of Ukraine. Within hours of the initial attack, families started fleeing their homes across the country—it's estimated that more than six million Ukrainians left to neighboring countries, with up to an additional ten million displaced internally. WCK quickly established operations on the western border with Poland, setting up warm, comfortable welcome stations, as well as in four other countries bordering Ukraine and two that accepted refugees.

In Przemyśl, a city in southeast Poland just a few miles from the Ukrainian border, we set up a huge cooking operation, one of the largest kitchens we'd ever run. We had chefs join us from around the world, including refugees from Ukraine and Polish locals who wanted to support their neighbors. Many of the refugees expressed the same thing: They wanted to feel busy, to make themselves useful. "If you're not busy, you think all the time about Ukraine and the people that stayed there. Work helps to think about something else," one of the volunteers at our kitchen told us.

In Ukraine, we worked with hundreds of restaurants to serve cities under siege, cook for towns that had been under Russian occupation, and feed families forced to flee their homes for safety. In cities like Lviv and Dnipro, both of which absorbed hundreds of thousands of displaced families, the local community of restaurants stepped up to take care of their fellow citizens, joining the fight the best way they could: by cooking. Chef Yurii, who runs one of WCK's partner restaurants in Lviv, in western Ukraine, told us that his brother joined the army at the beginning of the war—and that he decided to keep cooking. "It's more than just food and calories. When a person gets out of a train and tastes a warm cup of soup of their homeland, they feel they are needed and not forgotten—it's like a mother's hug," Yurii said.

———

In all of these cases, the work we do feels urgent and necessary. People don't leave their homes unless they have to—most migrants and refugees want nothing more than to stay in their communities. They are fleeing a host of issues—personal, political, economic, social—and carry more weight than just their bags. When we meet them on the road, it's just one step of the way on a very, very long journey—so we do the best we can to fill their stomachs and their hearts for the short time our paths cross.

In the middle of these sometimes horrific, always devastating crises, it can seem trite to think about the impact of a sandwich or arepa. But food is always a pressing concern, and relieving that concern improves a person's day. Sure, it gives them the calories they need to continue on, but more than that, it soothes them. It's a new, good memory. It's representation. We try to make meals that feel true to where we are, that have a connection to the community. People have been migrating forever, and many of these dishes have ancient ties for travelers—tamales have been around for 10,000 years and are one of the first on-the-go meals (with a biodegradable wrapper); arepas evolved from travel-friendly cornmeal patties dating back 2,000 years.

It's heavy stuff to contemplate, but understanding these dishes and their origins helps give context to the human condition as a whole. At the end of the day, if we make these recipes, reflect on their history, and consider what they mean to the people who created them and have kept them relevant, maybe our understanding for others—and our empathy—can grow.

AREPAS

This recipe comes from Gaby Maria Chirinos, a Venezuelan cook who joined WCK in Cúcuta, Colombia, on the border with Venezuela, to help us cook for refugees (see Refugees and Migration, page 100). Many Venezuelans and Colombians eat arepas every day—they're the perfect size for traveling and can be filled with whatever you like: ham, cheese, egg, carne mechada (shredded beef). The stuffing we most commonly made for Venezuelan migrants was the simplest: perfectly ripe avocado and stringy Venezuelan queso llanero, a mild aged cheese. Gaby says that "any Venezuelan who respects himself eats arepas with cheese and avocado"—but we won't judge if you want to stuff yours with the kitchen sink.

MAKES EIGHT 4-INCH AREPAS

DOUGH
2 cups (135 grams) **yellow** or **white masarepa** (see Note)
1 teaspoon **kosher salt**
2 to 3 cups **lukewarm water**
Vegetable oil, for forming and cooking the arepas

SERVING
4 tablespoons **unsalted butter**, at room temperature
2 **avocados**, sliced
2 cups **shredded cheese**, such as Venezuelan queso llanero, mozzarella, or queso Oaxaca
Kosher salt

1. MAKE THE DOUGH: In a medium bowl, combine the masarepa and salt. Slowly add the water (the amount of water needed depends on the brand of masarepa, so check the bag), mixing with your hands until you get a soft dough—it should have the consistency of wet sand or loose polenta, and you should be able to shape the dough without it cracking. When the mixture is smooth and lump-free, let it rest for about 10 minutes.

2. Divide the arepa dough into 8 equal portions and shape into balls. Oil your hands with some vegetable oil, then form each ball into a flat disk about ½ inch thick. The oil will help prevent the dough from sticking, so reapply as needed.

3. Heat a griddle or heavy skillet over medium-high heat and brush with oil.

4. Add the arepas to the griddle and sear over high heat until golden and crispy on both sides, 3 to 4 minutes per side. Reduce the heat to low and cook for another 5 minutes or so per side until they're slightly puffed up and cooked through—when you split one open, it should be dry all the way through, without too much dough sticking to the knife. (It may take some testing to understand when the arepas are cooked—one Venezuelan WCK team member says that describing the correct texture is like describing why a rainbow is beautiful . . . there are no words.) Alternatively, after searing, you can transfer the arepas to a baking sheet lined with foil or parchment paper and place them in a preheated 350°F oven until the outside is crisp and golden and the insides are cooked through, 7 to 8 minutes.

5. TO SERVE: Carefully split the arepas open with a wet knife. To serve the arepas as a true Venezuelan would, slather some butter inside each arepa and fill with slices of avocado and the shredded cheese. Sprinkle with a little kosher salt.

Note: Masarepa is precooked corn flour that's designed for arepas. It comes in yellow or white—either works for this recipe. We prefer the brand P.A.N.

MRS. OBAMA'S BREAKFAST TACOS

Once a week it's steak night at the Obama household: "It's a big part of our family tradition—and when our girls are around, sitting down for a meal means so much to all of us," Mrs. Obama says. The next morning there are usually leftovers, which can mean only one thing: breakfast tacos. This recipe, Mrs. Obama's favorite way to use the leftover steak, comes from chef Tafari Campbell, who worked for the Obamas in the White House and continued on with the family. It's a great dish for kids—Mrs. Obama says that the eggs and steak are healthy proteins that fuel our bodies, while the mushrooms add nutrients and an extra savory hit of umami. The WCK Relief Team has been happy to incorporate this dish into our rotation of breakfast options—sometimes we set it up as a station, inviting kids (and their parents) to add whatever toppings they like. We don't usually reveal whose recipe it is, but it's an honor to be able to share a meal from someone who knows as much about good food and nutrition as this former First Lady.

SERVES 4

PICKLES
6 **Fresno chiles**, seeded and sliced lengthwise in ¼-inch strips
1½ cups **distilled white vinegar**
¼ cup **sugar**
2 **garlic cloves**, smashed and peeled
1 **bay leaf**
1 medium **red onion**, sliced

STEAK
2 teaspoons **fine sea salt**
1½ teaspoons **chipotle chile powder** or **regular chili seasoning**
1½ teaspoons **granulated garlic**
1½ teaspoons **light brown sugar**
1 teaspoon **freshly ground black pepper**
1 teaspoon **mustard powder**
1 teaspoon **ground ginger**
⅛ teaspoon **ground cinnamon**
8 ounces **boneless rib-eye steak**, cut against the grain into ½-inch-thick slices

MUSHROOMS
2 tablespoons **extra-virgin olive oil** or **avocado oil**
2 tablespoons **unsalted butter**
8 ounces sliced stemmed **cremini, oyster, shiitake,** or a mix of mushrooms
1 medium **shallot**, halved and thinly sliced
1 **pasilla chile**, seeded and thinly sliced
1 medium **garlic clove**, minced
1 tablespoon chopped **chipotle pepper in adobo sauce**
Kosher salt and **freshly ground black pepper**

EGGS
6 large **eggs**
2 tablespoons **milk** or **water**
2 tablespoons **unsalted butter**
¼ cup shredded **Monterey Jack cheese**

TACOS
8 (6-inch) **corn tortillas**
Crumbled **Cotija cheese**
Chopped **fresh cilantro**

1. MAKE THE PICKLES: The night before you make the tacos, in a small saucepan, combine the chiles, vinegar, sugar, garlic, bay leaf, and ½ cup water and bring to a boil. Once the sugar has dissolved, remove from the heat and transfer the chiles and their pickling liquid to an airtight container. Add the onion to the container and refrigerate overnight.

(recipe continues)

2. PREPARE THE STEAK: In a small bowl, combine the sea salt, chipotle powder, granulated garlic, brown sugar, black pepper, mustard powder, ground ginger, and cinnamon. In a medium bowl, combine 2 tablespoons of the steak seasoning and the sliced steak and mix to coat the meat well. (You'll have a small amount of steak seasoning left over. Keep it in an airtight container at room temperature and use on a future steak.) Set aside while you start cooking the mushrooms. (Alternatively, do as the Obamas do and just use leftover steak!)

3. COOK THE MUSHROOMS: In a medium cast-iron skillet, combine 1 tablespoon of the olive oil and 1 tablespoon of the butter and set over medium-high heat until the butter is melted. Add the mushrooms, stir to coat them in the fat, and cook undisturbed until the mushrooms are beginning to get golden brown, 5 to 7 minutes. Stir them a few times with a wooden spoon, then add the shallot, pasilla, and garlic. Continue cooking until the mixture begins caramelizing, another 3 to 5 minutes. Add the chopped chipotle and season to taste with salt and black pepper.

4. Transfer the mushrooms to a heat-resistant bowl. Wipe the skillet clean and return it to the stove over medium-high heat. Add the remaining tablespoon each of olive oil and butter, then add the steak and sauté on both sides until browned and cooked to your desired temperature—between 1 to 2 minutes for rare and 3 to 5 for well done. Return the mushrooms to the pan with the steak for a quick reheat and set both aside.

5. MAKE THE EGGS: In a medium bowl, whisk together the eggs and milk until light and fluffy.

6. In a nonstick medium skillet, melt 1 tablespoon of the butter over medium heat and swirl to coat the skillet. Add half of the beaten eggs to the skillet and cook undisturbed until the eggs have set on top. Add half the cheese in a row perpendicular to the handle of the pan. Using a spatula, gently roll the eggs away from you while tipping the skillet down. The eggs will roll onto themselves into thirds. Roll the eggs onto a plate and repeat the process with the remaining butter, eggs, and cheese. Cut each omelet into quarters and set aside.

7. ASSEMBLE THE TACOS: In the cast-iron skillet (make sure to wipe it out first) or nonstick skillet, warm the tortillas over medium heat for 30 seconds to 1 minute on each side, until they start to get a little color to them.

8. Place one omelet quarter onto each of the tortillas. Top with the spicy mushrooms and a few pieces of the steak. Garnish each taco with the pickled Fresnos and onions, Cotija, and cilantro and serve immediately.

ADAPTATION

SHEET PANS, PAELLA PANS, AND VARIATIONS

You know what happened? We needed a restaurant, and they gave us their restaurant. We needed a car park, and [we] got a car park. And we began cooking sancocho, the best sancocho in the history of mankind. And we began making sandwiches, the best sandwiches with mayo in the history of humankind. And then in the parking garage we began getting food trucks. And we began getting paella pans. Paella pans! A crazy guy called Manolo came from Miami wanting to cook rice. He and his team have done hundreds of thousands of arroz con pollo, day in and day out.

—JOSÉ ANDRÉS, *WE FED AN ISLAND*

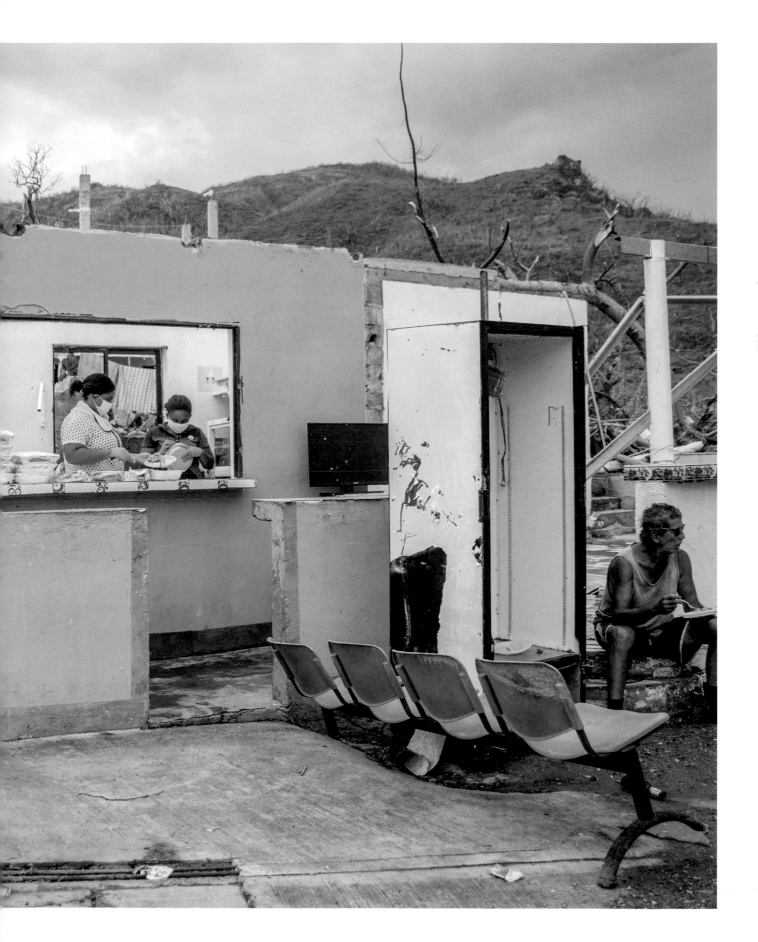

IT'S BECOME A BIT OF A JOKE AT WCK—WE DON'T HAVE MEETINGS. If we need to talk something over with colleagues, it's a chat, quick call, or grabbing a cup of coffee . . . never a meeting. This stems from something deep in the DNA of the organization: We adapt, we don't plan, and if you're in a meeting, you must be planning.

Instead, we are very comfortable reading the wind and reacting to the circumstances. We have to be. Earthquakes are completely unpredictable. Wildfires will jump a ridge and take off in a new direction. Volcanoes might be quiet one minute and spouting molten lava the next. As José has said, "Hurricanes don't listen—you can't tell them which way to turn." As disaster responders, we deal with nature—and have to do everything in our power just to keep up.

Adaptation is the ultimate unteachable skill, but it's right in the wheelhouse of professional chefs who are constantly jury-rigging broken appliances, discovering new sources for difficult-to-find products, and jumping in on any station in the kitchen that's lagging behind. It sets WCK apart from organizations that respond to disasters with a plan in place, hashed out through meetings—meetings!—all codified and structured. Some teams sit in an air-conditioned office and plan their response for days, weeks, months—and some just start cooking.

The nature of disaster really makes it impossible to plan before we hit the ground anyway. After Hurricane Dorian tore through the Abaco Islands in the northern Bahamas, we were the first relief organization to arrive. We flew in with boxes of sandwiches ready to distribute, and to gather intelligence about who needed what, and where, within hours of the storm passing. Our team quickly set up a base in an abandoned yacht club in Marsh Harbour where we could distribute meals that we flew in from Nassau twice each day.

Power was out across the island. There were generators, but they ran on diesel—and there was no diesel. But we were in a yacht club, which was full of grounded ships that ran on . . . diesel! So, with the permission of local shipowners, the team siphoned fuel from the ships to power the generators, quickly helping us get to work.

Loading meals to reach remote islands however we can from the Abaco Islands in The Bahamas, 2019.

The recipes in this chapter are a collection of dishes we've created and adapted over the years for a variety of situations, kitchens, and tastes. We can make them anywhere at any time—in fully equipped hotel kitchens and tiny middle school cafeterias. The outcomes may vary, but we always aim to make the best product we can, something we'd be proud to serve our families.

YOU CAN'T TELL A HURRICANE WHICH WAY TO TURN; ALL YOU CAN DO IS *REACT* TO THAT TURN.

Sometimes we'll take a classic recipe—enchiladas, for example—and we'll change the method to facilitate feeding a crowd, as with our lasagna-like Layered Vegetable Enchiladas (page 134) or the Venezuelan-esque Sheet Pan Pepito (page 143). Some dishes are infinitely adaptable: We've made some version of Classic Mac and Cheese (page 151)—a simple base recipe into which you can fold nearly any other recipe in this book—on many of our relief responses. You'll find recipes from two WCK friends and partners: Kafta Bil Bandora (page 141) from Reem Assil and Chicken Parmesan (page 148) from Ayesha Curry. And yes, you get to try the famous Arroz con Pollo (page 147) from Manolo—the "crazy guy" mentioned in the quote from *We Fed an Island* (page 114)—who came to Puerto Rico from Miami wanting to cook rice.

You can't tell a hurricane which way to turn; all you can do is *react* to that turn. For WCK, we want to ensure we're in the right place to start work once it does.

MOLLIE'S HERBED CHICKEN POT PIE
with Biscuits

———

Chicken pot pie became a go-to during our pandemic response in Washington, DC, where we had dozens of volunteers cooking at Nationals Park, the District's temporarily shuttered baseball stadium. This recipe, which comes from WCK chef Mollie Kaufmann (pictured on page 124), who has cooked in upscale restaurants throughout the city, is a superlative version—a simple but silky sauce coats shredded chicken, carrots, and peas, with a subtle herbal background from sage and thyme. The biscuits are made ahead of time and then refrigerated until it's all baked together. It's an easy recipe to multiply and great to share with neighbors or friends who need comfort—you can keep the filling and unbaked biscuits separate and give instructions for how to construct the final dish. "It somehow became my signature dish, and I'm not quite sure why," Mollie says. "But as long as everybody loves it, it can be mine."

SERVES 4 TO 6

BISCUITS
2 cups (240 grams) **all-purpose flour**, plus more for shaping

1 tablespoon **baking powder**

1 tablespoon **sugar**

½ teaspoon **fine sea salt**

6 tablespoons (85 grams) cold **unsalted butter**, plus 1 tablespoon, melted, for brushing

¾ cup (170 grams) **whole milk**

FILLING
4 tablespoons **unsalted butter**

1 small **yellow onion**, diced

2 medium **garlic cloves**, minced

1 tablespoon chopped **fresh sage**

3 **fresh thyme sprigs**

1 **bay leaf**

2 medium **carrots**, peeled and diced

2 **celery stalks**, diced

½ cup **whole milk**

3 tablespoons **cornstarch**

1½ cups **chicken stock**, homemade or store-bought

4 cups shredded **cooked chicken** (see Note on page 124), dark and white meat

1 cup **frozen peas**

1 teaspoon **kosher salt**, plus more to taste

1 teaspoon **freshly ground black pepper**, plus more to taste

1. MAKE THE BISCUITS: In a medium bowl, combine the flour, baking powder, sugar, and salt. Using the largest holes of a box grater, grate the cold butter into the bowl and work it into the dry mix with your hands until it has the texture of coarse sand. Add the milk and stir gently with a fork just until the mixture comes together into a wet dough.

2. Line a baking sheet with parchment paper. Turn the dough out onto a clean, lightly floured counter. Gently press it out with your hands into a rectangle about 1 inch thick. Fold into thirds like a letter and gently press it with your hands again to make a 1-inch-thick rectangle of dough. Using a 2- to 3-inch round biscuit cutter (or a clean glass about the same size), cut 6 to 8 biscuits (depending on the size of your cutter) from the dough—cut them out as close together as possible to minimize scraps. Place the cut-out biscuits on the lined sheet pan. Press the dough scraps together, reflour the surface if needed, and reroll into a 1-inch-thick sheet (refrigerate the dough for 10 or 15 minutes if it's too soft to work with). Cut out more biscuits, if possible, and discard any remaining scraps. Refrigerate the sheet pan of biscuits while you make the filling.

3. Preheat the oven to 450°F.

(recipe continues)

4. MAKE THE FILLING: In a large Dutch oven or heavy-bottomed ovenproof pot, melt the 4 tablespoons butter over medium heat. Add the onion, garlic, sage, thyme, and bay leaf and gently sauté, stirring regularly, until the onions are translucent and everything is fragrant, 4 to 5 minutes. Stir in the carrots and celery and sauté until fragrant, about 5 minutes.

5. In a small measuring cup, combine the milk and cornstarch with a fork or whisk and mix until smooth.

6. Add the chicken stock to the vegetables and bring to a simmer. Once the liquid is simmering, add the cornstarch mixture and bring to a boil. The mixture should start to thicken within a few minutes. Add the chicken, peas, salt, and pepper and stir to combine until everything is well distributed. Taste and season with additional salt and pepper, as needed. Remove the bay leaf.

7. Take the biscuits out of the fridge and arrange them on top of the filling, or you can bake them directly on the lined sheet pan. Brush the biscuits with the melted butter. Bake until the filling is hot and bubbling and the biscuits are golden brown and cooked through, 15 to 20 minutes.

8. Serve immediately in bowls, topping the chicken filling with a biscuit or two.

Note: **One 3-pound whole roasted chicken (or rotisserie chicken) should yield 4 cups of shredded meat. Or, you can poach 3 medium boneless, skinless chicken breasts or 5 to 6 boneless, skinless thighs in simmering salted water until they're cooked through, about 15 minutes for breasts and 12 minutes for thighs. Leftover turkey from Thanksgiving also makes a great pot pie!**

THE SPIRIT OF WCK

Sometimes you meet people whom you instantly feel like you've known forever. Such is the case with four women from different corners of the world, who have enmeshed themselves in WCK and who so profoundly understand and embody the mission. They have changed the course of the organization through their work and their hearts, always jumping in to do more.

Chef Elsa Corrigan (pictured on page 127, top) is a superstar volunteer who first worked with WCK in Hawaii in 2018, followed by stints in California (where she lives part-time, and has responded to more than a dozen wildfires), The Bahamas, Australia, Mozambique, and beyond. Elsa spent years running restaurants in Fiji and California—sushi is her specialty—but when her time running Mamasake near Truckee, California, started to wind down, she looked for a different way to dedicate her talents. Elsa saw that World Central Kitchen was active in Hawaii, responding to the eruption of the Kilauea volcano—and, remembering how Hurricane Katrina devastated parts of New Orleans, she wanted to use her skills to help communities during disasters and hopped on a plane for Hawaii.

"I started working in the kitchen and learned my first and most valuable lesson from the other volunteers that were around me," Elsa said. "We were not just there to make as much food as possible or as fast as possible, but WCK was providing a place for people who were impacted to feel useful, to distract them from the slow-moving disaster we were all a part of. We were there to take their minds off it for a while."

This is a theme we see everywhere: Communities want to get involved in WCK operations not just to feed people but to become part of their community's recovery. "My usefulness would not just be getting food to the people who were affected, but in helping people to help as well," says Elsa.

But don't let Elsa understate her usefulness at getting food to people—she's one of our stalwart kitchen team members. In fact, a few of her recipes have become famous on the wildfire frontlines, like her Chicken Chili Verde (page 167), which has wowed enough wildland firefighters throughout Northern California that they ask for it by name: "Is that Chef Elsa's chili . . . ?"

———

Rima Aritonang (pictured on page 127, bottom right), WCK's country lead in Indonesia, joined our team as a translator in 2018 when we responded to an earthquake and tsunami that struck Central Sulawesi, with major damage affecting the city of Palu. Rima had, until recently, been working as a teacher at the Alliance Française in Balikpapan, a city across the Makassar Strait from Palu. When the tsunami hit Palu, a friend called her to ask if she could help translate for a humanitarian aid organization coming to assess the damage. Rima is fluent in French—she's taught the language for nearly a decade and lived in southern France for two years—but she worried her English wasn't strong enough. When she learned that the WCK team needed her to help shop for ingredients and supplies at local markets, she agreed to do it—her mother is a chef and caterer, so Rima is familiar with the language of food.

The WCK team arrived and started working to source fresh ingredients in Balikpapan to send to Palu, where nothing was available in the aftermath of the storm. We quickly hit a snag—Indonesian officials wouldn't let us fly the products in. "It was not as simple as I would have imagined, even to help people, even when we wanted to help people, we were struggling," Rima remembers. The work was strenuous—by day Rima and the WCK team pleaded with local officials to let them bring aid, and by night they stocked up on more ingredients and supplies. After six days, we were told we could travel—as long as all the ingredients were locally purchased. "We felt like we won a lottery. We were very happy."

Since then, Rima has become WCK's lead for any crisis in Indonesia—from earthquakes to the Covid pandemic. "I've learned to be more grateful for the life I have, the family I have. For the food that my family has on the table," she says. Rima shared her mother's recipes for Sayur Gori (page 204), a savory vegan jackfruit curry, and a Beef Rendang (page 51), which is so famous that friends and family who travel away from Indonesia ask her to make a large batch to bring with them, for a familiar taste of home.

———

In 2017—when Hurricane María hit Puerto Rico—Chef Karla Hoyos (pictured bottom left) was working for Bon Appétit Management Company, a large institutional catering company, in Indiana. She was philanthropically minded, donating her time and skills to fundraising for nonprofits and foundations. Karla was raised in a family where giving was encouraged: When Santa Claus visited her family in Veracruz, Mexico, he would leave a note with her toys: "You have to pick one of the gifts you asked for and give it to a less fortunate child." She had also worked in disasters before; when a hurricane hit Veracruz, Karla, who was running a catering company at the time, cooked for a community of three hundred people who had been displaced by the storm.

So, when José called his friend Fedele Bauccio, the CEO of Bon Appétit, to recommend chefs to join the team in Puerto Rico, he knew who to turn to. Karla quickly packed and left for San Juan. When she arrived at our home base of El Choliseo, she became central to the operation, helping to run the kitchen and keeping things moving. It wasn't easy; power was out, days were long, and even getting a coffee was difficult. But Karla was relentless. "I was thinking, 'Do I really want to go back to my air-conditioned house and watch TV when there's so much help that needs to be done?'" She stayed for more than a month.

After the effort in Puerto Rico ended, Karla took on a new post: She joined José's kitchen team at The Bazaar in Miami as executive chef. She stayed close to WCK throughout her time at The Bazaar and after, traveling and cooking whenever possible. Karla has worked with our team in The Bahamas, Poland, Bangladesh, Haiti, Türkiye, and beyond. "Working in disaster relief isn't anything like cooking in a normal kitchen . . . 'adaptation' should be part of the job description for a relief chef," Karla says.

Karla's recipe for Creamy Curry Pasta (page 133) comes from her time working in Haiti after an earthquake hit the country's south in 2021. "When I activate a kitchen, I look at three things: What equipment do we have, how many meals are we cooking, and what product do we have to work with?" In Haiti, the answers were challenging: The kitchen she was working in only had three paella pans in which to cook 10,000 meals a day. There was limited cold storage, so everything would have to be delivered daily. Logistical complexity led to this beautifully simple one-pot dish.

———

Kim Stemple (pictured right) volunteered with WCK in early 2019 during the brief but intense Chefs For Feds response to the US federal government shutdown. Kim was full of life, with a personality that commanded a room. If she hadn't told us, we would never have known that she was in hospice care at the time, having been diagnosed a decade earlier with multiple autoimmune diseases. Regardless, Kim wanted to make sure that her final days were dedicated to keeping her neighbors fed. She was so excited on her first day of volunteering; as a former teacher, she loved connecting with the other volunteers. She returned every day she could, often with her son, Connor, to manage our kitchen's inventory.

Kim, an avid runner, founded an organization called We Finish Together, whose mission is to collect donated sports medals, add personal messages of hope, and distribute them to people who need a dose of kindness. She embodied many

values that World Central Kitchen holds dear—empathy, joy, and resilience. But above all, Kim believed in the power of hope. She wanted to be a source of spreading hope, ensuring people knew that in their darkest times, others were there beside them and that they were cared for. In her final days, and through her work with WCK, Kim was a steady source of hope, love, and compassion for everyone who worked with her. Though she is no longer with us, her bottomless well of empathy and care continues to inspire.

These women are emblematic of so many who have worked with us around the world, inspiring by their action and personifying the spirit and mission of World Central Kitchen.

CHILAQUILES

Teresa "Tere" Picos (pictured on page 121, top left) ran the WCK operation in Tijuana, Mexico, from 2018 to 2022, when we transitioned to a local partner to sustain the work. Tens of thousands of migrants and refugees from throughout Latin America and the Caribbean have come through Tijuana on their way to seek asylum in the US (for more about our work in Tijuana, see Refugees and Migration, page 100) and WCK was there to feed them. These chilaquiles came about one day when our chef team left for another emergency, putting Tere on the spot with the day's menu. It was a busy Monday, so she made the easiest thing she could think of: chilaquiles made from tortilla chips topped with red salsa and served with fried eggs, avocado, beans, and cheese. This version is perfect for a vegetarian brunch, but feel free to add some slow-cooked Braised Pork al Pastor (page 60) or Chicken Chili Verde (page 167) to make it a meatier meal.

SERVES 4

RED SAUCE
3 tablespoons **vegetable oil**
1 small **white onion**, finely chopped
3 **garlic cloves**, chopped
1 to 2 **serrano chiles** or small **jalapeños**, halved, seeded, and finely chopped
½ cup **chicken stock** or **vegetable stock**, or more as needed
1 pound **plum tomatoes**, quartered
3 small **dried guajillo chiles**, stemmed and seeded
3 small **pasilla chiles**, stemmed and seeded
2 cups canned or jarred sliced **nopalitos** (cactus pads), drained and chopped
2 cups **fresh spinach**, roughly chopped
½ cup finely chopped **fresh cilantro**
Kosher salt and **freshly ground black pepper**

CHILAQUILES
4 to 8 **sheet pan eggs** (from Basil Aioli Breakfast Sandos, page 96) or your favorite fried egg recipe
2 cups **Refried Beans** (page 296) or store-bought
24 ounces **tortilla chips**
½ cup **sour cream**
½ cup crumbled **queso fresco**
1 **red onion**, finely chopped
½ cup **fresh cilantro** leaves
2 **avocados** (optional), cubed

1. MAKE THE RED SAUCE: In a heavy-bottomed medium pot or Dutch oven, heat the vegetable oil over medium-low heat. Add the onion, garlic, and fresh chiles and sweat, stirring regularly, until the onions are translucent and the chiles are soft, about 10 minutes.

2. Add the chicken stock, tomatoes, and dried chiles to the pot. Bring to a simmer and cook, stirring occasionally, until the tomatoes are softened and broken down, about 20 minutes.

3. Using a hand blender, blend the sauce until smooth. (Alternatively, let the sauce cool for at least 15 minutes, then combine in a stand blender until smooth and return to the pot.)

4. Add the nopalitos, spinach, and cilantro and bring to a simmer over low heat. Simmer until thickened almost to the consistency of a Bolognese meat sauce, about 10 minutes. Season with salt and black pepper to taste. If the sauce gets too thick, add chicken stock or water.

5. ASSEMBLE THE CHILAQUILES: First, make the sheet pan eggs or fried eggs—one or two per person, depending on how hungry the crowd is.

6. Spread about ½ cup of refried beans in an even layer on each plate. On top of the beans, add a layer of tortilla chips. Spoon some red sauce on top, making sure you add nopalitos and spinach to each serving. Place 1 or 2 fried eggs on top. Garnish with a spoonful of sour cream, crumbled queso fresco, red onion, and cilantro. Top with avocado chunks if you'd like.

KARLA'S CREAMY CURRY PASTA

Chef Karla Hoyos developed this recipe while WCK was responding to an earthquake in southern Haiti in 2021; it's the epitome of adaptation (read more about Karla's story in The Spirit of WCK on page 125). The team had to create recipes that included protein, vegetables, and starch all cooked together in one paella pan. The result shows no sign of the restrictions placed on its creation, which were: limited cold storage and just three paella pans to prepare 10,000 meals daily. This is an ingenious one-pot dish where the pasta is cooked in the richly spiced broth, so there's no need to boil it beforehand (similar to our Turkey Bolognese, page 173). The combination of pasta starches and coconut milk makes for an extra creamy sauce, with meatiness from the fish and mussels. Karla only had access to frozen vegetables, which makes the recipe simple to execute, but feel free to chop some fresh carrots, zucchini, and cauliflower.

SERVES 6

½ cup **extra-virgin olive oil**
1 tablespoon minced **garlic**
1 tablespoon minced **fresh ginger**
1 (13.5-ounce) can **full-fat coconut milk**
2 tablespoons **curry powder**
12 ounces **mixed frozen vegetables**
Kosher salt
¾ cup **tomato paste**
1 pound **penne, rigatoni, farfalle,** or **fusilli pasta**
2 pounds **fish fillets** (such as snapper, halibut, or grouper), cut into 1-inch cubes
1 pound **mussels**, scrubbed
½ cup chopped **fresh cilantro**

1. In a Dutch oven, combine the olive oil, garlic, ginger, coconut milk, curry powder, and 8 cups water. Bring to a boil over medium heat.

2. Add the frozen vegetables and 1 teaspoon salt and return to a boil. Add the tomato paste and cook, stirring frequently, until dissolved, about 2 minutes. Add the pasta, stirring frequently so it doesn't stick to the bottom, and cook for 8 minutes.

3. Gently stir in the fish and mussels. Cover and cook until the pasta has absorbed all the liquid, the fish is cooked through and flaky, and the mussels have opened, 5 to 7 minutes. Discard any mussels that haven't opened. Season with salt to taste and serve sprinkled with cilantro.

LAYERED VEGETABLE ENCHILADAS

———

We've prepared enchiladas around the world with many different fillings. The trick in this version is in the construction: Instead of wrapping individual tortillas around filling, we layer them with the enchilada filling, almost like a lasagna. It saves so much time and allows the dish to be easily multiplied—if you want to feed more people, just build it in a bigger pan. We typically bake it in a standard hotel pan, which is enough to feed thirty, but a 9 × 13-inch baking dish is suitable if you're feeding your family (with leftovers, too). Meals like this one allow us to bake in a ton of vegetables without making it feel too wholesome—it's a cheesy, saucy, nourishing way to get kids (and everyone else) to eat the rainbow. You want high-quality tortillas here—if you can find an heirloom corn version, even better—to complement all those veg.

SERVES 6 TO 8

FILLING

3 tablespoons **extra-virgin olive oil**

1 tablespoon **unsalted butter**

1 large **yellow onion**, diced

1 **red bell pepper**, diced

1 **green bell pepper**, diced

½ pound **button mushrooms**, stemmed and sliced

4 medium **garlic cloves**, minced

1 **pasilla chile**, stemmed and seeded

1 medium **zucchini**, cut into ½-inch cubes

8 ounces **spinach**, roughly chopped

½ pound **plum tomatoes**, diced, or 1 (14.5-ounce) can diced **tomatoes**

½ cup **vegetable stock**

Juice of 2 **limes**

2 tablespoons **chipotle adobo paste** or sauce from a can of chipotle peppers in adobo

1 tablespoon **tomato paste**

1 tablespoon **ground cumin**

2 teaspoons **dried oregano**

1 (15.5-ounce) can **black beans**, drained and rinsed

1 cup **sour cream**

½ cup **fresh cilantro**, roughly chopped

2 tablespoons finely chopped **scallions**

1 tablespoon **kosher salt**, plus more to taste

2 teaspoons **freshly ground black pepper**

2 teaspoons **pimentón** (smoked paprika)

ASSEMBLY AND SERVING

16 to 18 (6-inch) **corn tortillas**

2 cups shredded **Monterey Jack cheese**

Guacamole, for serving

Sliced fresh **jalapeños**, for serving

Sour cream, for serving

(recipe continues)

1. Preheat the oven to 350°F.

2. MAKE THE FILLING: In a large saucepan, heat the oil and butter over medium-high heat until the butter is melted. Add the onion and sauté, stirring occasionally, until translucent, 3 to 5 minutes. Add the bell peppers and continue cooking and stirring until they start to soften, 2 to 3 minutes. Add the mushrooms, garlic, and pasilla chile and cook for 3 minutes, stirring occasionally, until the mixture starts to get aromatic. Add the zucchini and continue cooking until it starts to soften, about 2 more minutes.

3. Add the spinach and tomatoes in batches—you'll need to stir in some spinach to get it to wilt before adding another handful. Once the spinach has wilted and the tomatoes are getting soft, stir in the vegetable stock, lime juice, chipotle paste, tomato paste, cumin, and oregano and bring the mixture to a simmer. Reduce the heat to medium and simmer until it's starting to get fragrant, about 5 minutes. Add the beans and let it simmer for 5 more minutes—it should start to thicken a little bit. Discard the pasilla chile.

4. Remove the pan from the heat and stir in the sour cream, cilantro, scallions, salt, black pepper, and pimentón. Taste and adjust the seasoning if needed.

5. ASSEMBLE THE DISH: In a 9 × 13-inch baking dish or a half-size hotel pan, lightly and evenly spread about 1 cup of the enchilada filling over the bottom of the dish. Make a layer in this order: 4 or 6 tortillas (depending on the size of your dish—it's okay if they overlap a bit), 1 cup filling, and one-quarter of the shredded Jack cheese. Make two more layers the same way. Top with the remaining 4 or 6 tortillas and finish with the remaining filling. Set the remaining cheese aside.

6. Tightly cover the baking dish with foil and bake until the sauce is bubbling, about 15 minutes. Uncover, add the reserved cheese, and return to the oven, uncovered, for 5 more minutes to melt the cheese.

7. Let it rest for 5 minutes before serving. Serve with guacamole, sliced jalapeños, and sour cream.

THE WORLD IN A GRAIN OF RICE

If you took a random sample of ten WCK meals throughout the world, six of them would include the same starch: rice. From Indonesia to Madagascar, Ukraine to Louisiana, and throughout the Caribbean and Latin America, rice is the base of many of our meals. And it's obviously not just WCK: Almost half of humanity eats rice daily.

Rice was cultivated independently in two parts of the world: China *(Oryza sativa)* and West Africa *(Oryza glaberrima)*. The Asian species has become dominant nearly everywhere, and almost all varieties of rice you find in grocery stores—jasmine, basmati, glutinous, sushi—are cultivars of Asian rice. African rice still represents a portion grown in West Africa, and one particular strain that's well known in the US, Carolina Gold, very likely originated in Ghana. While a vast majority of the rice we make is Asian rice, the WCK team was able to serve Carolina Gold in North Carolina after Hurricane Florence in 2018.

We serve rice every way imaginable. Rice is often at the heart of the first dishes we make when we start working somewhere, and it's not unusual to have a large part of our operation dedicated to it. In Puerto Rico after Hurricane María, Arroz con Pollo (page 147) and other rice dishes, always cooked in massive paella pans that could make 500 servings at once, became part of our daily rhythm. Oil, sofrito, chicken, broth, rice; serve, clean, repeat. We went through up to 3,000 pounds of rice a day, enough to feed tens of thousands of people.

In Indonesia in 2018, after an earthquake and tsunami hit the island of Lombok, we had to build our kitchen from scratch because so many structures on the island were destroyed. We set aside an area for rice production, run by a local cook named Rozy who single-handedly made 500 pounds of rice a day in four big pots. It was a two-step process: First, the rice was boiled until partially cooked, then steamed to perfection. We served rice with nearly every meal, usually with a healthy dose of spicy Sambal (page 289).

In Madagascar, after a powerful cyclone hit the eastern coast in 2022, we learned how central rice is to life on the island. Every meal is served with it—people eat almost 2 cups of rice a day. Madagascar is near the top of rice-consuming countries in the world, and the grain's importance extends well beyond its place on the plate. It's embedded in the culture and agriculture of the country, too; in fact, if you ask someone to a meal, you "invite them to eat rice."

The crunchy scorched/crispy rice from the bottom of the pot shouldn't be overlooked either—it shows up around the world as a sought-after last bite or as an integral part of a rice dish: In Spain, it's socarrat; in Iran, tahdig; Puerto Rico has pegao; in Haiti, graten; and in Korea, nurungji. Madagascar also has a unique take on it: *ranovola,* which in Malagasy means "golden water." After the crispy bottom bits of rice are saved, water is added to the now-empty rice-cooking pot and boiled to make a toasty, nutty tea, which is served after meals either hot or cold. It helps with digestion and also effectively cleans the pot—a great two-for-one!

By serving rice around the world, we've seen the impact of globalization and the international agricultural system. The story of rice in Haiti is a cautionary tale about global inequity. For centuries, rice has been a major part of the Haitian diet, dating to the slave trade with West Africa; Haiti's rice production probably originated with the West African species. Throughout the nation's history, its farmers had the capacity to grow enough rice to feed the population. But that changed in the 1980s when the country was forced to start relying on imported American rice. There are a few reasons, but the most infamous one was President Reagan's Caribbean Basin Initiative in 1984, which aimed to open Haiti's economy and convert a third of the island's food production—which up until then was meant for local consumption—to export crops. That initiative, coupled with a flood of cheap subsidized rice that the United States started sending in, led to the near collapse of Haiti's rice industry. In turn, thousands of Haitian rice farmers plunged into poverty while industrial American rice farmers prospered. Effects of this policy still reverberate.

It may be humble, but rice is a common denominator connecting history and culture, colonialism and agriculture. We can see the world in a grain of rice: It's part of the best moments of humanity, eating together around a bowl, as well as some of the darkest stories of greed and plunder. We try to use rice as a lens through which to understand the communities where we work and to cook in a way that's respectful and reflective of that culture. It's a lesson we've learned everywhere we go: If you listen and learn and are flexible enough to adapt your system to the local context—and use the right rice!—you'll not only ensure people are fed, you'll do it with love and humanity.

REEM'S KAFTA BIL BANDORA

Growing up in the Boston area, baker and activist Reem Assil's favorite comfort food was kafta bil bandora—juicy meatballs in a spiced tomato sauce. "It was my mother's go-to on busy weekend nights, and she often served it with spaghetti to make us first-generation Arab kids feel a bit more like our American friends." Reem's California, an Arab bakery with locations in Oakland and San Francisco, was one of WCK's strongest partners throughout the pandemic. "We leaned heavily on this comfort dish to feed people who were underserved, overlooked, and food insecure leading up to the pandemic—who were also the ones most heavily impacted in the wake of it." Reem's kafta is not only a delicious adaptation of an Arab classic, it's a metaphor for immigrants' adaptation. Reem's parents came to the US from Palestine and Syria and looked for ways to embrace the familiar while also fitting in. This dish may look like meatballs in red sauce, but when you smell the warm spices, you know it's something special.

SERVES 4 TO 6

KAFTA

1 medium **yellow onion**

1 cup finely chopped **fresh flat-leaf parsley**, loosely packed (about 1 bunch)

1 tablespoon **kosher salt**

2 teaspoons **ground allspice**

1 teaspoon **sumac**

1 teaspoon **ground cinnamon**

1 teaspoon **freshly ground black pepper**

½ teaspoon **freshly grated nutmeg**

2 pounds **ground beef** or **lamb** (or a mix)

RUZ ARABI (SPICED RICE WITH FRIED VERMICELLI)

¼ cup **neutral oil**, such as sunflower or canola

1 cup **vermicelli** or **angel hair pasta**, broken into small fragments no larger than 1 inch

1 cup **basmati rice**, rinsed

2 teaspoons **baharat** (see Note, page 142) or ½ teaspoon **ground allspice** plus 1½ teaspoons **garam masala**

1 teaspoon **kosher salt**

RED SAUCE

1 tablespoon **extra-virgin olive oil**

1 medium **yellow onion**, medium-diced

2 medium **garlic cloves**, roughly chopped

1 (28-ounce) can **San Marzano tomatoes**, whole or diced, undrained

2 teaspoons **baharat** or ½ teaspoon **ground allspice** plus 1½ teaspoons **garam masala**

1 teaspoon **kosher salt**

½ teaspoon **freshly ground black pepper**

ASSEMBLY

2 tablespoons **vegetable oil**

1 teaspoon **sumac**

(recipe continues)

1. MAKE THE KAFTA: Grate the onion on the large holes of a box grater (or process in a food processor) until finely grated. Line a colander with cheesecloth and drain the onions or squeeze out the liquid by hand.

2. In a large bowl, combine the drained onions, parsley, salt, allspice, sumac, cinnamon, pepper, and nutmeg. Add the ground meat and, using your hands, knead the meat into the onion-spice mixture until evenly distributed. Roll the kafta mixture into meatballs the size of ping-pong balls and set aside on a plate or baking sheet.

3. MAKE THE RUZ ARABI: In a medium pot, heat the oil over medium heat. Once the oil is warm, fry the vermicelli, stirring often, until golden, 1 to 2 minutes. Add the rice, stir to coat, and fry, stirring frequently, until the rice smells toasty, about 3 minutes. Add the spice mix, salt, and 2½ cups water and bring to a boil over medium heat. Reduce the heat to low, cover, and continue cooking until all the water is absorbed, about 15 minutes. Uncover the pot and fluff the rice with a fork, then set it aside until ready to serve.

4. MAKE THE RED SAUCE: In a medium saucepan, heat the olive oil over medium heat. Add the onion and sauté until translucent, about 5 minutes. Add the garlic and cook until fragrant and soft, about 2 minutes. Add the tomatoes with their liquid, the spice mix, salt, and pepper. Bring to a simmer over medium heat and cook until slightly thickened, about 10 minutes. Use a hand blender and blend until smooth. (Or carefully transfer to a stand blender and blend with the steam vent open; return to the pan.)

5. ASSEMBLE THE DISH: Line a plate with paper towels. In a large skillet, heat the vegetable oil over medium-high heat. Working in batches, add the meatballs and cook until all sides are browned and the meat is cooked through, about 8 minutes. Remove the kafta to the paper towels to drain.

6. When all the meatballs are cooked, return them all to the pan. Add the sauce and toss to coat. Serve over the spiced rice and sprinkle the sumac over the top to garnish.

Note: Baharat is a spice blend used often in Arab cooking. It's often made with allspice, cumin, coriander, cardamom, cinnamon, cloves, and nutmeg—though exact amounts and spices change depending on who is making it. It can also be known as 7-Spice Mix in Middle Eastern markets.

SHEET PAN PEPITO

Pepito is a beloved Venezuelan street food, a sandwich found on city corners throughout the country. Every stall has its own version, but it's typically served on a big, soft roll; filled with Worcestershire-bathed meat, a tangy avocado relish called guasacaca, and shredded vegetables; and topped with crispy fried potatoes. We've reimagined those elements as a sheet pan meal. WCK first made it in our kitchen in Tijuana as we met Venezuelan families on their way to seek asylum in the US (see Refugees and Migration, page 100, for more). We served it with bread on the side so that homesick refugees could assemble the elements into something familiar. You can do that, too—just bring the whole pan to the table along with some bread or rolls for a DIY Venezuelan street food experience.

SERVES 4 TO 6

MARINATED STEAK
2 pounds **top sirloin**, cut into ½-inch-thick strips
3 medium **garlic cloves**, minced
3 tablespoons **Worcestershire sauce**
1 tablespoon **extra-virgin olive oil**
2 teaspoons **kosher salt**
½ teaspoon **freshly ground black pepper**

GUASACACA
1 large **avocado**
½ cup roughly chopped **green bell pepper**
½ cup roughly chopped **yellow onion**
3 tablespoons chopped **fresh cilantro**
2 tablespoons **apple cider vinegar**
2 tablespoons **fresh lime juice**
2 medium **garlic cloves**, peeled
½ cup **neutral oil**, such as canola
Kosher salt and **freshly ground black pepper**

ROASTED VEGETABLES
½ pound **fingerling** or **baby potatoes**
2 teaspoons **kosher salt**
½ medium head **green cabbage**,
    roughly cut into 2-inch chunks
½ medium head **red cabbage**,
    roughly cut into 2-inch chunks
4 medium **carrots**, peeled and
    cut into ½-inch rounds
1 bunch **scallions**, cut into 1-inch pieces
3 medium **garlic cloves**, minced
2 tablespoons **extra-virgin olive oil**
½ teaspoon **freshly ground black pepper**

SERVING
4 to 6 soft **hoagie rolls**

1. MARINATE THE STEAK: In a medium bowl, combine the sliced meat, garlic, Worcestershire, olive oil, salt, and pepper. Set aside at room temperature to marinate for 1 hour.

(recipe continues)

2. MAKE THE GUASACACA: Scoop the avocado into a blender or food processor. Add the bell pepper, onion, cilantro, vinegar, lime juice, garlic, and 3 tablespoons water and process on low speed while slowly drizzling in the ½ cup oil. Blend for about 3 minutes until very smooth. Season with salt and black pepper to taste. Refrigerate in a covered bowl until ready to serve.

3. Preheat the oven to 425°F. Line a large sheet pan with foil.

4. PREPARE THE VEGETABLES: In a medium pot of water, combine the potatoes and 1 teaspoon of the salt. Bring the water to a boil. Once it reaches a boil, reduce the heat to a simmer and cook the potatoes until they can just be pierced with a fork (you don't want them to be completely tender), about 5 minutes. Drain and let cool. Once cooled, slice the potatoes into ½-inch-thick rounds.

5. In a medium bowl, combine the green and red cabbage, carrots, parboiled potatoes, scallions, garlic, and olive oil. Season with the remaining 1 teaspoon kosher salt and the pepper and toss to combine.

6. Spread the vegetables out on the prepared sheet pan and roast until they begin to soften and become browned and caramelized, about 15 minutes—no need to stir.

7. Remove the sheet pan from the oven and add the marinated meat on top of the roasted vegetables. Return the sheet pan to the oven and roast until the meat is almost cooked through, about 10 minutes longer. Turn on the broiler and place the sheet pan on the upper-middle rack under the broiler until the meat begins to caramelize, about 2 minutes.

8. Serve alongside the prepared guasacaca and soft sandwich rolls, toasted or untoasted.

ARROZ CON POLLO A LA MANOLO

If you can cook arroz con pollo for four people, you can just as easily make it for four hundred. That's the attitude of Manolo Martínez, the chef behind the business Paellas y Algo Más (Paellas and More) and one of the original members of WCK's Chefs For Puerto Rico team (see page 177). Manolo, his family, and dozens of volunteers crewed a circle of huge paella pans—four feet in diameter, large enough to serve five hundred people each—and cooked pan after pan of arroz con pollo, singing songs, both traditional and invented, as they went. At the team's peak, they were cooking more than 10,000 pounds of chicken and 3,000 pounds of rice a day—feeding tens of thousands of people following Hurricane María. You probably don't need to feed quite that many, so we've scaled his recipe way back. It works best in a Dutch oven or other deep pot, but you could pull it off in a 14-inch paella pan. And don't forget the singing . . . it adds a little extra sazón.

SERVES 6

3 tablespoons **extra-virgin olive oil**

1 medium **yellow onion**, diced

5 **garlic cloves**, minced

1 cup **Sofrito** (page 294)

1 **plum tomato**, diced

½ cup pitted **green olives**

3½ pounds **boneless, skinless chicken thighs and breasts**

1 pound (2¼ cups) **medium-grain white rice**, such as **Arroz Rico** or **Botan**

5 cups **chicken stock**, warmed

6 **culantro leaves** (see page 31) or 1 bunch **cilantro**, roughly chopped

Kosher salt and **freshly ground black pepper**

1 cup fresh or thawed **frozen green peas**

1 (12-ounce) jar **roasted red peppers**, drained and diced

Pique (optional; page 293), for serving

1. In a Dutch oven or other heavy-bottomed pot (or if you're feeling ambitious, in a 14-inch paella pan), heat the oil over medium heat. Add the onion, garlic, and sofrito and cook, stirring regularly, until fragrant and the onion is translucent, 4 to 5 minutes. Add the tomato and olives and cook until the tomato is soft, about 5 minutes.

2. Increase the heat to medium-high, add the chicken, and cook, turning once or twice, until it's mostly gone from pink to white on all sides, about 5 minutes. Add the rice and stir until all ingredients are well combined.

3. Add the warm chicken stock, culantro, 1 to 2 teaspoons of salt (depending on how salty your stock is), and a few grinds of black pepper. Bring to a boil over medium-high heat and let cook, uncovered, until all the liquid has evaporated, about 15 minutes.

4. Reduce the heat to low, cover with a lid or foil (carefully crimped around the edges to create a tight seal), and cook until the rice is plump and tender with no crunch at the center, about 20 minutes.

5. Stir the rice to fluff it, then add the peas and roasted peppers and let stand for 2 minutes, until they're warmed through. If you're lucky, you'll have some golden-burnt crunchy rice at the bottom—in Puerto Rico it's called pegao, and it's a treat for the cook (or their lucky children).

6. Serve the arroz con pollo warm, with some pique on the side if you want.

AYESHA'S CHICKEN PARMESAN

Cookbook author and restaurateur Ayesha Curry's chicken parmesan is warm, saucy, cheesy, and absolutely delicious. Ayesha and her husband, NBA's Golden State Warriors superstar Steph, run the Oakland, California-based foundation Eat. Learn. Play., a community organization focused on supporting the youth of Oakland with programs centered on nutrition, education, and physical activity. When the pandemic took our team to hundreds of cities across the nation, ELP became one of World Central Kitchen's closest partners in the area. When the Currys moved to town after Steph was drafted, this chicken parm was the first thing Ayesha made, and it's become a favorite comfort food for the family. Ayesha, like Steph, works best in threes: She sets up bowls for flour, eggs, and bread crumbs for dredging and dunking the chicken before a shallow fry, then bakes it with fresh mozzarella and some marinara. Linguine is the Currys' go-to pasta, but the ball's in your court on that decision.

SERVES 4

¼ cup **all-purpose flour**
Kosher salt and **freshly ground black pepper**
2 large **eggs**
½ cup **whole milk**
1 teaspoon **Dijon mustard**
1¼ cups **panko bread crumbs**
¼ cup grated **parmesan cheese**
4 **boneless, skinless chicken breasts**
Extra-virgin olive oil, for pan-frying
2 cups **marinara sauce**
1 (8-ounce) ball **fresh mozzarella cheese**, cut into 8 slices
Chopped **fresh basil**, for garnish
Fresh **linguine** or your favorite pasta, cooked to al dente, for serving

1. Preheat the oven to 425°F.

2. Set up a dredging station: Place three shallow bowls on the counter. In the first bowl, combine the flour, 1 teaspoon salt, and ½ teaspoon pepper and mix with a fork. In the second bowl, whisk together the eggs, milk, and mustard. In the third bowl, mix the panko with the parmesan.

3. Put each chicken breast between two pieces of plastic wrap or parchment paper and use a kitchen mallet to carefully pound it until it's about ½ inch thick. Pat the chicken dry on both sides with a paper towel and sprinkle each side with a pinch of salt. Dredge the chicken breast through the flour mixture so both sides are lightly coated, patting to remove any excess. Dip the chicken into the egg mixture to coat and finally dredge in the panko mixture, pressing on both sides to get a good crust. Place the breaded chicken on a separate plate and repeat with the remaining 3 pieces.

4. Line another plate with paper towels. Pour 1 inch of olive oil into a large skillet and heat over medium-high heat until shimmering, about 350°F.

5. Using tongs, carefully add 2 of the chicken breasts to the pan (you cook them in batches so they brown properly) and cook until golden brown on the outside but not quite cooked through, 2 to 3 minutes per side. Remove them and place on the paper towels to drain. Repeat with the remaining breasts.

6. Spread half of the marinara sauce in a 9 × 13-inch baking dish. Place the chicken in the dish in a single layer. Spoon the remaining sauce evenly over the chicken. Top each piece of chicken with 2 mozzarella slices.

7. Bake until the mozzarella starts to brown and the chicken is cooked through, 15 to 20 minutes. Serve garnished with chopped basil and over the hot pasta.

CLASSIC MAC AND CHEESE

This simple stovetop mac and cheese recipe has gotten the WCK team out of many tight spots—last-minute requests, higher meal needs than anticipated—and it can do the same for you. Simple, quick, and delicious, it can be revelatory for hungry children more accustomed to boxed versions—but the real magic lies in how adaptable it is (see Variations). Livening it up with chiles—fresh, canned, or pickled—is a natural. Add a spicy ferment like kimchi and create something entirely new. You can serve it with Chicken Chili Verde (page 167) or Firefighter Chili (page 42), or add some leftover Beef Rendang (page 51) or Haitian Griot (page 52); in fact, you'd be hard-pressed to find a savory recipe in this book that doesn't taste good folded into this classic mac and cheese.

SERVES 4 TO 6

Kosher salt

1 pound **pasta**, such as elbows or shells

6 tablespoons **unsalted butter**

2 tablespoons **all-purpose flour**

2 cups **whole milk**

1 teaspoon **freshly ground black pepper**

1 tablespoon **Dijon mustard**

1 pound **sharp cheddar cheese**, shredded

1. In a large pot, bring 4 quarts water and about 2 tablespoons kosher salt to a boil. Add the pasta and cook just to al dente according to the package directions. Drain and set aside.

2. In a medium pot, melt the butter over medium heat. Add the flour and mix constantly with a wooden spoon or silicone spatula until it forms a thick paste (called a roux). Slowly add the milk while stirring to combine the milk and roux, scraping the bottom of the pan (now you're making a béchamel). Keep stirring the béchamel over medium heat until it starts to bubble but not boil, then reduce the heat to low. Add 1 teaspoon salt, the pepper, and mustard and continue to cook until the sauce thickens, about 5 minutes; it should be creamy and coat the back of the spoon.

3. Remove the béchamel from the heat and slowly mix in the cheddar, a handful at a time, stirring to incorporate as it melts before adding another handful. This cheese-enriched béchamel is called a mornay sauce.

4. Add the cooked pasta to the sauce, stir until it's well coated, and serve.

Variations

KIMCHI MAC AND CHEESE (PICTURED LEFT)

Drain 12 ounces **kimchi** and chop. Fry it in the melted butter before adding the flour to make the béchamel. Complete the recipe as directed. Garnish each serving with 1 tablespoon chopped scallions and 1 tablespoon toasted sesame seeds.

JALAPEÑO MAC AND CHEESE

Drain a 7-ounce can of **pickled jalapeños** and chop. Dice 2 fresh jalapeños (reserve some of the fresh jalapeños for garnish). Fry the chiles, both pickled and fresh, in the melted butter before adding the flour to make the béchamel. Complete the recipe as directed. Serve garnished with the reserved fresh jalapeños.

LEFTOVERS MAC AND CHEESE

Complete the recipe, then fold in 2 cups of warmed leftover **Beef Rendang** (page 51), **Braised Pork al Pastor** (page 60), or **Firefighter Chili** (page 42) before serving.

HOPE

STEWS, SOUPS, AND WARMING MEALS

Small ripples of hope can become mighty waves of change.

—ROBERT EGGER

OF ALL THE THINGS YOU CAN LOSE, THE SADDEST MAY BE HOPE: hope for the future, for your family, for yourself. But in the face of a cataclysmic disaster, it's an easy thing to lose. When everything you own and cherish is gone, why would there be reason left to hope? Worry and fear take over: What comes next?

Robert Egger, the founder of DC Central Kitchen and a longtime member of World Central Kitchen's board of directors, preaches the power of hope to bring profound change during these moments (read more about Robert in A New Hope, page 186). To Robert, and to José as well, there is hope in a plate of food. For people trying to figure out how to rebuild, the fuel you get from food is more than a form of calories; it's a chance to change a perspective. When you've been trapped in your own head reliving a trauma, finding a friendly face and a warm meal may not solve your biggest problems, but it can be the difference that improves your day and mindset enough to get you going in the right direction.

BUT HOUSES CAN BE REBUILT, AND MEMORIES LAST FOREVER. THE SUN WILL RISE AGAIN.

We see it everywhere we go. During wildfires, many of the people we meet are living in shelters, not even knowing if their house is still standing. After a hurricane, entire neighborhoods may return to find their roofs ripped off and treasured belongings underwater. Farmers want to know if their crops survived; families don't know what happened to their pets; livelihoods are in question.

But houses can be rebuilt, and memories last forever. The sun will rise again. This is the root of hope, and sometimes a conversation over a warm meal, prepared with care and love, affirms that.

Recipes in this chapter are designed to be warming and comforting, to bring hope even in the darkest times. They're mostly stews and soups, the kind of hearty dishes that satisfy to the core. Sancocho (page 181), the first dish we served to hungry Puerto Ricans after Hurricane María, became a blueprint for much of what we do (see Chefs For Puerto Rico, page 177). José's Red Snapper Suquet (page 157), a dish he prepared in Mozambique after a devastating cyclone, originated with

Catalan fishermen who craved a taste of home while at sea. Soupe Joumou (page 163), a national dish of Haiti that we've served after multiple disasters, is a pumpkin soup emblematic of freedom and hope and the centerpiece of many families' meals on the country's Independence Day. Our recipe for Ukrainian Borsch (page 164) was on the weekly menu at our kitchen in Poland, on the border with Ukraine, where we fed hundreds of thousands of refugees fleeing war, hoping for peace and continued freedom.

Hope is a catalyst. It inspires the feeling that tomorrow is going to be better than today, that things are looking up. With food, we can create a small ripple of hope in someone's day—and you can, too, for a neighbor, friend, or family member. And from there, who knows what mighty waves of change will come?

JOSÉ'S RED SNAPPER SUQUET

Suquet is a classic Catalan fisherman's stew. This version is José's take on the dish, one he made for the team's family meal in Mozambique after Cyclone Idai hit in 2019. He describes it as a "Mozambican-Spanish-Catalan-American fish stew," a dish that could only be made by José, who was once a cook in the Spanish navy. The secret is the Catalan trick of adding picada, a dense paste of almonds, toasted bread, garlic, and olive oil, which thickens the stew. Everything else is more or less negotiable—in Mozambique, José used red snapper, though Catalans like to use monkfish. If you start with a whole 3-pound snapper, you should have enough bones to make a fumet (fish stock) with fillets saved for the soup. If you don't want to make the fumet, use fish stock and about 2 pounds of fillets instead.

SERVES 4 TO 6

1 (3-pound) whole **red snapper** or 2 pounds **red snapper fillets**

PICADA
¼ cup blanched **almonds**
1 tablespoon **extra-virgin olive oil**
3 slices (½-inch-thick) **baguette**
2 medium **garlic cloves**, peeled

SUQUET
4 medium **plum tomatoes**
2 tablespoons **extra-virgin olive oil**
2 medium **garlic cloves**, minced
2 cups **Fumet** (recipe follows) or store-bought **fish stock** (water will do in a pinch, just up the salt)
1 cup **dry white wine**, such as Albariño
1 pound **waxy potatoes**, such as Red Bliss, cut into 1-inch cubes
1 teaspoon **pimentón** (smoked paprika)
Sea salt
Crusty bread, for serving

1. If you are making the fumet (recipe follows), fillet the fish and save the bones and head for the fumet. Cut the fillets into 1-inch chunks and refrigerate until ready to use.

2. MAKE THE PICADA: In a small skillet, toast the almonds over medium-low heat, stirring regularly to make sure they don't burn, until they're starting to brown and release some oil, 3 to 4 minutes. Remove them from the pan and set aside. Add the olive oil to the pan and heat it for 30 or so seconds until it's hot, then add the bread and toast it until golden brown on both sides, about 1 minute per side. Set aside.

3. In a small mortar, crush the garlic with a pestle until it's broken down into a smooth paste. (Or do this in a small food processor.) Add the almonds and pound them together until the almonds are smooth. Add the bread and continue to crush until you have a loose paste. Leave it in the mortar until you're ready to use it.

4. MAKE THE SUQUET: Cut the tomatoes in half and, using the large holes of a box grater, grate the flesh of each half over a small bowl to make a loose tomato sauce, discarding the skins.

5. In a heavy-bottomed pot or large pan, heat the olive oil over medium heat. Add the garlic and sauté until it's fragrant and sizzles, 1 to 2 minutes. Add the grated tomatoes and keep cooking, stirring regularly, until the sauce thickens a bit, 8 to 10 minutes.

6. Add the fumet, wine, potatoes, and pimentón and stir to combine. Cook over medium heat until the potatoes are tender and the liquid has reduced by one-third, 15 to 20 minutes.

7. Taste and add sea salt if needed. Add the chunks of fish and all of the picada and stir to incorporate. Cook until the fish is cooked through, 3 to 5 minutes. Serve warm with crusty bread.

(recipe continues)

Fumet

MAKES ABOUT 2 CUPS

Bones from a 3-pound red snapper, including head if desired
½ tablespoon **kosher salt**
1 medium **yellow onion**, diced
1 tablespoon **black peppercorns**
3 **bay leaves**

1. Rinse the snapper bones and head under cold water. Put them in a medium pot with the salt, onion, peppercorns, bay leaves, and 4 cups cold water. Bring to a low simmer over medium heat and cook until the liquid has been reduced by half, 45 to 60 minutes—skim any foam that rises to the surface.

2. Strain the fumet through a fine-mesh sieve and set it aside. If you use a snapper head, make sure to pick any meat from it and save it for adding to the dish.

THE POT THAT WILL FEED THE WORLD

José Andrés

I'm a dreamer, and I have a very, very big dream, one that could change the entire course of humanity. Let me tell you about it.

There is a famous children's story about an old woman named Strega Nona, who lives in a small Italian village. She has this magical pot in her home that, on her command, makes pasta. Not just a little pasta, but a lot—it makes more and more pasta, until she tells it to stop. The story is funny for children because, one day, her assistant tries to use the pot but doesn't understand the magic and ends up creating so much pasta that it threatens to take over the entire village and wash it away in a sea of noodles. But luckily Strega Nona comes back and stops the pot just in time, then forces her assistant to eat all of the pasta as punishment . . . funny, right?

There are some obvious morals for children in the story, but I'm more interested in that magical pot itself. Where can I get one?! Why have we not invented this pot? Is it a question of physics, a chemical one, a biological one? Or are we just not asking the right questions? Are we not making the right demands of our scientists, our politicians, our farmers, and our technology to get us there?

I can see it clearly in my head, this pot. Think about it: We produce more than enough food on this planet to feed all the people on it. Every day around the world, our farmers grow enough calories for every single woman, child, and man—but still, people go hungry. This is not only unjust, it is inhumane. I believe that food is a universal human right, but the forces of our food systems, of our agriculture, of our politics keep this dream from becoming a reality. Can you believe that in the twenty-first century, there are almost a billion people in the world who go to sleep hungry?

To me, as a proud son of Spain, it's clear that the pot should be filled with paella, but I can imagine all sorts of things that will be filling it: sancocho from Puerto Rico, soupe joumou from Haiti, borsch from Ukraine. It's a culturally adaptive pot; wherever it goes, it makes the foods that are the most comforting, filling, nutritious, hopeful. And sure, maybe if we are in Italy it can make some pasta.

Maybe it's not about the pot at all, but more about what goes *into* the pot. Maybe it's more like the story of Stone Soup than the one about the old Italian lady. Maybe the question is not about science at all, but about humanity . . . if we each bring something small, a little piece of ourselves, coming together to each help in our own way, we can be working together to fill any pot in the world, wherever there's a need.

SOUPE JOUMOU

Soupe joumou is a Haitian celebration of emancipation and independence. During Haiti's long period of colonization, the French forced enslaved Haitians to grow—but wouldn't let them eat—pumpkins. On January 1, 1804, the Haitian people finally gained their freedom through rebellion, and this hearty pumpkin-and-meat soup is served on Independence Day to commemorate the victory. It's also regularly served for Sunday breakfast, but the New Year's version is a little more special, often including the bone from the previous week's Christmas ham. This recipe—which comes from chef Mi-Sol Chevallier, who ran WCK's École des Chefs (see Bringing Haitian Culinary Traditions into the Future, page 55)—works best with calabaza, a flavorful pumpkin found throughout the Caribbean, but kabocha squash is a fine substitution (and butternut will work in a pinch).

SERVES 4 TO 6

1 (3-pound) **calabaza** or **kabocha squash**, peeled, seeded, and cut into rough 2-inch pieces

1 pound **beef brisket**, cut into 1-inch cubes

1 pound **beef shin**, meat separated from the bone and cut into 1-inch cubes (reserve the bone)

1 **ham hock** (optional)

¼ cup **Épis** (page 290)

1 **Scotch bonnet pepper** or **habanero chile**

2 **scallions**, thinly sliced

1 medium **leek**, thinly sliced

1 small **yellow onion**, minced

2 medium **garlic cloves**, minced

½ cup **fresh flat-leaf parsley**, finely chopped

1 teaspoon **kosher salt**, plus more as needed

2 medium **carrots**, peeled and cut into 1-inch rounds

6 **waxy potatoes**, such as Red Bliss, peeled and cut into 1-inch cubes

3 medium **taro roots**, peeled and cut into 1-inch cubes

½ small head **green cabbage**, shredded

1 bunch **fresh thyme**

4 ounces **vermicelli** or **angel hair pasta**, broken in half

Juice of 1 **lime**

1. In a large pot, bring 8 quarts unsalted water to a boil over high heat and add the pumpkin pieces. Boil until the pumpkin is soft enough for a fork to easily pierce it, 20 to 25 minutes. Remove the pumpkin with a slotted spoon and transfer to a food processor, leaving the water in the pot. Carefully puree the pumpkin until smooth, adding a little of the water from the pot if needed, and set aside.

2. Reduce the heat under the pot of water to medium to bring to a gentle simmer. Add the beef brisket, shin (including the bone), ham hock (if using), épis, Scotch bonnet, scallions, leek, onion, garlic, parsley, and salt. Simmer, skimming off any gray foam that rises to the top, until the soup has reduced a bit and is fragrant, about 40 minutes.

3. Add the pumpkin puree, carrots, potatoes, taro, and cabbage and cook until the vegetables are soft, another 20 to 30 minutes.

4. Tie the thyme sprigs with kitchen twine to make a little bundle. When the vegetables are soft, add the vermicelli and thyme bundle to the pot, give it a stir to distribute the noodles, and cook until the noodles are al dente, 4 to 6 minutes. If the soup gets too thick from the noodles absorbing liquid, add another cup of water and stir.

5. Remove the pot from the heat and stir in the lime juice and more salt as needed. Discard the thyme bundle and remove the Scotch bonnet (or make sure your guests don't eat it whole!). Serve hot.

UKRAINIAN BORSCH

Ukrainian borsch—commonly spelled "borscht" outside of Ukraine—is the classic, bright-red, slightly sour beet soup, chock-full of vegetables (and sometimes meat) and topped with a dollop of sour cream and a sprinkle of dill. There are as many recipes for borsch as there are babusias (grandmothers), and at our kitchen in Poland, right on the border with Ukraine, we made many different versions, depending on who was cooking and what recipe their grandmother taught them (for more about our work in Ukraine, see Sharing Joy in a Brutal World, page 270). This hearty vegetarian version quickly became a favorite, full of potatoes, cabbage, and pickles—all of which get beautifully stained by the beets. Some cooks use canned beets as a shortcut, but most babusias insist on starting with raw. It takes longer, but the result pays off in a beautifully crimson, earthy-sweet stock.

SERVES 4 TO 6

3 pounds **red beets**, scrubbed, 2 pounds left whole and 1 pound peeled and diced
3 tablespoons **vegetable oil**
1 large **yellow onion**, finely diced
1 **red bell pepper**, finely diced
3 medium **garlic cloves**, minced
2 **carrots**, peeled and medium-diced
1 tablespoon **Hungarian paprika**
1 **bay leaf**
1 tablespoon **kosher salt**, plus more to taste
¼ teaspoon **freshly ground black pepper**
2 medium **russet potatoes**, peeled and medium-diced
1 small head **green cabbage**, shredded
1 large **dill pickle**, cut into ½-inch cubes, plus ½ cup **pickle juice**
1 cup **sour cream**, for garnish
1 bunch **fresh dill**, chopped, for garnish

1. In a food processor fitted with the shredding blade, shred the 2 pounds whole beets. (If you don't have a food processor, roughly chop them.)

2. Transfer the shredded beets to a 6- to 8-quart stockpot and add 10 cups water. Set the stockpot over high heat and bring to a boil. Once boiling, reduce the heat to low and simmer until the beets are extremely soft and the liquid is deep red, about 2 hours. Strain the liquid through a sieve into a large bowl or container, pressing the cooked beets against the side of the sieve to extract as much liquid as possible. Discard the pulp. Measure the beet stock (it should be 4 to 6 cups) and add enough water to come to 10 cups. Set aside.

3. Rinse out the stockpot. Set over medium heat and add the vegetable oil. Add the onion, bell pepper, and garlic and sauté until softened, 5 to 7 minutes. Add the carrots, paprika, bay leaf, salt, and black pepper and continue to cook until the carrots start to soften, 2 to 3 minutes.

4. Add the beet stock mixture to the pot along with the potatoes and diced beets and bring to a boil. Reduce the heat to medium-low, cover, and cook until the potatoes and beets are fork-tender, 10 to 15 minutes.

5. Add the cabbage and pickle and return to a simmer over medium heat. Cook until the cabbage has wilted, 3 to 5 minutes. Add the pickle juice and cook for 2 to 3 minutes to warm through. The soup should now have a rich red color. Taste and add salt, as needed. Remove the bay leaf.

6. Serve garnished with a dollop of sour cream and chopped dill.

CHICKEN CHILI VERDE

This is a WCK classic. We've served it all over the US, from Eagle Pass, Texas (for migrants and refugees coming north), to Fremont, Nebraska (for families affected by floods), to Redding, California (for wildland firefighters). The glowing reviews are unanimous. That's thanks to its creator, chef Elsa Corrigan (see The Spirit of WCK, page 125). It's super simple to make, has a nice balance of acid and heat (skip the jalapeño to keep it mild), and is versatile enough to serve with rice, warm tortillas, or folded into Classic Mac and Cheese (page 151). In Santa Cruz, California, our team was on the frontlines of a wildfire, bringing bagged meals to firefighters working twenty-four-hour shifts. A guy in front said, "We met your team at the last fire. Is it the green chili? That stuff was incredible." So don't take our word for it . . . this chili has a reputation.

SERVES 4 TO 6

5 **scallions**, trimmed and roughly chopped

1 (28-ounce) can whole or crushed **tomatillos**, drained if whole

1 (27-ounce) can whole **fire-roasted green chiles**, drained

1 **jalapeño** (optional)

4 medium **garlic cloves**, peeled

¼ cup roughly chopped **fresh cilantro**, plus more for garnish

1 tablespoon **olive oil** or **canola oil**

2 pounds **boneless, skinless chicken breast**, cut into 1-inch pieces

1 medium **yellow onion**, diced

Kosher salt and **freshly ground black pepper**

2 cups low-sodium **chicken stock**

1 (15.5-ounce) can **chickpeas**, drained and rinsed

1½ teaspoons **ground cumin**

1½ teaspoons **dried oregano**

1 teaspoon **ground coriander**

Juice of 1 **lime**

¼ cup crumbled **Cotija** or shredded **Monterey Jack** cheese, for garnish

Cooked **white rice** and/or **tortillas**, for serving

1. Measure out ½ cup of the scallion greens and set aside for garnish. Place the remainder in a blender and add the tomatillos, fire-roasted chiles, jalapeño (if using), garlic, and cilantro and puree until just smooth.

2. In a medium pot, heat the oil over medium heat. Add the chicken and onion, season with salt and pepper, and cook, stirring occasionally, until the onion is just translucent and the chicken has lightly browned and isn't sticking to the bottom of the pot, about 10 minutes. Add the chicken stock and scrape the bottom of the pan to deglaze it, then add the tomatillo puree, chickpeas, cumin, oregano, and coriander and stir to combine. Bring to a boil, then reduce to a simmer, cover, and cook until the chili is flavorful and thickened, about 2 hours.

3. Taste and add salt and pepper if needed, then stir in the lime juice before serving. Top each bowl with the reserved scallion greens, cilantro, and cheese. Serve with rice and/or tortillas.

UNIVERSAL COMFORT FOODS

Wherever we cook, we work with local chefs, use local ingredients, and prepare local dishes—it's part of our DNA. World Central Kitchen is nothing without these relationships that guide and support our work as we integrate into a community and respectfully reflect the local culture in our cooking.

We build these partnerships with great intention. And it results in something that's become another critical piece of our DNA, one that happened more organically: The dishes we cook tend to be warming and comforting. You might have already noticed this throughout the book, and—spoiler alert—you'll be reading comforting recipes all the way to the last page. If you want to think of this as a global comfort foods cookbook, you wouldn't be wrong. We're sharing recipes for the dishes that are the most meaningful to families, cultures, and souls in many of the places we've worked. Ingredients, spices, and cooking techniques may vary from place to place, but the search for comfort after a disaster—and hope for the future—is universal.

Comfort food provides a sort of gustatory nostalgia, triggering positive associations and warm memories. Sure, there's the hit of brain-pleasing salt and fat that rushes in with a bite of chicken parm or mac and cheese, but the effect of comfort food goes so much deeper than brain chemistry. It brings us back to a moment of safety and security—feelings often in short supply in the face of difficult times.

And while specific ideas of what comfort food is may differ from place to place, we've found that some dishes have universal appeal, even if they aren't attached to a culture. Wherever we are in the world, unfamiliar flavors and presentations are instantly accepted if a plate is warm and cozy. Suddenly, a food that's a favorite in one place becomes a new go-to halfway around the world, and we find more common ground through the power of the table. Dishes like this make up our canon of comfort foods; a Comfort Food Hall of Fame, maybe.

Bolognese, the famous Italian meat sauce, is a great example. We've cooked versions of Bolognese in nearly every place we've worked, and it's always a hit. Whether it's the classic made with beef and pork, one made with turkey (see page 173), or our vegetarian version with profoundly meaty mushrooms, everyone likes it. "It's rich, it's satisfying, it has everything you'd ever want in a dish," says WCK's chef Fatima Castillo, who lives in Guatemala and has made the dish in at least half a dozen countries. "To me, it's really the most universally comforting food, no matter where you grew up."

We find comfort food all over the map. In Indonesia, Beef Rendang (page 51) is a crowd-pleaser that's easy to adapt for new audiences around the world; we've even folded it into our creamy Classic Mac and Cheese (page 151), combining two hits to make a third. From our very first days in Puerto Rico, Arroz con Pollo (page 147) was a regular part of our kitchen rotation and has become a favorite wherever we cook. Braised Pork al Pastor (page 60) or barbecued pork are dependably comforting for much of the world, even if you didn't grow up in Mexico or the American South. Baker and activist Reem Assil's recipe for Kafta bil Bandora (page 141)—spiced meatballs in a rich tomato sauce—hits some serious childhood memories for kids who grew up in the United States *or* the Levant, and is a prime example of a dish that quickly joins the Hall of Fame.

We're all human and our differences make us unique, special, and interesting. But isn't it comforting when we discover a few similarities as well?

WCK team members in Mananjary, Madagascar, sit together to enjoy family meal, 2022.

TURKEY BOLOGNESE

We have dozens of pasta dishes in our playbook, but this one is our ace in the hole. It's infinitely adaptable, stealthily healthy, and enjoyed by all ages everywhere we serve it. It showcases a simple water-efficient technique: You cook the pasta directly in the sauce (similarly to Karla's Creamy Curry Pasta on page 133), which starts loose and ends up enriched by the pasta's starch—your pasta cooking liquid essentially becomes your sauce. Meaning one less pot to wash—saving time, effort, and precious water.

SERVES 4 TO 6

3 tablespoons **extra-virgin olive oil**

1 medium **yellow onion**, finely diced

2 medium **garlic cloves**, finely chopped

1 small **carrot**, peeled and cut into ¼-inch dice

1 small **eggplant** or 1 large **zucchini**,
    cut into ½-inch cubes

1 teaspoon **ground fennel**

1 teaspoon **ground coriander**

1 **bay leaf**

1 teaspoon **dried oregano**

½ teaspoon **crushed red pepper flakes**

¼ teaspoon **freshly ground black pepper**

Kosher salt

1 pound **ground turkey** (or ½ pound **ground beef**
    and ½ pound **ground pork**)

2 tablespoons **tomato paste**

1 (14.5-ounce) can diced **tomatoes**

4 cups **chicken stock** or **water**

12 ounces **penne pasta**

1 cup grated **parmesan cheese**, for serving

½ cup finely chopped **fresh flat-leaf parsley**,
    for serving

1. In a medium pot, combine 2 tablespoons of the olive oil and the onion and cook over medium heat, stirring frequently, until translucent, about 5 minutes. Add the garlic and carrot and cook, stirring frequently, until the carrots are softened but still crunchy, about 3 more minutes. Add the eggplant or zucchini and cook, mixing well, until the vegetables soften, about 2 more minutes. Add the fennel, coriander, bay leaf, oregano, pepper flakes, black pepper, and ½ teaspoon salt and stir to combine.

2. Add the remaining 1 tablespoon oil and the ground meat and cook, stirring occasionally and breaking the meat up into small crumbles, until no longer pink, about 5 minutes. Add the tomato paste and cook for 2 minutes, mixing to incorporate it into the meat and vegetables. Add the canned tomatoes and stock and bring the sauce to a boil over high heat. Reduce the heat to medium and simmer, uncovered, until the sauce is somewhat reduced and starting to thicken, 25 to 35 minutes. It should have the consistency of a loose chili. Taste and add salt, if needed.

3. Add the pasta to the pot of sauce and mix well to coat and disperse the pasta. Cook, uncovered, stirring every few minutes so that the pasta cooks evenly and doesn't stick to the bottom of the pot, until it's al dente and the sauce is thickened, about 15 minutes. Remove the bay leaf.

4. Taste and add salt and pepper, if needed. Serve with a shower of parmesan and parsley.

FIRE ENGINE

The Bahamas' famous Fire Engine stir-fry of canned corned beef, vegetables, and chiles has two plausible etymologies. The most straightforward is that the name comes from the dish's bright red color, courtesy of a healthy amount of tomato paste. More dramatically, imagine a metaphorical fire engine that's on call to quench the fire caused by an abundance of searingly hot Bahamian goat peppers. This dish was on rotation in our kitchens on Abaco and Grand Bahama, two of the islands devastated by Hurricane Dorian in 2019. We cooked it by the paella panful. To get an idea of how much we were making on the daily, multiply this recipe by a thousand, then do it twice a day . . . for three months. When you make it, you're welcome to use more chiles—just make sure to have the fire department on speed dial! And, yes, canned corned beef might not be standard on your shopping list, but give it a try—it's an inexpensive, shelf-stable protein popular in the Caribbean and around the world.

SERVES 4

2 tablespoons **vegetable oil**

2 cups roughly chopped **green cabbage**

1 medium **yellow** or **white onion**, diced

1 small **red** or **green bell pepper**, diced

2 medium **garlic cloves**, chopped

1 (12-ounce) can **corned beef**

1 **Bahamian goat pepper** or **habanero chile**, stemmed and carefully minced (or substitute serrano or jalapeño for less heat)

2 tablespoons **tomato paste**

1½ teaspoons **ketchup**

1 teaspoon **dried thyme**

½ teaspoon **ground cumin**

1 **bay leaf**

¾ to 1 cup **chicken stock** or **water**

Kosher salt and **freshly ground black pepper**

Cooked **white rice**, for serving

Pique (page 293) or other hot sauce, such as D'vanya's, for serving

1. In a large skillet, heat the vegetable oil over medium-high heat. Add the cabbage, onion, bell pepper, and garlic and cook, stirring regularly, until the onion is translucent, about 5 minutes.

2. Add the corned beef, goat pepper, tomato paste, ketchup, thyme, cumin, and bay leaf and stir to combine. Stir in ¾ cup chicken stock and simmer for 10 to 15 minutes. It will thicken as it simmers. Add the rest of the chicken stock if needed—in the end it should be saucy like Bolognese and not too dry. Season with salt and black pepper to taste. Remove the bay leaf.

3. Serve over rice with hot sauce.

CHEFS FOR PUERTO RICO

There's a photo that holds a central place in the lore of World Central Kitchen. It was taken in Puerto Rico in the days immediately following the destruction caused by Hurricane María, and it features José, Puerto Rican chef Jose Enrique, and a small crowd in front of a bright pink building, serving up clear plastic bowls of stew. In the background is a sign that reads "¡Hay Sancocho!" The restaurant was Jose Enrique's, located in the Santurce neighborhood of San Juan. His regular menu—creative takes on island classics highlighting local ingredients—had to be suspended so the restaurant could shift all of its energy to the production of sancocho and other stews and rice dishes to feed people in the wake of the storm. The team made one dish per day, and they served it until they ran out.

Those early days after María marked a turning point for WCK. José, along with his friend Nate Mook, a documentary filmmaker who became the organization's CEO for five years, flew to San Juan on the first commercial flight to the island after the storm. Beginning with a few chef friends, José got cooking. Soon, a troupe of Puerto Rican chefs, restaurateurs, and food truck owners formed a team

within WCK: Chefs For Puerto Rico (usually stylized, appealing to José's love of social media, as #ChefsForPuertoRico). They started cooking outside Enrique's restaurant, but quickly grew out of the location. They were granted access to El Choliseo, the city's coliseum, enabling them to increase their output to more than 100,000 meals a day.

A new path was set for WCK. "Usually when people think about first responders, in their minds they're thinking firefighters, police officers, people like that," said Yamil Lópcz, one of the core team members. "But they never think that a cook can be a first responder. María changed that perspective." There wasn't much precedent for a project like Chefs For Puerto Rico. José created WCK in the aftermath of the devastating 2010 Haiti earthquake, and he and his team worked to feed people after Hurricane Matthew in Haiti, Hurricane Sandy in New York, and Hurricane Harvcy in Texas, but those were minor undertakings compared to what Puerto Rico needed.

For more than six months after the hurricane, the team cooked, reaching every municipality on the island and serving almost 4 million meals. A staggering 20,000 volunteers worked out of 20 kitchens and 10 food trucks around the island, delivering meals wherever they were needed. It was a feat of passion, perseverance, community, love, and hope for a future that every Puerto Rican could be proud of. (For a deeper dive into the tireless work of the Chefs For Puerto Rico team, read *We Fed an Island*, José's book with Richard Wolffe, published in 2018.)

———

If that photo symbolizes the mission and identity of WCK, the dish being served in it does the same for the specific effort in Puerto Rico. Sancocho is a stew that gets better and better the bigger the batch, so when José and the team went from making sancocho for dozens in a city square to making it for thousands outside of the city's coliseum, the quality didn't suffer—in fact, it actually improved. You can taste it for yourself—our recipe, based on the one we made in those early days after the hurricane, is on page 181. WCK's chef Alejandro Perez, one of the Chefs For Puerto Rico, says a good sancocho is basically "every single root vegetable in Puerto Rico thrown into a pot with corn and pig's feet." This version is more limited in scope—it calls for yuca and potatoes, and the protein comes from pork shoulder and chicken—but feel empowered to dig up as many root vegetables as you can. Throw in a couple of trotters if you have them handy—it will only add to the experience.

The team also made rice—lots of it. They had access to huge paella pans, and Manolo Martínez, owner of Paellas y Algo Más (Paellas and More), a Puerto Rican-based catering company specializing in rice dishes, became the team's go-to for Arroz con Pollo (page 147).* The team cooked in paella pans that spanned four feet. Each yielded about 500 servings and included 175 pounds of chicken and 50 pounds of rice. Daily, they cooked 10,500 pounds of chicken and 3,000 pounds of rice—enough to serve 30,000 people.

"When the paella operation started, we only had a limited amount of produce that we could add to the rice, which led us to be creative in our flavor profiles," remembers Christian Carbonell, a chef on the team. "Going from simple canned vegetables and meat paella to more complex paellas using local produce, herbs, and meats was very satisfying. We always worked with pride in our food no matter the ingredients we had on hand, because the people depended on us. We wanted to brighten their day." It's that small ripple of hope that can become a mighty wave of change, a lesson we learned day in and day out in Puerto Rico.

"The Chefs For Puerto Rico team came together for the same cause," said Stephanie Ortiz, another team member. "We all came from different areas of the island with different situations, but we were united by the same mission." Each of the members of the team, some of whom went on to join World Central Kitchen's staff, were affected by the work they did after María. "We will forever remember that we did something we will always be proud of."

Years later, the group continues to meet up to reminisce and share updates on their lives. They get together at the Miramar Food Truck Park, a circle of food trucks serving a range of cuisines a mile west of where they originally cooked together. It was founded in the years after María by Yareli Manning, one of the original team members, to bring together some of the food trucks that were part of the mission: Yareli's own Meatball Company, Yummy Dumplings (co-owned by Yareli's sister Xoimar and Michael Sauri), Peko Peko, El Churry, Piscolabis, Lemon Submarine, Açai on the Go, and Ocean Deli.

"It would be impossible to remember Hurricane María without going back to the memories and moments we experienced with chef José and WCK," said Yareli. "My profound gratitude for keeping us working to help our Puerto Rican brothers and sisters in one of the most difficult moments of our history. However, it was the family that we built—between volunteers and people from all over the world—that has given us the strength and hope to continue rebuilding the Puerto Rico that we deserve."

A note for anyone concerned about the cavalier use of the word paella here: To a hammer, everything is a nail; to a paella pan, everything is a paella. You may have learned from none other than José Andrés that the one true paella is paella Valenciana, the revered rice dish from coastal Spain that includes chicken, rabbit, and beans. Everything else, to a Valencian, is an arroz con cosas—"rice with things."

SANCOCHO

Sancocho, a hearty stew of meat and root vegetables, was the first dish served by the Chefs For Puerto Rico team after Hurricane María and one we made hundreds of times in the following months (read more in Chefs For Puerto Rico, page 177). The recipe calls for cilantro, but if you want a more robust herbal flavor, look for culantro (aka recao) instead (see page 31). For the full experience, serve this stew with white rice, avocado, limes, and an abundance of hot sauce.

SERVES 6

¼ cup **extra-virgin olive oil**

1 large **sweet onion**, such as Maui or Vidalia, roughly chopped

4 **scallions**, cut into ¼-inch pieces

3 medium **garlic cloves**, roughly chopped

1 (28-ounce) can diced **tomatoes**, drained, or 6 **plum tomatoes**, blanched, peeled, and diced

1 tablespoon **achiote powder** or **sweet paprika**

2 green or half-ripe (closer to yellow) **plantains**, peeled (see Note, page 288) and cut into 1-inch pieces

2 pounds **yuca**, peeled and cut into 1-inch pieces

2 ears **corn**, shucked and cut into thirds

4 **bone-in, skinless chicken thighs**

1 pound **boneless pork shoulder**, cut into 1½-inch chunks

2 cups chopped **fresh cilantro** (including stems) or **culantro**, plus more for garnish

1½ tablespoons **kosher salt**, plus more to taste

4 medium **Yukon Gold potatoes**, peeled and cut into 1-inch pieces

Cooked **white rice**, for serving

2 **avocados**, sliced

2 **limes**, quartered

Pique (page 293), or other hot sauce

1. In a large Dutch oven, heat the olive oil over medium-high heat. Add the onion and scallions and cook until softened and golden brown, 12 to 15 minutes, stirring regularly so they don't burn. Add the garlic and cook until softened and fragrant, about 3 minutes. Add the tomatoes and cook until the tomatoes have broken down, the liquid is reduced, and they are beginning to stick to the bottom of the pot, 8 to 10 minutes.

2. Stir in the achiote and cook for 1 to 2 minutes to combine. Add the plantains, yuca, corn, chicken, pork, 1 cup of the cilantro, and the salt. Add enough water to cover and bring to a boil. Reduce the heat to a simmer and cook, uncovered, until the meat is tender and cooked through, about 30 minutes.

3. With a slotted spoon, transfer the chicken to a plate. Check the pork and if it's tender, add it to the chicken. Otherwise, leave it in while you cook the potatoes. Add the potatoes to the pot and simmer until tender, about 20 minutes.

4. Meanwhile, when the chicken is cool enough to handle, pull the meat from the bones. Chop the meat into small pieces or shred it with your fingers.

5. Return the meat to the pot and stir in the remaining 1 cup cilantro. Cook for 3 minutes more, giving it a good stir so everything blends together. Taste and add salt if needed.

6. Serve the stew hot with the rice, avocado, cilantro, limes, and hot sauce.

LAMB MASSAMAN CURRY

This recipe comes from chef Kelly Eastwood, who runs a cooking school and kitchen in Bermagui, Australia, on the country's far southeast coast. During the 2020 bushfire season—the region's worst on record—WCK partnered with Kelly to cook meals for the many small communities up and down the coast that were affected. Working in Australia during a wildfire presents its own unique situations; at one point, Kelly and the WCK team delivered meals to a wildlife refuge in the small town of Mallacoota, where they were asked to help operate on a frustrated, bandaged-up koala injured in the fire. "You don't want to be attacked by their claws," Kelly says. The koala—and the day—was saved. Kelly cooked with the team for months during the bushfires, and this warming, spiced curry became a favorite. Thai food is very popular in Kelly's community and around Australia, so she regularly made curries as a familiar dish—some of the neighborhood kids even started calling it "muscle-man curry." Fragrant lime leaves (see page 32) are key to the dish, as is a hint of fish sauce at the end.

SERVES 4

CURRY

1 tablespoon **vegetable oil**

1 medium **yellow onion**, medium-diced

4 ounces (about ½ cup) **Thai massaman curry paste**, such as Maesri or Mae Ploy

4 medium **garlic cloves**, minced

2-inch piece **fresh ginger**, peeled and minced

2 (6-inch) **lemongrass stalks**, tough outer part removed, finely chopped

10 fresh or frozen **makrut lime leaves** (dried leaves will also work)

1 **cinnamon stick**

1 **bay leaf**

½ teaspoon **ground cardamom**

½ teaspoon **ground coriander**

½ teaspoon **ground cumin**

2 (13.5-ounce) cans **full-fat coconut milk**

¾ cup **chicken stock**

1½ pounds **lamb shoulder**, cut into ¾-inch pieces

1 pound **white potatoes**, peeled and cut into ¾-inch cubes

1 tablespoon **fish sauce**

1½ tablespoons **light brown sugar**

1 teaspoon **kosher salt**

SERVING

Cooked **white rice** (preferably jasmine)

1 bunch **Thai basil**, roughly chopped

1 bunch **fresh cilantro**, leaves only, roughly chopped

½ cup **unsalted roasted peanuts**, roughly chopped

1 **lime**, cut into wedges

1. MAKE THE CURRY: In a large heavy saucepan or Dutch oven, heat the oil over medium-high heat. Add the onion and cook, stirring regularly, until it begins to soften, 2 to 3 minutes. Add the curry paste, garlic, ginger, lemongrass, lime leaves, cinnamon stick, bay leaf, cardamom, coriander, and cumin and stir constantly for 2 minutes to combine. Add the coconut milk—it may separate, but that's okay. Continue to cook over medium-high heat for another 2 minutes, stirring regularly. Add the stock and lamb, reduce the heat to medium-low, partially cover (lid cracked about an inch), and simmer for 1½ hours; it'll be reduced and aromatic.

2. Add the potatoes and continue to simmer, uncovered, until the potatoes are cooked through, 20 to 25 minutes. You may want to skim some oil off the top of the curry, depending on how fatty your lamb was.

3. Remove from the heat, then stir in the fish sauce, brown sugar, and salt. Remove the lime leaves, bay leaf, and cinnamon stick before serving.

4. TO SERVE: Spoon the warm curry into bowls with rice. Garnish with the Thai basil, cilantro, peanuts, and a lime wedge.

On the eastern coast of Australia, 2020 bushfires devastated communities—WCK worked with local restaurants to feed neighbors in need.

A NEW HOPE

"I'm not in the nonprofit business . . . I'm in the *bravery* business." A conversation with Robert Egger (pictured right), the founder of DC Central Kitchen and a long-time member of WCK's board of directors, is laced with riddles, truth bombs, and nuggets of wisdom honed by a lifetime of both learning and teaching.

When Robert speaks, it's wise to listen. He planted the seed that led to World Central Kitchen's creation. Some might even call him the Obi-Wan Kenobi to José's Luke Skywalker. When José was a young padawan—er, *chef*—in Washington, DC, soon after leaving Spain, he volunteered at Egger's nonprofit DC Central Kitchen. DCCK was founded in 1989 with two major goals: keep food from being wasted, and more importantly, keep *people* from being wasted. The organization functions as a virtuous circle: Formerly incarcerated, jobless, and unhoused men and women are trained in the culinary arts, cooking with "seconds"—imperfect fruits and vegetables that are normally plowed under—to feed unhoused DC residents. The program expanded to institutional catering, keeping itself in business by serving DC public schools and hospitals. It's always had volunteerism at its heart, welcoming anyone and everyone to help with the mission, cooking shoulder to shoulder with people from all walks of life. That's what José saw when he got involved after arriving in DC in the early 1990s.

Fast-forward twenty years. "I'm thinking of calling it World Central Kitchen," José told Robert in 2010 as he schemed up a new nonprofit organization to reinvent how food aid and disaster relief should be done. "So I get DC, and he gets the rest of the world!?" Egger chuckled as he remembers the conversation. The two organizations have different models, but the spirit of DCCK drives WCK: the hope of treating everyone with dignity and empathy, working together to lift up humanity.

Egger now lives in Tatooine-esque New Mexico, where he took on a role as food-security advisor to the mayor of Santa Fe. He got involved in WCK's relief work during the pandemic in 2020, enlisting the help of culinary students at the Santa Fe Community College to cook for their neighbors. Green Chile Posole (page 189), which his team served during the pandemic, is a dish with a long history in the area. Its origins date to pre-Columbian Mexico, and it features the beautifully warming local Hatch chiles. "The posole is a Trojan horse; they don't see it coming." Another riddle from Robert. What he means is that they're not just serving calories or a hot meal to the community, but also culture, history, and local tradition. It's everything good in one bowl, food medicine at a time when it's most needed.

One of José's favorite quotes from Robert is about charity: "Too often, charity is about the redemption of the giver, when it should be about the liberation of the receiver." You just nodded when you read that, didn't you? Because everyone does. *Of course that's what charity is.* How does that fact so often get lost? It's a line that a Jedi could believe in, treating everyone throughout the galaxy with dignity and respect.

ROBERT'S GREEN CHILE POSOLE

"We're fighting hunger with tradition." Robert Egger, a former WCK board member and the founder of the food nonprofit DC Central Kitchen, made this dish with a team of culinary students in a community college kitchen in New Mexico during WCK's pandemic response. (To read more about Robert Egger, see A New Hope, page 186.) This New Mexican take on posole is all about the chiles: True green chiles from New Mexico's Hatch Valley will make this dish the best version of itself, so see if you can find them (they're available frozen online but can get pricey out of season). Hominy, sometimes called posole, is field corn that's gone through the ancient process of nixtamalization (see Hominy, page 31). It's best bought dried and then rehydrated, but you can substitute canned. Plan to use both mild and hot chiles, but Robert says be judicious: "A good posole doesn't burn when you eat it, it just brings up your internal temperature."

SERVES 4 TO 6

1 pound dried **posole/hominy** (see Notes)

1 tablespoon **extra-virgin olive oil**

1 pound **pork shoulder**, trimmed of excess fat and cut into ¾-inch cubes

Kosher salt

1 medium **yellow onion**, chopped

2 large **garlic cloves**, minced

1 tablespoon **dried oregano**, preferably Mexican, plus more for serving

2 small **tomatillos**, husked and chopped

1 teaspoon **freshly ground black pepper**

6 cups **chicken** or **vegetable stock**, preferably low-sodium, or **water**

4 to 6 **fresh green Hatch chiles**, roasted and peeled (seeded if you don't want it too spicy), or 3 (4-ounce) cans chopped Hatch green chiles (see Notes)

Lime wedges, for serving

1. In a large bowl, combine the dried posole with 6 cups water and soak at room temperature for at least 8 hours, or overnight. Drain.

2. In a large heavy-bottomed pot, heat the oil over medium-high heat. Add the pork and ½ teaspoon salt and sauté until well browned, turning the meat regularly, 7 to 10 minutes.

3. Add the drained posole, onion, garlic, oregano, tomatillos, black pepper, stock, 1 teaspoon salt (use less if your stock is not low-sodium), and the green chiles. Bring to a boil, then reduce the heat to medium-low and simmer, uncovered, until the posole has "bloomed" (the individual kernels will appear to have burst open) and is tender, about 3 hours. Taste the stew every 30 to 45 minutes and add salt as needed.

4. Serve hot with lime wedges and more dried oregano, which will add a beautiful floral note.

Notes:

- You can substitute three 20-ounce cans of hominy for the dried posole. Skip the soaking step, then follow the recipe as written, adding the drained hominy when you would have added the soaked posole, and simmer only until the pork is tender, 1 to 1½ hours.

- If you're using canned Hatch chiles, use a blend of hot and mild to give the posole a nice warm heat—double up on the hot if you want it spicier.

QORMA-E-NAKHOD
Stewed Chickpeas with Spinach and Goat Cheese

Sometimes, WCK finds we can provide the most help thousands of miles away from the disaster we're responding to. This was the case in 2021 when the political situation in Afghanistan abruptly changed, forcing thousands of Afghans to flee their homes and homeland. Our teams met them with nourishing plates of food at airports in Qatar, Madrid, and Washington, DC. Many hadn't had a warm meal in days. In Madrid, we worked with Nadia Ghulam, a writer and cook who fled Afghanistan years earlier after having studied and worked for a decade disguised as a boy (for more about Nadia's story, see Refugees and Migration on page 100). This was one of the recipes she shared with our Relief Team—a warm, comforting vegetarian stew of chickpeas and spices, topped with a creamy cumin-flecked goat cheese sauce. "I'm so glad I can do something for the people of my country," Nadia said about cooking for the new arrivals. "Even if they've come a far way, they aren't feeling alone."

SERVES 4

GOAT CHEESE SAUCE
½ cup **whole milk** or **heavy cream**
4 ounces **fresh goat cheese**, crumbled
½ teaspoon **ground cumin**
Kosher salt

STEW
¼ cup **extra-virgin olive oil**
1 large **yellow onion**, finely chopped
2 **garlic cloves**, minced
1 small **red bell pepper**, finely chopped
1 small **green bell pepper**, finely chopped
1 medium **carrot**, peeled and cut into ¼-inch dice
1 cup **tomato puree**
1½ teaspoons **ground cumin**
1 teaspoon **sweet paprika**
½ teaspoon **cayenne pepper**
½ teaspoon **ground turmeric**
Kosher salt
8 ounces **spinach leaves**, roughly chopped
2 (15.5-ounce) cans **chickpeas**, undrained
1½ cups **vegetable stock** or **water**
Freshly ground black pepper
½ cup chopped **fresh parsley**, for garnish

1. MAKE THE GOAT CHEESE SAUCE: In a small saucepan, combine the milk, goat cheese, and cumin. Bring to a simmer over low heat and cook, stirring regularly, for 15 minutes. Don't let it boil. It may break a bit, which is okay. Let the sauce cool to room temperature while you make the stew. Mix it well before serving—it should be thick and creamy. Taste and add salt as needed.

2. MAKE THE STEW: In a medium saucepan, heat the oil over medium heat. Add the onion and garlic and sauté until translucent, 5 to 7 minutes. Add both bell peppers and continue cooking until they soften, about 3 more minutes. Add the carrot and cook for 5 minutes. Add the tomato puree, cumin, paprika, cayenne, turmeric, and ½ teaspoon salt and mix well. Add the spinach in batches, stirring to get it to wilt into the mixture. Add the chickpeas and their liquid and the stock and increase the heat to medium-high. Simmer for 15 to 20 minutes to thicken the stew. Taste and add salt and pepper if needed.

3. Divide the stew into four bowls and top each with a dollop of goat cheese sauce and a sprinkle of parsley. Serve warm.

COMMUNITY

—

DISHES TO SHARE WITH FAMILY AND FRIENDS

We the people, not I the person.

—JOSÉ ANDRÉS

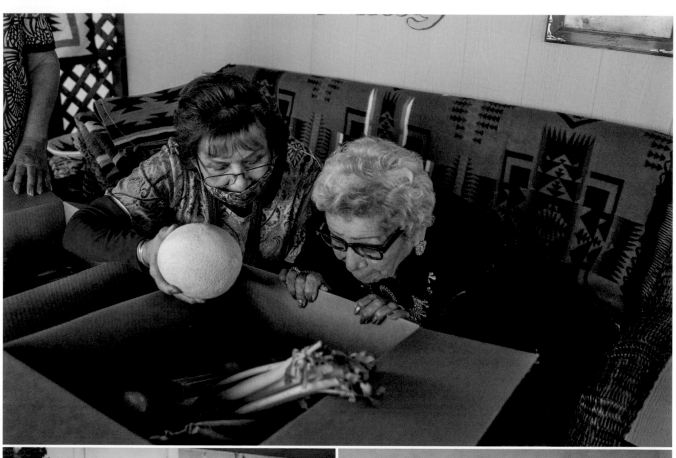

ONE OF THE MOST POWERFUL THINGS EVIDENT TO THE WCK TEAM AFTER ANY DISASTER IS THE ENDURING IMPORTANCE OF COMMUNITY. It shows up in different ways wherever we are, but it's always there, right at the root of healing.

We see communities showing up to help one another—especially their most vulnerable—in the difficult weeks and months after a crisis. In Guatemala after a deadly volcanic explosion, women from the town of Ceilán set up an operation to make sure rescue crews were fed and taken care of during long, dusty days.

In Northern California, where wildfires get more intense each season, volunteers from affected communities have jumped at the opportunity to make sandwiches with us. When we've delivered our meals, we see signs: "Paradise Strong," "Love Whiskeytown forever," "Thank you fire heroes."

In Beirut, after an explosion rocked the city's port in the summer of 2020, we saw a massive outpouring of civic service—thousands of people, from all walks of life, organized themselves to take care of each other and to clean up the city. It was like a family coming together to collectively solve something too overwhelming for any one individual.

On the Navajo Nation, in the depths of the pandemic, the community showed up to protect themselves, especially their elders. Many households have multiple generations living together. The nation decided to conduct "blitz testing"—health workers would go from home to home, testing every member of each family. Families quarantined together while they waited a few days for test results. WCK, with its entirely Diné (Navajo) team, delivered food boxes with enough food for the family to get through the quarantine. This mindset exemplified the best of humanity: We'll make it through—*together*.

In Ukraine, during our response to the Russian invasion in 2022, WCK helped mobilize more than 4,000 chefs, cooks, drivers, logistics specialists, and more—Food Fighters, as José calls them—to make sure that the country was able to feed itself through the war. This massive network ensured that towns and cities across the country—even on the frontlines of the conflict—had critical food support, a nationwide community feeding everyone who needed a meal.

The word *community* shares its root with *commensality*—the act of eating together. You don't need to have been through a crisis to know that sitting around a table and breaking bread with friends and loved ones can uplift and heal—remember, longer tables, not higher walls. Feasting and sharing food are intrinsic to humanity; to dine together is to be human. The recipes in this chapter are meant for sharing—at a potluck, a party for friends, a community supper, or when extended family is coming over for dinner. Most of the offerings here are vegetarian, so should be welcoming to all. You can turn them into an entire menu or serve them with others from the book—if you have dedicated carnivores coming over, add a meat or fish dish.

José shares a recipe for Sòs Pwa Nwa (page 203), which he learned about in his earliest visits to Haiti after the 2010 earthquake—a dish that was nothing short of an epiphany for him. You'll also see recipes from a few members of WCK's Chef Corps. Brooke Williamson—*Top Chef* winner and LA restaurateur—shares a recipe for a picnic-ready farro salad made with carrot juice. Guy Fieri—yes, that guy—and Tyler Florence share Thanksgiving recipes inspired by the feast we served for the Northern California town of Paradise after the 2018 Camp Fire. Emeril Lagasse, who worked with us in Florida and whose team provided support in New Orleans, offers a recipe for Gumbo z'Herbes (page 215), an underappreciated but delicious Louisiana classic that cooks pounds of greens into a rich, velvety stew. During the pandemic, Sanjeev Kapoor, one of the biggest culinary names in India, shared with José his recipe for Dal Tadka (page 223), spiced split pigeon peas—and now he shares it with you. You also get a deep dive into WCK's salad game, broken down into how we think about building salads that will stay fresh through challenging conditions.

World Central Kitchen is a community, too. Everyone who wants to get involved is central to the cause. Every volunteer who shows up to cook and make deliveries; every donor who contributes whatever they can to fund the work; every kid who hosts a lemonade stand to raise money; every restaurant that steps up to feed its neighbors in need—and even the restaurants who haven't been tapped yet.

"We are the biggest organization in the history of mankind," José says. "Because in my eyes, every restaurant is WCK, every cook and chef in the world is WCK . . . they just don't know it yet."

That isn't hyperbole. José is following a straight line from where we've been to where we're going. We don't know which communities will be hit with a disaster next, but we know that the community will be instrumental in its own healing.

Consider this your invitation to get involved. Cook for a neighbor with a newborn. Volunteer at your local animal shelter. Help a refugee family get settled. You know what your community needs best—do that. *"We, the people" means you, too.*

And if you happen to bring a pot of black beans or green gumbo with you, you might be surprised at how much longer that table can grow.

BRIAM

Briam is Greece's answer to a dish that can be found throughout southern Europe, one similar to Spain's pisto manchego, Catalan samfaina, and Provençal ratatouille. Our take on the Greek version features a garlicky oregano- and thyme-infused olive oil to flavor the roasted vegetables. We served it after wildfires ripped through the island of Evia, east of Athens. The WCK team worked with restaurants in the island's mountainous north, preparing food for elderly residents who stayed at home despite the fires. We brought meals to small villages of fifty to one hundred residents, then volunteers in the community walked up narrow cobblestone paths to deliver them to each household. Roasting the vegetables fanned out in alternating colors makes a beautiful presentation, and it's equally delicious warm or at room temperature. Be sure to have some crusty bread on hand to soak up that aromatic infused oil.

SERVES 4

½ cup **extra-virgin olive oil**

2 medium **garlic cloves**, thinly sliced

1 tablespoon **fresh oregano leaves** or 1 teaspoon dried

1 teaspoon **fresh thyme leaves** or ½ teaspoon dried

1 pound **Yukon Gold potatoes**, cut into ⅜-inch-thick slices

1 pound **zucchini** or other summer squash, cut into ⅜-inch-thick slices

1 teaspoon **kosher salt**

½ teaspoon **freshly ground black pepper**

1 (14.5-ounce) can diced **tomatoes**

8 ounces **red onions**, halved and cut into ⅜-inch-thick slices

8 ounces fresh **tomatoes**, cut into ⅜-inch-thick slices

Crusty bread, for serving

1. Preheat the oven to 400°F.

2. In a small saucepan, combine the olive oil, garlic, oregano, and thyme and cook over medium heat, stirring occasionally, until the garlic starts to tan and become aromatic, 4 to 5 minutes. Remove from the heat and let it cool slightly, 3 to 4 minutes.

3. In a large bowl, combine the potatoes, zucchini, salt, and pepper. Spoon in half of the infused oil, including the garlic and herbs, and toss well until all of the vegetables are coated.

4. Spread the canned tomatoes in a 9 × 13-inch baking dish. Start layering the vegetables in rows, alternating vegetables (and colors), overlapping them as you go. You may need to double up on squash and potatoes—squash, potato, onion and then squash, potato, fresh tomato—and so on, until you've used all of the vegetables. You'll probably have three or four rows of vegetables, depending on how wide they are. Drizzle the remaining infused oil evenly over the vegetables, as well as any remaining liquid from the bowl that held the potatoes and zucchini.

5. Bake until the potatoes are browned and fork-tender and the onions are getting soft, 45 to 60 minutes.

6. Serve warm or at room temperature with some crusty bread—and don't leave a drop of that infused oil behind!

BLACK BEANS AND THE ART OF LISTENING

José Andrés

Many years ago, when I first went to Haiti after the terrible earthquake in 2010, I had a lot to learn. Well, I *still* have a lot to learn, but I had even more to learn back then. I had heard about the horrors of what was happening in and around Port-au-Prince after the disaster, and I thought I could help somehow. I knew that at my restaurants, I was able to feed the few, the ones who could afford to come eat. But in a place like Haiti, maybe I could also feed the many.

I had never been to Haiti, and I had never really tried Haitian food. It was all new to me. But I knew I could cook. I had restaurants in Washington, DC, and Los Angeles and was about to open places in Las Vegas. I had a TV show on PBS about Spanish cuisine. I had even just been named Chef of the Year by *GQ*! After all, *I am José Andrés!*

I went to Haiti full of ideas of how to change the world, to use my skills as a cook and a chef to bring food to people in need. We brought a solar cooker so we could cook anywhere there was sunshine. Some days, if the sun wasn't out, we couldn't feed anyone; other days, we cooked for hundreds of people in the beautiful, bright Caribbean sunshine.

There was a shelter outside of Port-au-Prince where I met a group of women who were cooking for their community. We joined them for a day, planning to make some amazing black beans and rice, comforting food. Some of the women in the camp were helping me, cutting onions, peeling potatoes. I didn't speak French or Kreyòl, and they didn't speak Spanish or English, but I started to understand something from the way they were looking at me, with a smile, almost a laugh. I started to see what they were telling me with their faces: The way I was making the beans was not the way they liked to eat them!

When I finally understood, I put the tools in their hands and said, *Show me how you like to eat the beans*. We gathered burlap sacks and used them to sieve the black beans, pushing them through the sacks slowly, with muscle, to make sure that what was coming out on the other side was a smooth, creamy puree. A sauce! I finally saw it, this sòs pwa nwa, a black bean sauce to be eaten next to steamed white rice. It ended up so beautiful and rich and velvety, this perfect texture that I had never seen before from beans.

This may sound like a small thing to you. *Why are you telling me so much about these beans, José?* But this is everything there is to know about me today, and about World Central Kitchen. This is a moment when I truly learned to *listen*. Not to come in and tell people what they want, but to really understand what I am being told. If you like your beans to be smooth, why should anyone serve you anything else?

Since that day, I have hoped to make World Central Kitchen the same way. When we go into a community, we never tell them, *This is what you need to eat, this is what you want.* Instead we come with open ears and a deep hunger to learn from them, to collaborate on making meals that are comforting and familiar to everyone there. You'll see it throughout our work: Wherever we are, we are talking to local chefs, visiting the markets, tasting the dishes to understand what we should be cooking.

To me, this dish, sòs pwa nwa, is absolutely delicious. It's so savory, garlicky, smooth, and creamy . . . and it reminds me to be humble and always, always listen to what the community is telling you.

SÒS PWA NWA
Black Bean Sauce

When José made black beans and rice for a group of women in Haiti after the 2010 earthquake, he learned two lessons: First, they wanted their beans smooth, without skins; and second, the Big Name Chef had a lot to learn about listening (more on that, straight from José, on page 200). These are the beans that changed everything: pureed and sieved until creamy and rich, perfect with a side of rice and good conversation. The dish he was unknowingly making was *sòs pwa nwa*, Kreyòl for *"sauce pois noir,"* or "black bean sauce" in English. Haitian chef Mi-Sol Chevallier tells a story about the dish: Growing up, before her family had a blender, they would peel each bean by hand. Hopefully you have a blender at home, but if not, you'd better start peeling!

SERVES 4 TO 6

1 cup **dried black beans**
8 **whole cloves**
1 medium **yellow onion**, peeled but whole
2 tablespoons **Épis** (page 290)
1 teaspoon **kosher salt**, plus more to taste
Cooked **white rice**, for serving

1. In a medium saucepan, combine the beans with enough water to cover by 1 inch. Soak for 4 hours or up to overnight.

2. Bring the beans and soaking liquid to a boil over medium-high heat. Reduce the heat to medium and cook until the beans are very soft, 1 to 1½ hours, adding water as needed to keep the beans covered—keep a close watch and stir occasionally so the beans don't burn.

3. When the beans are soft enough to easily mash, drain them in a sieve set over a medium bowl. Reserve the cooking liquid and transfer the beans to a high-powered blender. Puree the beans until they're very, very smooth, adding a little of the cooking liquid if needed to get the blender going. If you don't have a high-powered blender and your puree still has some texture from the skins, you can press the puree through a fine-mesh sieve with the back of a wooden spoon over a medium bowl. Return the puree to the saucepan.

4. Insert the pointy end of the cloves into the surface of the peeled onion until it's studded all over (this is an *oignon clouté*, or "studded onion," a traditional French flavor booster). Add the épis, salt, and 1 cup of the reserved cooking liquid to the bean puree and stir to combine. Add the clove-studded onion and cook over medium-low heat, stirring regularly, for 20 to 30 minutes, to get the right consistency—you want the final dish to be smooth, creamy, and the texture of a thick soup. Add more of the cooking liquid or water as needed.

5. Taste for seasoning and add more salt as needed. Remove the oignon clouté and serve hot with white rice.

SAYUR GORI
Jackfruit Stew in Coconut Milk

This recipe comes from our superstar team leader in Indonesia, Rima Aritonang, who has been on the ground with us for every major natural disaster that has struck Indonesia over the past few years, including earthquakes, tsunamis, and floods. "A lot of beautiful things actually happen in disaster," Rima says. "You really can see the best of people." (For more of Rima's story, see The Spirit of WCK, page 125.) Sayur gori, which we regularly serve as a vegetarian dish along with rice and sambal, is young jackfruit cooked in coconut milk with chiles and spices. If you've never cooked with jackfruit before, it's a delicious and easy replacement for meat. The final dish has a toothsome texture and soaks up the richly spiced coconut milk.

SERVES 4

SPICE PASTE
1 large **shallot**, roughly chopped

1 head **garlic**, cloves roughly chopped

2 to 3 fresh **Lombok chiles** or **cayenne peppers** (seeded if you want it less spicy) or **serrano peppers**

¼ cup **macadamia nuts**

1½-inch piece **fresh turmeric**, peeled and roughly chopped, or 1 tablespoon **ground turmeric**

1 teaspoon **ground coriander**

¼ teaspoon **kosher salt**

STEW
3 tablespoons **canola** or other **neutral cooking oil**

1 **lemongrass stalk**, bruised with the back of a chef's knife, and tied in a knot (see Note)

1-inch piece **galangal**, peeled and bruised

3 **makrut lime leaves**

2 **bay leaves**

2 (20-ounce) cans **green jackfruit** (see page 32), drained

1 tablespoon **dark brown sugar**, plus more to taste

1 teaspoon **kosher salt**, plus more to taste

1 (13.5-ounce) can **full-fat coconut milk**

Cooked **white rice**, for serving

Sambal, homemade (page 289) or store-bought, for serving

1. MAKE THE SPICE PASTE: In a mortar, combine the shallot, garlic, chiles, macadamia nuts, turmeric, coriander, and salt and grind with a pestle until it becomes a rough-textured thick paste. (Or do this in a small food processor.)

2. MAKE THE STEW: In a wok or deep skillet, heat the oil over medium-high heat. Add the spice paste and sauté, stirring frequently to make sure it doesn't burn, until fragrant, 2 to 3 minutes. Add the lemongrass, galangal, lime leaves, and bay leaves and cook, stirring, for 1 minute to coat them in the spice paste.

3. Add the jackfruit, brown sugar, and salt and mix well. Add the coconut milk and 1 cup water and bring to a boil, stirring frequently but gently. Once the mixture boils, reduce the heat to a simmer and cook for 30 to 40 minutes, continuing to stir frequently, to thicken the stew.

4. Taste and add brown sugar or salt, if needed. Serve hot with rice and sambal.

Note: Bruising lemongrass helps release its aromatics into the stew. Using the back of a heavy knife, smack the stalk a few times to break it apart a bit without entirely cutting it. Tying the lemongrass in a knot will make sure that the stringy lemongrass doesn't break apart as the stew cooks.

Habib stays up through the night to keep watch over the horizon in case of another tsunami in Banten, Indonesia, 2018.

BROOKE'S CARROT-FARRO SALAD

This colorful salad tastes like spring and fall at the same time; it's bright and refreshing, nutty and rich, and makes a great addition to a picnic basket in any season. Chef Brooke Williamson cooks the farro in carrot juice so the grains soak up the earthy-sweet essence of carrot and retain a satisfying bite. Brooke has been a partner and friend of WCK for years. Her restaurant, Playa Provisions, has supported our efforts in Southern California, and Brooke herself is always game to show up at our kitchens and unpack her knives. "Having had mainly neighborhood-driven restaurants, my husband, Nick, and I are keenly aware of how important community is, not only for the purpose of receiving support, but also for how important it is to give. Our community is our extended family . . . our neighbors and staff are who we turn to in the best and worst of times."

SERVES 4

4 tablespoons **extra-virgin olive oil**
1 medium **yellow onion**, finely chopped
2 medium **garlic cloves**, finely chopped
2 cups **farro** (see Note), rinsed
2 tablespoons **light brown sugar**
3 cups **pure carrot juice**
Kosher salt
2 medium **carrots**, peeled and diced
Grated zest and juice of 2 medium **lemons**
1 **shallot**, minced
6 **red radishes**, thinly shaved
¼ cup roughly chopped **fresh cilantro** leaves
1 **avocado**, diced
2 tablespoons toasted **sesame seeds**
Freshly ground black pepper

1. In a large saucepan, combine 2 tablespoons of the olive oil, the onions, and garlic and sweat over medium heat until they're translucent, 3 to 5 minutes. Add the farro and toast for 2 minutes, stirring frequently to make sure the onions and garlic don't brown. Add the brown sugar, carrot juice, and 1 teaspoon salt and simmer over medium-low heat, stirring occasionally, until the farro is al dente—chewy but still firm, 20 to 30 minutes.

2. Add the diced carrots and continue to cook, stirring often, until the farro is cooked through and the carrots are tender, 10 to 15 minutes.

3. Taste the farro and season with salt, if needed, then drain in a colander (save any leftover cooking liquid in the refrigerator to use in a salad dressing). Spread the farro out on a large sheet pan and drizzle with the remaining 2 tablespoons olive oil, stirring to coat it well. Let it sit at room temperature until cool.

4. Place the cooled farro in a large bowl and toss with the lemon zest, lemon juice, shallot, radishes, and cilantro. (The salad can be made to this point up to 1 day ahead and refrigerated.)

5. When ready to serve, add the diced avocado, gently stir, and finish with the sesame seeds and a few twists of black pepper.

Note: Look for farro from brands like Bob's Red Mill or Earthly Choice. Make sure your farro isn't "quick-cooking" or that the package doesn't say "cooks in 10 minutes."

HOW TO MAKE A SALAD

Dressing your salad right before serving is ideal, but what do you do if you're serving *a lot* of people? If you take away anything from this guide, make it this: If you're not serving your salad immediately, *start with your dressing at the bottom*. It's upside-down logic, but think: no soggy greens until you toss the salad, and those pesky bottom leaves actually become the best dressed! That's how we do it when we're serving individual salads in brown paper bags. Remember that next time you pack your kids' lunch.

THE DRESSING (FOR ABOUT 1 CUP)

Green Goddess Dressing: The classic. Puree 1 cup mixed herbs, 1 cup baby spinach, 1 clove garlic, 1 teaspoon onion powder, 2 tablespoons lemon juice, 1 tablespoon white wine vinegar, ⅓ cup mayo, and salt and freshly ground pepper to taste.

Cauliflower Ranch Dressing: WCK food-waste fave. Braise cauliflower stems in milk and puree them (and save the milk). Combine 3 tablespoons puree, 3 tablespoons sour cream, 2 tablespoons buttermilk, 1 tablespoon cauliflower-braising milk, 1 tablespoon mayo, 1 teaspoon red wine vinegar, ½ teaspoon onion powder, ½ teaspoon parsley flakes, ¼ teaspoon garlic powder, and ¼ teaspoon ground black pepper.

Red Wine Vinaigrette: ½ cup olive oil, 3 tablespoons red wine vinegar, 2 teaspoons Dijon mustard, 1 teaspoon honey, and ½ teaspoon each garlic powder, dried oregano, parsley flakes, salt, and ground black pepper.

Creamy Cilantro Dressing: Puree ¼ cup mayo, ⅓ bunch cilantro, 2 tablespoons sour cream, 1 tablespoon milk, 2 teaspoons lime juice, 1 small garlic clove (minced), ½ teaspoon salt, ½ teaspoon ground coriander, ¼ teaspoon ground cumin, and ¼ teaspoon ground black pepper.

Honey Mustard Dressing: ¾ cup mayo, ⅓ cup honey, 3 tablespoons Dijon mustard, 2 tablespoons lemon juice, ½ teaspoon salt, and ½ teaspoon ground black pepper. Doubles as a pretzel dipping sauce.

Leftover Cooking Liquid: Anytime you have flavorful leftover cooking juices, like from the Carrot-Farro Salad (page 209), think of it as a potential salad dressing!

THE HEFT

Leafy greens are great, but so are vegetables with a little extra body to them.

Romaine / **Mesclun mix** / **Spinach** / **Shredded cabbage** / **Shredded broccoli and cauliflower stems** / **Kale**

SOME COLOR ON TOP

Most people will tell you that lettuce alone does not a salad make. It's the rainbow of add-ons that make a salad vibrant and special.

Cherry tomatoes / **Roasted red peppers** (roasted out of a jar is easy) / **Roasted beets** (most markets carry roasted vacuum-packed beets) / **Pickled onions** / **Shredded carrots** / **Mandarin orange slices** / **Fresh corn** (sauté it with some cumin and toss with lime juice before serving) / **Broccoli** / **Fresh or frozen peas** / **Roasted squash or Brussels sprouts** / **Apples or pears** / **Hard-boiled eggs** / **Shredded cheese** / **Chickpeas** (try them roasted in some olive oil at 425°F for 30 minutes or so) / **Pitted black or green olives** / **Beans** (black, pinto, navy . . .)

ADD A SALAD TO A SALAD!

Coleslaw / **Ham, tuna, or chicken salad** / **Pimiento cheese** / **Tabbouleh**

AND A CRUNCH

This is where everything comes together, that last little touch of texture on top.

Tortilla chip strips / **Roasted pumpkin seeds** / **Dried fruit** / **Toasted sesame seeds** / **Croutons** / **Chia seeds** / **Cooked quinoa** / **Cooked fonio** / **Crunchy fried onions**

HOW TO REDUCE FOOD WASTE, WHETHER COOKING FOR 4 OR 4,000

While the recipes in this book are written for 4 to 6 people, in the field our recipes serve anywhere from 400 to 4,000. (If you want to scale any of the recipes up to serve that many people, see How to Scale a Recipe, page 35.) As a result, we end up with *a lot* of excess—peels, scraps, bones, and more. So we're always looking for ways to thoughtfully use them and not give away our beautifully biodegradable scraps to the trash heap, which only contributes to climate change (not to mention all of the energy and resources used to grow and transport the food in the first place).

The EPA offers a hierarchy for reducing food waste. The best solution is to repurpose it for human consumption. If that's impossible, then use it to feed animals. And, as a last resort, compost it. So when we start cooking in a new kitchen, that's how we draw up our strategy: Can we reuse scraps in our meals? Can we make connections with local farmers? What are the composting options?

One of our favorite tricks with vegetable scraps is to incorporate them into salad dressing. WCK chef Elyssa Kaplan, volunteer chef Matt Masera, and team member Dan Abrams perfected the technique in The Bahamas. They would poach broccoli and cauliflower stems in milk to soften them, then blend the poached stems into all of our dressings—one of Elyssa's favorites is Cauliflower Ranch Dressing (page 210). This technique reduces the number of scraps the kitchen produces, helps stretch portions, and most importantly, adds bulk and nutrients to a dressing. We love recipes like this—see chef Emeril Lagasse's Gumbo z'Herbes (page 215) for the perfect way to use up an abundance of green tops and stems.

We're also tapped into a network of food rescue organizations, which is especially important when the number of meals we need to prepare fluctuates day-to-day. In many situations, the number of people sheltered and in need of meals can change by hundreds or thousands, and we might not know what the day's final number will be until the morning that we're cooking. If there are more people than expected, we'll be resourceful and stretch our ingredients. If there are fewer people, we'll have a surplus. That's when organizations like Copia, the Food Rescue Alliance, and Food Rescue US are great friends to have; they pick up excess meals and donate them to others in the community.

For scraps that can't be repurposed into our meals, animals are the next best recipients. On the Caribbean island of Saint Vincent, after a volcanic explosion displaced thousands of people, we established our kitchen at a culinary institute that was temporarily out of session (read more in Vincy Stew Chicken and the Art of Listening, page 64). The institute grounds were also home to a family of goats

struggling to find food in the ashy landscape. The goats gratefully ate our scraps, which had two outcomes: happy animals and a perfect on-site waste management solution. We created a similar arrangement in Kentucky after a series of tornadoes: We established a relationship with a local pig farmer, who gladly accepted our scraps . . . and then sent us photos of the pigs enjoying their meals!

Compost is the trickiest solution, but it's getting easier as more facilities become available around the world. It would be great if it were more accessible on the fly—we'd love to just set up a mobile composter outside of a kitchen. Maybe one day that technology will be available.

Food waste isn't just a challenge for WCK; food is the *number one item* Americans throw away—and an estimated *one-third* of food produced is never eaten! It's either plowed under on farms, discarded by grocery stores, or thrown away in people's homes—due to both structural issues and personal choices. The numbers are daunting, but each of us has the power to make a difference, like buying "seconds" (imperfect produce) at the farmers' market. You'll get a better price—plus the farmers make money instead of composting slightly bruised or overripe items.

The destructive consequences of climate change can feel overwhelming and may seem impossible to reverse on our own. Whether you're thinking global or local, act hyperlocal—starting in your own kitchen—and make a critical impact to change the course of the environment for the better.

EMERIL'S GUMBO Z'HERBES

It may not be as well known as its meatier cousin, but this green gumbo is a Louisiana classic. The recipe comes from legendary chef Emeril Lagasse, who has worked with the WCK team in New Orleans and the Florida panhandle after Hurricane Michael in 2018. It's a flexible recipe—swap in other smoked meats for the pork, or add some salted butter if you want to keep it luxuriously vegetarian. The only nonnegotiable element: plenty of greens. "Old timers will tell you that if you enjoy it on New Year's Day, you will gain a new friend for each type of green used in the gumbo," Emeril says. "So try to use as many types of greens as you can find." Bonus points if you can use stems and tops from other vegetables you may otherwise discard, like beet greens, carrot tops, and herb stems—it's a perfect recipe to keep your kitchen food-waste-free.

SERVES 4 TO 6

¾ to 1 pound **salt pork**, **smoked ham**, or **smoked turkey** (optional)

1 teaspoon **kosher salt**, or to taste

½ teaspoon **cayenne pepper**

2 **bay leaves**

2 quarts **vegetable stock**, **chicken stock**, **smoked pork stock**, or **water**, plus more as needed

2 tablespoons **vegetable oil**

1 large **yellow onion**, chopped

1 medium **green bell pepper**, chopped

1 large **celery stalk,** chopped

4 medium **garlic cloves**, minced

2 pounds (about 3 bunches) **assorted greens** (such as collards, mustard greens, turnip greens, spinach, chard, and kale), trimmed, tough midribs and stems finely chopped, greens washed and roughly chopped

½ teaspoon **dried thyme**

¼ teaspoon **dried oregano**

¼ teaspoon **dried basil**

¼ teaspoon **crushed red pepper flakes**, to taste

¼ cup chopped **fresh parsley leaves**

½ cup finely chopped **scallions**, green tops only

2 tablespoons **butter**, optional

Cooked **long-grain white rice**, for serving

Louisiana hot sauce, such as Crystal or Red Rooster, or **Pique** (page 293)

1. If you're using meat, start here; if not, jump directly to the next step: In a large, deep pot, combine the meat, salt, cayenne, bay leaves, and stock. Bring to a boil over medium-high heat. Reduce the heat to a simmer, partially cover, and cook until the broth is flavorful and the meat is tender and falling from the bones, 30 minutes or longer. With a slotted spoon, remove the meat from the broth and chop it into bite-size pieces or remove it from the bones (discard bones and skin). Set the meat aside and transfer the broth to a large container.

2. Wipe out the pot and return it to medium heat. Add the oil, onion, bell pepper, and celery and cook, stirring often, until the vegetables are wilted and golden, about 10 minutes. Add the garlic and cook until fragrant, 1 to 2 minutes. Add the reserved meat (if using) and stock or broth (if you're not using meat, add the salt, cayenne, and bay leaves here), along with the greens, thyme, oregano, basil, pepper flakes, and parsley. Bring to a gentle boil over medium heat and simmer until the greens are meltingly tender, 1 to 1½ hours. If the gumbo gets too thick during cooking (it should be brothy), add a bit more water or stock.

3. When the greens are very tender and the broth is rich and flavorful (this may vary depending on the type of greens you used), stir in the scallion greens, taste, and adjust the seasoning, if needed. Remove the bay leaves (if you can find them!) and allow the gumbo to cook another 5 to 10 minutes. If you made the gumbo without meat, add the butter to the pot just before removing from the heat. It adds a richness that might be missing.

4. Serve the gumbo in deep soup bowls over rice with hot sauce on the side.

HOLIDAYS WITH WORLD CENTRAL KITCHEN

WCK has cooked every single day, 365 days a year, somewhere around the world, since September 2017. And we don't take holidays off. Whenever a special day approaches, our team puts together a celebration fitting the moment. We know these feasts provide an opportunity for the community to come together and celebrate something universal, even in times of crisis.

Our first big holiday was Thanksgiving in Puerto Rico after Hurricane María in 2017. José, his wife, Tichi, and their three daughters, Carlota, Inés, and Lucía, went to San Juan to host—along with the team from Chefs For Puerto Rico (see page 177)—a special holiday meal delivery for 40,000 Puerto Ricans. It was a traditional Thanksgiving meal with a local twist: Along with mashed potatoes, corn, stuffing, cranberry sauce, and gravy, there was pavochón, a distinctly Puerto Rican mashup of *pavo* (turkey) and *lechón* (slow-roasted pork). The team seasoned turkeys with lechón spices—salt, black pepper, fresh garlic, oregano, and cumin—and roasted them. This was no easy feast—even two months after the storm, many communities were still without power and the electricity in the kitchen was still spotty; as the team cooked, the lights flickered. The meal itself was as necessary as it was celebratory. Tichi remembers it as a revelatory moment: "It was the first time for me that I could see how WCK wasn't just feeding the body. It was feeding the soul, creating community, giving people an opportunity to heal after disaster."

One of our most ambitious holiday get-togethers happened a year later, weeks after the Camp Fire destroyed the town of Paradise, California. Along with local officials and the neighboring city of Chico, we invited everyone impacted by the fire to a Thanksgiving feast cooked by a team of chefs and restaurateurs, including Chef Corps members Guy Fieri (pictured right) and Tyler Florence (see pages 219 and 220 for recipes from their Thanksgiving tables). We called it Thanksgiving Together and prepared food for 15,000 people, serving 7,000 pounds of turkey, 2 tons of mashed potatoes and green beans, 500 pounds of fresh cranberries, and 1,000 pumpkin pies.

The most surprising thing about the meal was that so many members of the community didn't want to be served dinner—they wanted to be the ones *serving* it, behind the buffet line. We had over 1,000 volunteers help out, working in the kitchens, serving meals in the dining hall, or delivering food to families who couldn't make it. The hall seemed only half-full much of the day, not because there wasn't enough food or enthusiasm but because so many of the guests volunteered to help! We truly felt the power of community that day, when people whose lives had been turned upside down chose not to receive a meal but to serve one. The most moving

moment of the day was when thirty California state firefighters walked into the hall to serve meals; the hall erupted in a standing ovation. Firefighters who had risked their lives to save the town, community members who escaped with only the clothes on their backs, business owners who lost everything—everyone came together to give back to their neighbors.

Since then, we've celebrated Thanksgivings, Christmases, Eids, Easters, and more all around the world. One particularly memorable Christmas was in The Bahamas in 2019 after Hurricane Dorian a few months earlier. By December, we had established a kitchen on the island of Great Abaco and prepared a feast of smoked ham with green beans and yams for the island's residents who were in the process of rebuilding their homes and their lives. But it wasn't just about the food: Santa Claus (with the help of Relief Team member Sam Bloch) showed up to bring gifts to the kids, and we prepared a surprise for a few young children who had lost their belongings in the storm. WCK's Sandie Orsa gave them each a wrapped present and told them to open it: bike locks. They looked a bit confused, at least until the rest of the team rode in with their brand new bikes!

Wherever we are, we try to honor holiday traditions with our menus and celebrations. For Guatemalan Christmas, we made tamales wrapped in banana leaves (a recipe you can find on page 83) and had a piñata for kids. The chefs had a little fun in Kentucky for Christmas in 2021, serving maple green beans with cranberry and bacon and a broccoli-and-potato-puff casserole. And in the midst of an ongoing war in Ukraine on Orthodox Easter, we worked with partners to prepare traditional paska, a sweet egg-enriched bread that has a profound significance to Ukrainians— you can find our recipe on page 274.

Holidays mean something different for everyone. For some, they're about family and togetherness; for others, solitude and reflection. Some treat a holiday as an excuse to feast; others keep things simple. Each time we've hosted a holiday celebration in a community recovering from a disaster, though, there's one thing in common: a shadow of tragedy and encouraging signs of resilience. It's not a time to forget the challenges, but an opportunity to take a deep breath and renew a commitment to making it through, to waking up the next day and continuing the hard work.

And most of all, it's a time for community. When a group comes together to prepare food and then serve it to neighbors and friends at long tables, it's a form of therapy, of working through the pain and trauma of disaster. We don't have to wait until the rebuilding is complete to celebrate with one another; togetherness is a key part of healing.

GUY'S GREEN BEAN CASSEROLE

Guy Fieri is not just the Mayor of Flavortown. He's also an active citizen of another community, Northern California, where he grew up and lives with his family. Whenever WCK responds to wildfires in the area, Guy is usually somewhere to be found, often firing up his traveling smoker rig (complete with flat-screen TV) to help feed firefighters and evacuees. The morning of Thanksgiving Together (see page 216), Guy and his team were up at 4 a.m. to start smoking turkeys—they cooked over 7,000 pounds of meat for the feast. This rich and delicious green bean casserole, a Fieri family (and Flavortown) favorite, is a worthy adaptation of the classic Thanksgiving dish: Tender blanched green beans are enrobed in a creamy mushroom sauce and topped with crispy fried shallots.

SERVES 4 TO 6

Kosher salt

1½ pounds **green beans**, ends trimmed, halved

2 tablespoons **unsalted butter**

1 tablespoon **vegetable oil**, plus more for shallow-frying

1 pound **mixed mushrooms** (such as shiitakes, creminis, and oyster), cleaned, trimmed, and quartered

½ teaspoon **fresh thyme leaves**

2 **garlic cloves**, minced

¼ teaspoon **cayenne pepper**

¼ teaspoon **ground nutmeg**

Freshly ground black pepper

1 cup plus 2 tablespoons **all-purpose flour**

1 cup low-sodium **chicken stock**

1 cup **sour cream**

½ cup **heavy cream**

¼ cup grated **parmesan cheese**

4 medium **shallots**, thinly sliced and separated into rings

1. Preheat the oven to 450°F.

2. Bring a large pot of salted water to a boil. Fill a large bowl with ice and water. Line a large platter with clean towels.

3. Add the beans to the boiling water and cook until they turn bright green, 2 to 3 minutes. Use a slotted spoon to transfer them to the ice water. Let them cool for a couple of minutes, then drain and dry them on the towel-lined platter.

4. Set a large cast-iron skillet over medium-high heat. Add the butter and 1 tablespoon oil. When the pan is hot, add the mushrooms and cook, undisturbed, until the mushrooms sear, about 1 minute. Add the thyme and garlic and continue cooking until the mushrooms brown, 4 to 5 minutes. Season with the cayenne, nutmeg, and salt and black pepper to taste. Cook 2 to 3 minutes more, then dust with 2 tablespoons of the flour as the mushrooms release their moisture. Stir with a wooden spoon to incorporate the flour and gradually add the chicken stock. Bring to a simmer, then reduce the heat to low and add the sour cream and heavy cream. Stir gently and cook over low heat until the sauce thickens, 5 to 6 minutes.

5. Add the blanched beans to the skillet and toss to mix well. Evenly spread the mixture in the pan. Sprinkle the beans with the parmesan and transfer the skillet to a sheet pan. Bake until the casserole is bubbling and the top is golden, about 15 minutes.

6. Meanwhile, pour about ½ inch of oil into a deep skillet and heat to 350°F. Line a plate with paper towels. In a large bowl, mix together the remaining 1 cup flour and a generous sprinkle of salt and pepper. Toss the shallot rounds in the seasoned flour, then place them in a fine-mesh sieve and shake off excess flour. Working in small batches, fry the shallots until golden brown, 3 to 5 minutes. Transfer the shallots to the paper towels and season with salt while still hot; repeat to fry the remaining shallots.

7. To serve, top the casserole with the fried shallots.

TYLER'S CORN BREAD STUFFING

Tyler Florence and his wife, Tolan, have been on the frontlines with World Central Kitchen several times, jumping in to support our wildfire work in Northern California and helping feed federal workers in the Bay Area during the 2019 US federal government shutdown. They opened their home as a makeshift WCK headquarters and rallied their friends to make sure the region's federal employees—from NASA physicists to EPA scientists—could eat. In 2018, after an eighteen-hour day of cooking and serving, the Florences invited the WCK crew for a late-night dinner prepared by the chef and his team. This classic stuffing recipe tastes best if you make your own corn bread, but six large corn bread muffins from the grocery store will work, too.

SERVES 4 TO 6

CORN BREAD
1 cup (120 grams) **all-purpose flour**
1 cup (156 grams) **coarse cornmeal**
¼ cup (53 grams) packed **light brown sugar**
1 teaspoon **baking powder**
½ teaspoon **baking soda**
2 teaspoons **kosher salt**
1 cup (227 grams) **buttermilk**
¼ cup (84 grams) **honey**
2 large **eggs**
8 tablespoons (1 stick/225 grams) **unsalted butter,** melted
¼ cup (50 grams) **canola oil**
Softened butter for greasing the skillet

STUFFING
2 tablespoons **unsalted butter**
2 medium **yellow onions,** diced
1 bunch **fresh sage leaves,** finely chopped
Kosher salt and **freshly ground black pepper**

¼ cup **heavy cream**
¼ cup **chicken stock**
1 large **egg**
Softened butter for the baking dish

1. MAKE THE CORN BREAD: Preheat the oven to 400°F.

2. In a large bowl, combine the flour, cornmeal, brown sugar, baking powder, baking soda, and salt. In a medium bowl, whisk to combine the buttermilk, honey, and eggs until smooth. Pour the buttermilk mixture into the flour mixture and whisk well to combine until no lumps remain. Whisk in the melted butter and the canola oil. Let sit for about 10 minutes so the cornmeal can soften a bit before baking.

3. Butter a 10- to 12-inch cast-iron skillet and add the batter. Bake until a toothpick inserted in the center comes out clean, 12 to 15 minutes. Leave the oven on but reduce the temperature to 375°F.

4. Let the corn bread cool to room temperature, then cut it into 1-inch cubes—either in the skillet or carefully invert the skillet to remove the corn bread and cut it on a cutting board. Set the cubes aside.

5. MAKE THE STUFFING: In a medium skillet, melt the butter over medium heat. Add the onions and cook, stirring occasionally, until soft and browned, about 15 minutes. Add the sage and cook while stirring for another 1 to 2 minutes, until the sage is fragrant. Scrape the contents of the skillet into a large bowl. Add the corn bread cubes, season well with salt and pepper, and give it a good toss with a wooden spoon until it's well combined.

6. In a separate small bowl or measuring cup, whisk together the cream, stock, and egg until well combined. Pour the mixture over the corn bread and stir until the stuffing is evenly coated.

7. Butter a 2-quart or 9 × 9-inch baking dish. Spoon the stuffing into the dish. Bake until hot and crusty on top, about 30 minutes.

SANJEEV'S DAL TADKA

Sanjeev Kapoor was the star of *Khana Khazana*, one of the most popular cooking shows in Asia for almost twenty years (with 500 million viewers in 120 countries!). He has written more than 140 cookbooks, runs dozens of restaurants around the world, and co-owns a twenty-four-hour cooking channel. A member of WCK's Chef Corps, he's also a humanitarian and philanthropist, supporting initiatives combating hunger in India and raising money for NGOs that support people with autism. "I don't want to be capable only for myself but for others, too," he says. "If you can't make an impact with the kind of position you have, then what's the point? Food has given me so much and if there's anything to do with food, I feel I should give back." During India's Covid surge in 2021, Sanjeev connected WCK with kitchens and teams throughout the country to cook for doctors, nurses, and support staff working around the clock. During a quiet moment in one of his kitchens, he taught José how to make this recipe for dal tadka—creamy split pigeon peas that are mixed with onion, garlic, chiles, and spices tempered in ghee.

SERVES 4

1 cup **toor dal** (split pigeon peas; see page 32), soaked in room temperature water for 1 hour

¼ teaspoon **ground turmeric**

¼ teaspoon **asafoetida** (optional; see page 29)

1 tablespoon **ghee**

1 teaspoon **cumin seeds**

1 tablespoon finely chopped **fresh ginger**

1 tablespoon finely chopped **garlic**

1 medium **yellow onion**, finely chopped

1 to 2 **green chiles**, thinly sliced

1 medium **tomato**, finely chopped

½ teaspoon **ground red chiles**

1 teaspoon **garam masala**

Kosher salt

Steamed **basmati rice**, for serving

Chopped **fresh cilantro leaves**, for garnish

1. In a medium pot, combine the soaked dal, turmeric, asafoetida (if using), and 4 cups water. Bring to a boil over medium-high heat and cook until the dal are soft and creamy, 45 to 60 minutes—add more water if the peas dry out before they're soft. (Alternatively, you can also cook the soaked dal in an Instant Pot—use 2½ cups water and cook on high pressure for 8 minutes, then let the pressure release naturally.)

2. In a deep nonstick pan with a lid, heat the ghee over medium heat. Add the cumin seeds, ginger, and garlic and cook for 2 to 3 minutes, stirring regularly, until they get fragrant. Add the onion and green chiles and sauté until the onions turn translucent, 3 to 5 minutes. Stir in the tomato, then cover the pot and cook until the tomato starts to break down, about 5 minutes. Add the ground red chile and garam masala, mix well, and cook uncovered for a minute, until everything is fragrant.

3. Add the cooked dal and mix well. Stir in ¼ cup water and ½ to 1 teaspoon salt and simmer for 2 to 3 minutes, until everything is incorporated.

4. Serve hot with the rice and garnished with cilantro.

RESILIENCE

DISHES TO SUPPORT FARMERS, FISHERS, AND SMALL FOOD PRODUCERS

La agricultura es la espina dorsal de un pueblo. (Agriculture is the backbone of a nation.)

—EUGENIO MARÍA DE HOSTOS

La destinée des nations dépend de la manière dont elles se nourrissent. (The future of nations depends on how they feed themselves.)

—JEAN ANTHELME BRILLAT-SAVARIN

JEAN ANTHELME BRILLAT-SAVARIN'S FAMOUS APHORISM COULDN'T FEEL MORE RELEVANT, NEARLY TWO HUNDRED YEARS LATER. How do we choose to feed ourselves? And who is allowed in the room to make those choices?

While WCK is most visible during our disaster response work, from Day 1, the vision has always been bigger: We want to make sure that those communities aren't just fed today, but that their food systems are resilient enough to withstand future shocks tomorrow.

After the devastating 2010 earthquake in Haiti, José and his nascent team worked to update school kitchens and helped train staff. We built a bakery and fish restaurant attached to an orphanage, which led to a project supporting tilapia farms and deep-sea fishers. These projects weren't necessarily part of a grand strategy, but they did trace a path for the future. Moments of crisis can become opportunities for the biggest change, inflection points for a new trajectory.

Hurricane María in Puerto Rico changed the way WCK looked at post-disaster food systems. During our response, the Relief Team worked with small farmers in communities across the island to source ingredients for our kitchens, and we got to know them and their needs. We realized they weren't getting support from government agencies, private companies, or the nonprofit sector—and we also learned that Puerto Rico had been importing 85 percent of its food before the storm. We saw an opportunity to help. Through a grant and training program, we directed aid to farmers, fishers, and food producers, hoping to help the island's food system come back even stronger than its pre-María levels of food production. This eventually became WCK's Food Producer Network and soon expanded to Guatemala, The Bahamas, and the US Virgin Islands.

From 2018 to 2022, the program invested over $5 million through 300 projects, leading to significant and measurable increases in production and revenue for grantees—more than half of whom are women—as well as increased food access for many Puerto Ricans and overall stronger food sovereignty on the island.

Beyond grants, WCK programs have supported a variety of projects. École des Chefs (now called Atelier des Chefs) was an early project led by chef Mi-Sol

Chevallier to raise the standard of cooking and hospitality in Haiti. Kitchen Skills and Safety was a program to train school and community cooks in Haiti, Guatemala, Honduras, and Costa Rica in food handling—more than 700 cooks completed the training. And Clean Cooking, a project José worked on in Haiti even before the founding of WCK, aimed to bring modern cooking technologies to communities to improve household health, access to education, and beyond.

"Small food producers account for a third of the world's food supply," said Mikol Hoffman, the former director of the Food Producer Network. "Our work uplifts these producers by strengthening food production with practices that are economically viable, socially just, and environmentally sound."

Over the years, WCK has met hardworking people whose work and lives and livelihoods reflected the longer-term goals of the organization. Alex Maldonado, who lost his boat motor in Hurricane María, became an advocate for his fishing community in northern Puerto Rico by supporting the growth and success of other fishers. ASPROC in southern Guatemala is an association of over ninety Kaqchikel Mayan farmers who specialize in greenhouse production of organic tomatoes, as well as supporting the development of regenerative agriculture among other farmers in their communities. In The Bahamas, Vashti Johnson-Joseph of Sunflower Farms, who learned to farm at age six from her grandparents, teaches primary school students about farming, animal care, and sustainable food production.

There are hundreds more stories to highlight about people who have benefited from these programs—enough for another book.

In this chapter, you'll find recipes both from the regions in which our Resilience programs worked and from two WCK partners, Eric Adjepong and Kamal Mouzawak. Eric shares a recipe (page 235) that celebrates the importance of shrimp farmers in Mozambique, which was rocked by Cyclone Idai in 2019. Kamal, who founded Souk el Tayeb, the first modern farmers' market in Lebanon, gives his preparation for the smoky wheat known as freekeh (page 246).

The importance of resilience in a food system isn't just critical for developing nations hit by catastrophe—it's important for all of us in a chaotic world. Climate change, political discord, and corporate bottom lines make agriculture and food systems increasingly vulnerable to shocks, both natural and man-made; we saw the terrible effects in the early months of the pandemic, and again during the Russian invasion of Ukraine. When we face crises, we must also see the opportunity for dramatic change. We need to focus our efforts and our resources on resilient food systems, on sustainability, on promoting local solutions embedded in community.

Our future depends on it.

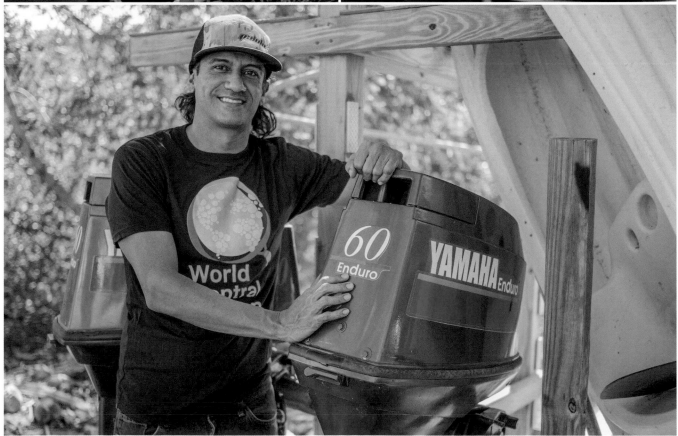

PASSION FRUIT GLAZED SKIRT STEAK

This recipe comes from Yaritza García Ortiz, a farmer in Corozal, Puerto Rico, about thirty minutes southwest of San Juan. Yaritza grows vegetables and roots, like yuca and taro, on her farm, Finca Inarú, since they are resistant to hurricanes and provide a vital source of nutrition after storms. Through WCK's Food Producer Network, she received funding for an all-terrain utility vehicle to help with the farm work. In addition to what she harvests for sale, she has passion fruit vines growing along a fence for cooking at home. She uses the fruit to make a sweet-tart glaze for skirt steak, which hits all the sweet-acid-salt-umami notes. If you can't find fresh passion fruit, look for pulp in the refrigerator or freezer section of your grocery store or Latin market.

SERVES 4

8 **passion fruits** or ½ cup **passion fruit pulp** (strained of seeds)
½ cup **balsamic vinegar**
¼ cup **sugar**
Kosher salt and **freshly ground black pepper**
2 pounds **skirt steak**, about ¾ inch thick

1. Halve the passion fruits and scoop out the pulp with a spoon, adding it to a fine-mesh sieve set over a small bowl. Push the pulp through the sieve with the back of a spoon, making sure to get as much pulp out as possible (discard the seeds).

2. In a small saucepan, combine the passion fruit pulp, vinegar, sugar, and a pinch each of salt and pepper. Cook over medium heat, stirring occasionally, until it starts to thicken, about 20 minutes—it will be a little runnier than jam, but with a nice glaze consistency. Set aside until serving or refrigerate in an airtight container for up to 1 week.

3. About 1 hour before you plan to cook, bring the steak to room temperature: Set it on a plate and sprinkle each side of the steak with ½ teaspoon kosher salt.

4. Prepare an outdoor grill to medium-high direct heat. (Or preheat a grill pan over medium-high heat. Make sure to have your exhaust fan running!)

5. Grill the steak for 2 to 3 minutes per side for medium-rare. Take the steak off the heat, put it on a cutting board, and spoon the glaze over it, enough to make sure the meat is well coated on both sides. (Any leftover glaze makes an excellent sweet-tangy accompaniment for a cheese board.) Let the steak rest for 10 minutes, then cut it against the grain and with the knife at an angle to the cutting board into ½- to ¾-inch-thick slices.

BAHAMIAN STEW FISH
with Grits

The Bahamas, an archipelago of over seven hundred islands, has always had a vibrant fishing industry. When Hurricane Dorian struck the northern islands of the Abacos and Grand Bahama, as many as 90 percent of fishers lost their boats, decimating the industry. After WCK's emergency response, during which we served more than 3 million meals, our Food Producer Network worked for three years supporting dozens of small fishers by providing grants that helped buy new engines, freezers, and other vital equipment. During our time on the islands, our chefs learned to make this breakfast stew made from turbot, a local white fish. (Fire Engine, page 174, is another common breakfast.) Stew fish shares its roots with Creole dishes like gumbo—the toasty brown roux may look familiar, but the tangy-spicy marinade known as Old Sour is all Bahamian.

SERVES 4 TO 6

FISH

1 **habanero chile**, thinly sliced (for less heat, use a serrano or cayenne chile instead)
3 medium **garlic cloves**, peeled
2 tablespoons **fine sea salt**
1 teaspoon **freshly ground black pepper**
4 portions **skinless firm white fish** (6 ounces each), such as turbot, grouper, or snapper

OLD SOUR

Juice of 6 **limes**
Juice of 2 **lemons**
1 **habanero**, **serrano**, or **cayenne chile**, thinly sliced (depending on how spicy you want it)
10 **allspice berries**
1 medium **yellow onion**, halved and thinly sliced

STEW

½ cup **vegetable oil**
1 medium **celery stalk**, finely diced
1 medium all-purpose **potato**, such as Yukon Gold, peeled and medium-diced
1 medium **carrot**, peeled and sliced into ½-inch-thick coins
3 **fresh thyme sprigs**
2 tablespoons **tomato paste**
½ cup **all-purpose flour**
4 cups **fish stock**
Kosher salt and **freshly ground black pepper**
2 tablespoons **dry sherry**
Grits (recipe follows), for serving

1. PREPARE THE FISH: In a mortar, puree the chile, garlic, salt, and black pepper with a pestle until a paste forms. (Or do this in a small food processor or blender.) Place the fish in a medium bowl and, using gloves, massage it with the rub.

2. MAKE THE OLD SOUR: In a small bowl, combine the lime juice, lemon juice, chile, and allspice berries. Pour half the marinade over the fish, cover the fish with the onion slices, and set aside for 20 to 30 minutes to marinate. Reserve the remaining marinade.

3. MAKE THE STEW: Remove the fish and onions from the marinade and discard the marinade. In a medium Dutch oven or deep skillet, heat the vegetable oil over medium-high heat until very hot. Working in batches, fry the fish until browned, about 2 minutes per side (keep a close eye on it to make sure it doesn't burn). Remove the fish from the oil with a slotted spoon or spatula and set aside.

4. Reduce the heat to medium, add the onions to the pot, and cook, stirring occasionally, until translucent and fragrant, 3 to 5 minutes. Add the celery, potato, carrot, and thyme and sauté, stirring regularly, until the vegetables start to soften, 5 to 7 minutes. Stir in the tomato paste

(recipe continues)

1. PREPARE THE PIRI-PIRI SHRIMP: To ensure proper emulsification, make sure all of your ingredients are at room temperature before you begin. In a high-powered blender (don't try this in a food processor), combine the garlic, chiles, lemon juice, cilantro stems, bell pepper, vinegar, tomato, oregano, paprika, and salt to taste. Blend on high until it starts to become a uniform paste. With the machine running, add chunks of the softened butter, about 1 tablespoon at a time, until the piri-piri marinade is emulsified.

2. Place the shrimp in a medium bowl and pour the marinade over the top. Marinate for 2 hours at room temperature, or transfer to an airtight container and marinate in the fridge for up to 8 hours.

3. MAKE THE CILANTRO-GARLIC CHILI SAUCE: In a small food processor, combine the garlic, cilantro leaves, jalapeño (with some of the seeds if you want it spicier), cumin, sea salt, and pepper flakes. Process until the mixture is very finely chopped. With the machine running, slowly drizzle in the olive oil and blend until the sauce is mostly smooth. Scrape down the sides of the food processor, transfer the mixture to a medium bowl, and fold in the roasted red peppers, shallot, and pine nuts. Add the vinegar and salt to taste.

4. MAKE THE XIMA: In a medium pot, combine the coconut milk and 1 cup water and bring to a boil over high heat. Slowly whisk in the cornmeal and stir constantly to avoid sticking. Reduce the heat to low once it starts to thicken, add the kosher salt, and continue whisking until the xima is smooth and supple, 3 to 5 minutes.

5. In a cast-iron skillet, cook the shrimp and its marinade over medium-high heat until fully cooked and pink throughout, about 2 minutes per side.

6. Spoon the warm xima into four bowls. Place some of the shrimp and marinade in each bowl, top with a few spoonfuls of the cilantro-garlic chili sauce, and serve.

MARINATED QUESO FRESCO

De la Crema is the cheesemaking project of sisters Glorimel Torrado and Carmen Rivera, two entrepreneurs in Hatillo, Puerto Rico, the center of the island's dairy industry. Glorimel and Carmen set up their operation next door—literally footsteps away—from Hatillo Dairy and its more than 250 cows, meaning that their milk is as fresh as can be. The women make a variety of fresh and aged cheeses and yogurts, including an incredible aged tetilla with Spanish black truffles. (Carmen completed a PhD thesis in Spain about the science of growing truffles.) This easy recipe highlights de la Crema's Queso Fresco Blanco, a mild, semisoft, slightly tangy cheese that tastes of sweet cream and grass. The cheese sits in an aromatic marinade for a day before being served and is a perfect addition to an appetizer plate with some bread and a cold beer. If you're not lucky enough to have access to de la Crema's cheeses, look for queso fresco or mild French feta.

SERVES 4

1 small **green bell pepper**, diced
1 small **red bell pepper**, diced
1 small **yellow bell pepper**, diced
½ small **yellow onion**, diced
⅓ cup **extra-virgin olive oil**
⅓ cup **distilled white vinegar** or **apple cider vinegar**
¼ cup chopped **fresh cilantro**
1 teaspoon **kosher salt**
1 teaspoon **freshly ground black pepper**
10 ounces **semisoft white cheese**, such as **queso fresco**, cut into ½-inch cubes
1 **baguette**, sliced, or **crackers**, for serving

1. In a large jar, combine all of the bell peppers, the onion, olive oil, vinegar, cilantro, salt, and black pepper. Cover tightly and shake vigorously until well combined.

2. Place the cheese cubes in an airtight container and pour the marinade over the top. Cover and marinate in the refrigerator for at least 8 hours or overnight—though it'll be delicious over the next 2 to 3 days.

3. Serve with a sliced baguette or crackers.

CHOJÍN
Guatemalan Radish and Chicharrón Salad

This refreshing salad originated in Antigua, Guatemala, a city in the central Sacatepéquez department, which has a heavy influence from its Spanish colonizers—including a deep love of pork. It combines the crunch of fresh radish with cool mint leaves and tangy lime, plus a hefty dose of chicharrones, which soak up the dressing and add a salty, fatty crackle. We served it alongside meaty main dishes and warm tortillas in shelters after the 2018 eruption of Volcán de Fuego, which destroyed villages outside Antigua. We also offered it without the crispy pig skin as a vegetarian dish; if you prefer to serve it this way, you can call it *picado de rábano* ("chopped radishes"). Caoba Farms, one of WCK's Food Producer Network grantees, grows peppery, colorful radishes organically in the volcanic soil of Antigua and sells them at local markets. This salad would be perfect with some locally grown radishes and freshly fried chicharrones, if you can find them!

SERVES 4

1 bunch (about ½ pound) **radishes**, finely chopped

1 medium **yellow onion**, halved and finely diced

2 **plum tomatoes**, finely chopped

Juice of 4 **limes**, plus more to taste

2 tablespoons finely chopped **fresh parsley**

2 tablespoons finely chopped **fresh mint**

Kosher salt and **freshly ground black pepper**

1½ cups **fried pork rinds**, freshly fried if possible, and broken into ½- to 1-inch pieces

2 ounces **dry salty cheese** that crumbles easily (see Note)

Corn tortillas (optional), warmed, for serving

2 teaspoons finely chopped **fresh or dried chiltepin chiles** or **fresh jalapeños** (optional)

1. In a large bowl, add the radishes, onion, tomatoes, lime juice, parsley, mint, and salt and pepper to taste and toss to combine—tasting to balance the bright lime and the salt. Right before serving, toss in the pork rinds and crumble in the cheese.

2. If desired, serve the salad over warm tortillas and add some chiles on top for heat. Eat immediately while the pork rinds are still crunchy.

Note: Queso seco and queso Cotija work best (Fud, Tropical, or el Centroamericano brands are available at many Latin markets), or use queso fresco or queso llanero. Feta works in a pinch.

PRESSURE COOKER GUATEMALAN RED BEANS *with Beef Short Ribs*

This recipe comes from a short cookbook that WCK published in 2022 as part of our Clean Cooking program in Guatemala, *Recetas para olla de presión con tradición* (*Traditional Pressure Cooker Recipes*). The goal of the cookbook, and the program, was to teach families how to prepare nutritious meals using less energy-intensive methods than cooking over a wood fire, which is how beans are traditionally prepared in Guatemala. In a pressure cooker, they are done much faster and use a lot less energy. We've included directions for both traditional pressure cookers and electric pressure cookers (such as the Instant Pot); whichever you use, you'll have dinner on the table in under an hour.

SERVES 4 TO 6

1 pound **dried red beans**

4 tablespoons **canola oil**

2 pounds **bone-in beef short ribs**

1 medium **yellow onion**, finely chopped

1 medium **red bell pepper**, finely chopped

4 medium **garlic cloves**, thinly sliced

2 **plum tomatoes**, quartered

4 small **tomatillos**, husked and halved

1 **pasilla chile**, seeded and cut into thin ribbons

1 **dried guajillo chile**, seeded and cut into thin ribbons

2 tablespoons **roasted pumpkin seed powder** (see Note)

2 teaspoons **ground cumin**

1 teaspoon **achiote powder**

Kosher salt and **freshly ground black pepper**

Cooked white rice, for serving

1. For at least 3 hours before cooking (overnight is fine), soak the beans in water in a large bowl. Drain before cooking.

2. In the pressure cooker, heat 2 tablespoons of the oil over medium heat. (If using an electric pressure cooker, set to sauté.) Sear the short ribs in batches until lightly browned, about 2 minutes per side. Set them aside.

3. Add the remaining 2 tablespoons oil to the pot. When the oil is hot, sweat the onion until softened, about 3 minutes. Add the bell pepper and garlic and cook, stirring constantly, until the bell pepper softens, about 2 minutes. Add the tomatoes and tomatillos and cook, stirring constantly, until the tomatoes start to break down, about 2 minutes. Add ¼ cup water, the dried chiles, pumpkin seed powder, cumin, and achiote and cook until the sofrito is fragrant, 2 to 3 more minutes. (On an electric pressure cooker, cancel sauté.)

4. Add the drained beans, reserved short ribs, and 8 cups water. Mix well. Season with 2 teaspoons salt and pepper to taste and stir. Cover the pot and lock the lid.

5. Set the pot over high heat and bring the mixture to a boil without the weighted gauge. When steam consistently rises from the opening, place the weighted gauge on top. When the hissing gets very loud, turn the heat down so the gauge maintains a steady rhythm and cook for 30 minutes. For either type of cooker, the total time should be about 45 minutes, including the time it takes to come to pressure.

6. Carefully release the pressure using a quick-release method, then open the pressure cooker, taste, and add more salt and/or pepper, if necessary.

7. Serve hot with white rice on the side.

Note: Pumpkin seed powder can be found at some Latin markets, or you can make your own. Roast 2 heaping tablespoons of raw hulled pumpkin seeds in a 350°F oven for 10 to 12 minutes, then pulverize them in a spice grinder until they're a fine powder.

PAPAS ARRUGADAS CON MOJO ROJO

During WCK's response to an island-splitting volcanic eruption on La Palma in Spain's Canary Islands, we supported local farmers by buying and serving thousands of salty, earthy *papas arrugadas*—"wrinkled potatoes." They're traditionally made by boiling potatoes in seawater (we compensated by cooking them in *very* salty water, which gives them their wrinkles) and then serving alongside a garlicky classic mojo rojo made from local red chiles. Mojo recipes differ from household to household in the Canaries. This beautifully rich and smooth version comes from WCK chef Olivier de Belleroche.

SERVES 4

POTATOES

2 pounds small **new potatoes**,
    no larger than 2 inches in diameter
Kosher salt or **coarse sea salt**

MOJO ROJO

1 **red bell pepper**, left whole
1 teaspoon **cumin seeds**
4 medium **garlic cloves**, peeled
1 teaspoon **sea salt**
1 tablespoon **white wine vinegar**
1 teaspoon **pimentón** (smoked paprika)
¾ cup **extra-virgin olive oil**

1. Preheat the oven to 450°F.

2. COOK THE POTATOES: In a large pot, combine the potatoes with water to cover by about 3 inches. Set over high heat and add enough salt to make it as salty as the ocean—start with ¼ cup (!) and stir it in, then add more as needed (as the water warms up, the salt will dissolve more easily). Bring the water to a boil, then reduce the heat to a simmer and cook until the potatoes are tender and able to be pierced to the center with a paring knife, 25 to 30 minutes total. The potatoes will begin to wrinkle (arrugar) as they cook.

3. MEANWHILE, START THE MOJO ROJO: Place the red bell pepper on a small sheet pan and roast, turning it every few minutes with tongs, until the skin is charred and the pepper is soft, 10 to 15 minutes. Remove the pan from the oven and allow the pepper to cool for a few minutes. Carefully remove the skin; if you have difficulty, you can put the pepper in a paper bag for a few minutes to steam it, then try again. Remove the stem and seeds and set it aside.

4. When the potatoes are tender, carefully pour out almost all of the water, leaving just enough to cover the bottom of the pot, about ¼ inch. Reduce the heat to medium-low, return the pot to the heat, and cook, regularly shaking the pot to shake the potatoes, until the remaining water has evaporated and the salt starts crystallizing, 8 to 10 minutes. Remove the pot from the stove, then cover it with a kitchen towel so the potatoes steam and continue to wrinkle until ready to serve.

5. FINISH THE MOJO: In a small skillet, toast the cumin seeds for 1 to 2 minutes over low heat, until fragrant. Transfer the seeds to a small food processor and add the roasted pepper, garlic, salt, vinegar, and pimentón and blend until it's a uniform color and texture. Slowly drizzle in the olive oil and keep blending until you have a smooth, bright red paste—if it emulsifies, great; if it doesn't, it's not a problem (some may argue it's more traditional that way). Taste the mojo and adjust for salt, knowing that you're about to dip a very salty potato in it.

6. Serve the potatoes in a large bowl with the mojo rojo in another small bowl on the side for dipping. If you're not serving the potatoes immediately, you can put the mojo in a bowl and keep it in the fridge to firm up a little before serving.

KAMAL'S FREEKEH
with Caramelized Onions

Freekeh, an ancient grain from the Levant, is wheat that hasn't yet turned from green to straw yellow. Since green wheat rots quickly, farmers throw it in open fires in the field to dry and preserve it. The grains maintain their green color and develop a smoky flavor from the fire. Kamal Mouzawak, the founder of Lebanon's first modern farmers' market, Souk el Tayeb, explains that freekeh is a taste of a peaceful Lebanon: "For me, freekeh is about the time after the civil war, when Lebanon was no longer divided into impenetrable regions anymore, we could move around and taste the 'other' again." Freekeh was a regional specialty of the southern part of the country, so he had never tasted it before opening the market in 2004. But now it's popular throughout the country and has been introduced to the rest of the world. Freekeh is easy to cook and very adaptable—it can be served fully cooked and as separate grains, like bulgur, or creamy and soupy, almost like a risotto. This recipe from Kamal is simple and delicious—just make sure to give the onions enough time to fully caramelize. Serve the freekeh with meat, fish, or roasted vegetables.

SERVES 4

¼ cup **extra-virgin olive oil**
3 medium **yellow onions**, finely chopped
1 cup **coarse freekeh**
2 cups **chicken**, **vegetable**, or **fish stock** or **water**
Kosher salt

1. In a large sauté pan with a lid or a Dutch oven, heat the olive oil over medium-low heat until shimmering. Add the onions, stir to coat, cover, and cook, stirring every 5 minutes or so, until they're a deep caramel-brown confit, almost resembling marmalade, 45 to 60 minutes. If there's still any moisture left in the pan, cook uncovered for about 5 minutes, or until it's mostly evaporated.

2. While the onions are cooking, put the freekeh in a medium bowl and rinse with water, discarding anything that floats. Don't soak the grains too long—you don't want to lose the smoky flavor.

3. When the onions are caramelized, add the freekeh and toast, stirring constantly, for 5 minutes. Add the stock and salt to taste and bring to a boil over medium-high heat. Once it boils, reduce the heat to low and cook, uncovered, until the grains are tender, 25 to 30 minutes.

BUY LOCAL

In the United States, traditional food relief after a disaster tends to rely on food that's quick and easy to distribute. That usually means "meals ready to eat," or MREs. If you've never tasted an MRE, consider yourself lucky. They're designed to be deployed to battlefields and engineered to be just as edible on Day 100 as Day 1, whether they've been left in the desert heat or jungle humidity for weeks or months (or years!). They're known to be passable soccer balls in a pinch. José's R&D culinary team—the minds also behind multiple Michelin stars—experimented for days on MREs and couldn't tweeze any life into them.

Anyone who's lived on MREs for days at a time knows one key thing about them: They stop a body up. Sure, they're edible, and some of the varieties might taste good to select palates (macaroni and chili—aka chili mac—is a particularly sought-after MRE). But they're tough on the stomach and designed for battlefield conditions—not a natural disaster. In the early days after a traumatic event, when the soul needs to be nourished, who wants a meal calibrated to survive a war? Why do relief agencies turn to the MRE to feed people in need and then ship them all over the world?

The short answer is a bureaucracy that prioritizes American products, even when local ones are available. It's the reason you'll find bags of American corn and wheat distributed around the world, despite local availability. It's the reason that American rice was distributed for free in Haiti after the 2010 earthquake, driving down the market price for rice and pushing local farmers out of business. Until recently, American agencies were *legally required* to distribute American products, and some still do—though many are starting to source locally now that the legal constraint has been removed.

World Central Kitchen isn't obligated to follow these rules. It would never occur to us to ship resources halfway around the world when those ingredients exist locally. Chefs know: The best product doesn't come from a factory farm across the country—it comes from the family farm in the next town over. In restaurant kitchens, buying local usually makes the most sense. Even if the economy of scale doesn't work in your favor, the quality tends to be higher with lower transportation costs. And the local investment helps your neighbors stay in business, keeping the economic health of the community strong. Though we've also learned not to monopolize the market by buying too much of the local produce; the community also needs to be able to shop.

On Hawaii's Big Island after the 2018 explosion of Kilauea, a local farmer realized he needed to harvest his entire crop of purple Okinawan sweet potatoes before they were destroyed by falling ash. He knew our kitchen was one of the only ones operating in the area, so he offered us his harvest; we bought many of his potatoes and made beautiful multilayered Haupia Bars (page 262), an island favorite.

On the island of Providencia in the Caribbean, which was in the path of back-to-back hurricanes that damaged 98 percent of its infrastructure in November 2020, José embraced the "buy local" mentality. He found a local fisherman—one whose equipment survived the storms—who was bringing spiny lobsters to shore. José bought everything the fisherman offered and put a deposit on the next day's catch (for a taste of the island's cuisine, try the Rondón on page 251).

In eastern Kentucky in the summer of 2022, in partnership with chef Edward Lee's LEE Initiative, we bought produce from small farmers whose markets and storage space were wiped out by floods. We set up a farmers' market to give away the produce to families who were also dealing with the disaster. By offering local products—including ham and cornmeal milled in the area—we provided not only culturally appropriate foods but also agency. Many families in rural eastern Kentucky live off the land; they have small garden plots to feed themselves and rarely visit a grocery store. By giving them access to products they were familiar with, they could go home and cook for themselves, regaining a sense of normalcy in a difficult time.

It's a lesson we learned early in the pandemic when we distributed grocery boxes to families across the Navajo Nation. Along with produce and dry goods, the team—which was entirely Diné (Navajo), led by production manager Ollie Arviso—included a Diné specialty, neeshjizhii, or dried steamed corn, in the deliveries. Neeshjizhii, the result of an intensive three-day process of cooking in an underground oven, is profoundly smoky, and when stewed with lamb or mutton represents comfort and food medicine to many members of the community. We bought and distributed almost 16,000 pounds of neeshjizhii from two local producers, along with more than 1,500 tons of other food. When we can work closely with a community and offer meaningful products, it's just common sense—why would we ship something inferior that has no connection when we can keep the money, and the spirit, local?

"Buy local" has become something of a cliché. But it taps into something bigger that can't fit on a bumper sticker. It's not just about supporting local farmers or fishers, not just about keeping dollars in the local economy. It isn't just about finding better products or discovering new ingredients. It's not even just about countering the effects of climate change. It's all of those things and more: a shift away from a destructive way of looking at the world, one rooted in imperialism, Western paternalism, and protectionism. It's a new paradigm, one that can generate positive change at local and global levels—for ourselves and generations to come.

RONDÓN

Our team was introduced to rondón, a specialty of the Colombian islands of San Andrés and Providencia, off the coast of Nicaragua in the Caribbean, after Hurricanes Iota and Eta hit the islands in November 2020. Rondón is a process-intensive dish made on the beach for community gatherings—it's not typically served in restaurants. To learn how to make it, we drove 4×4s to a small beach hotel where a local cook walked José and the team through the process: Grate coconuts to make coconut milk, then simmer it over an open fire with fish and shellfish, root vegetables, yuca dumplings, and aromatics until you have a rich, thick stew. This recipe is simplified to make it easier for those far from the white sand beaches of San Andrés, but it's still a project—we may not start with grating coconuts by hand, but a few difficult-to-source ingredients like conch and pig tail (see Notes, page 252) are important to the final dish and are included in our version. The service is also important: Traditionally, each ingredient is composed on the plate and topped with the coconut-rich cooking liquid as a sauce. Serve with hot sauce like Pique (page 293) and a beer or Rum Sour (page 281).

SERVES 4 TO 6

MARINATED FISH

2½ pounds **fish fillets** (such as sea bass, red snapper, grouper, or turbot), cut into 3-inch-wide strips
Juice of 2 **lemons**
1½ tablespoons **fine sea salt**
¼ teaspoon **freshly ground black pepper**

DUMPLINGS

3 cups (450 grams) **cassava flour** or **corn flour**, plus more for rolling
1 tablespoon **baking powder**
1 tablespoon **fine sea salt**
1 cup **full-fat coconut milk**

STEW

1 small head **garlic**, separated into cloves and peeled
2 (13.5-ounce) cans **full-fat coconut milk**
1 large **yellow onion**, diced
2-inch piece **fresh ginger**, peeled
1 pound **yuca**, peeled and cut into 2-inch pieces
1 pound **ñame** (see page 32) or **sweet potato**, peeled and cut into 2-inch pieces
3 **green plantains**, peeled (see Note, page 288) and each cut into thirds
1 (15-ounce) can **conch** (see Notes), drained and cut into 2-inch pieces
1 pound **unsalted pig tail** (see Notes), cut into 2-inch pieces
½ cup roughly chopped **fresh basil**
½ cup roughly chopped **fresh oregano**
1 tablespoon **black peppercorns**
Fine sea salt

1. MARINATE THE FISH: In a large bowl, combine the fish strips, lemon juice, salt, and pepper and set aside to marinate at room temperature while you prepare the rest of the dish.

(recipe continues)

2. MAKE THE DUMPLINGS: In a large bowl, mix the cassava flour, baking powder, and salt. Gradually pour in the coconut milk and stir until a smooth dough forms. Knead for 10 minutes until smooth and pliable, then cover and let rest at room temperature for 20 minutes.

3. MAKE THE STEW: Add the garlic cloves to a mortar and mash into a paste with a pestle (or process in a small food processor). In a large pot with a lid or Dutch oven, combine the coconut milk, 4 cups water, the garlic paste, onion, and ginger and bring to a boil over medium-high heat. Boil for 3 minutes. Reduce the heat to medium, add the yuca, ñame, and green plantains and simmer until they start to soften, about 10 minutes.

4. Add the marinated fish with its liquid, the conch, and pig tail and simmer for 5 more minutes. There won't be much excess liquid in the pot, and some ingredients will not be fully covered—stir gently to make sure everything gets cooked. After 5 minutes, add the basil, oregano, and peppercorns. Taste the broth and adjust the seasoning if needed with salt.

5. While the broth simmers, roll out the dumpling dough on a large cutting board dusted with flour into a thin rectangle about 15 × 5 inches and ⅛ to ¼ inch thick. Cut the dough into strips that are about 1 × 5 inches.

6. Check the yuca and ñame by piercing them with a fork; they should be soft almost all the way through. Place the dough strips on top of the cooking stew, making sure to not overlap them. Cover the pot with the lid and let it simmer until they cook fully, 10 to 15 minutes. When the dumplings are done, they'll look soft, smooth, and a bit glossy and will lose their raw taste.

7. SERVING THE RONDÓN IS AN ART: With a slotted spoon or tongs, remove the stew elements and dumplings (being careful not to break them) and place them in four separate medium bowls: vegetables and plantains in one, dumplings in another, fish and conch in a third, pig tails in a fourth. Serve each person with a few pieces from each bowl, finishing with the coconut broth as a sauce instead of as a soup.

Notes:

- Pig tails are often available at Latin or Caribbean markets. If you can only find salted pig tails, boil them in water for 30 minutes, then drain and set them aside to cool before using.

- Canned conch can be found in some specialty stores or online; you may find it by its Italian name, scungilli.

JOY

SWEETS, DRINKS, AND RECIPES FOR CELEBRATING

No hay mal que por bien no venga. (There is no chaos that good cannot come from.)

—PUERTO RICAN SAYING

MOMENTS OF JOY CAN BE FEW AND FAR BETWEEN DURING A CRISIS. People go through a wide range of emotions, and happiness is rarely among them.

One of our goals is to bring brief pleasure to people through a hug, a friendly word, and of course with food. While we can't change the reality of a situation, we can at least bring a touch of joy to the moment. Food is a source of hope, food is dignity, food is empathy . . . we've talked about all those things.

But one thing in particular can truly bring actual *joy* to people in even the darkest times: sweets.

WCK usually doesn't serve dessert with meals, though we almost always include a piece of fruit. There's nothing wrong with sweets; we just spend our energy and resources cooking holistically nutritious meals and don't usually have the facilities to provide desserts that don't add significant nutritional benefit.

But that doesn't mean we *never* serve them. Especially when we're feeding children, we like to include a treat now and again. Cooking for kids brings our teams special joy, too. In Venezuela, we served very young children and their parents as they came to our dining room; some of them, like two-year-old Camila, were in danger of malnutrition when they started visiting. Over days, weeks, and months, we saw her grow up and get healthier and healthier with regular meals. The Torta de Cambur (page 261) is the banana bread we served in the dining room, a favorite with the kids there.

COOKING FOR KIDS BRINGS OUR TEAMS SPECIAL JOY, TOO.

In this chapter you'll find a brightly colored, multilayered Hawaiian Haupia Bar (page 262), made with coconut and bright purple sweet potato, appropriate for breakfast or a festive holiday dessert; a Tres Leches (page 265) that became one of our go-tos when celebrating birthdays for the youngest residents in the border-crossing camps of Matamoros in Mexico; and Guatemalan Buñuelos (page 266), little fried doughnuts served with a sweet honey-citrus syrup that make an appearance in early December throughout the country for the Quema del Diablo, a traditional holiday.

Easter in Ukraine is a big deal, which is why even in the midst of war, we worked with partners to serve tens of thousands of Easter cakes, or pasky (see recipe for Paska, page 274), to families around the country, along with colored eggs. Our recipe came from the family of one of our Ukrainian team leads. You'll also find an incredible Lemon Olive Oil Cake (page 269) from Meghan, The Duchess of Sussex. You'll want to have it on the kitchen counter at all times, available for a slice with your afternoon coffee.

At the end of the chapter are three cocktail recipes, two of which can be served without alcohol for young ones and nondrinkers. Coquito and Kremas are Puerto Rican and Haitian variations, respectively, of a creamy holiday drink. They bring joy both as a drink and as a gift; it's common in both places to exchange bottles with friends and family throughout the holiday season, bringing people together and lifting spirits no matter the situation. And finally, José's favorite rum sour is a delicious basil-infused version of the classic Caribbean cocktail. With the recipe, he shares his thoughts about the drink and its importance in the early days of WCK's work in Puerto Rico, a punctuation mark between a long day and a productive night.

During and after a crisis, children often don't comprehend the enormity of the situation they're in. That innocence allows for unexpected moments of pure joy. Sharing something sweet, throwing a birthday party, listening to live music, dancing—these are the times we love to see, when kids (and their parents!) can forget the troubles around them and just have fun. These are the moments that recharge our batteries.

TORTA DE CAMBUR
Venezuelan Banana Bread

—

We served millions of bananas, called cambures in Venezuela, to children who received hot meals out of our kitchen in Caracas. From 2019 until 2022, we cooked for Venezuelan families in the capital, as well as refugees fleeing the economic situation in the country (see Refugees and Migration, page 100, for more about our work on the Venezuelan-Colombian border). When the kitchen had too many ripe bananas—and for holidays like Children's Day—we would bake torta de cambur for the kids. And don't worry too much about the rum if you're baking for kids because the alcohol bakes off, or you can just leave it out and add another splash of vanilla.

MAKES A 1½-POUND LOAF (SEE NOTE)

TOPPING
2 tablespoons **unsalted butter**, at room temperature
2 tablespoons **light brown sugar**
2 tablespoons **all-purpose flour**
1 tablespoon **ground cinnamon**
1 ripe medium **banana**, peeled and
   cut lengthwise into thirds

BATTER
Softened butter and **flour** for the pan
2 cups (240 grams) **all-purpose flour**, sifted
½ cup (107 grams) packed **light brown sugar**
1 teaspoon **table salt**
2 teaspoons **baking powder**
½ teaspoon **baking soda**
1 teaspoon **ground cinnamon**
3 ripe medium **bananas**, peeled
1 cup (312 grams) **sweetened condensed milk**
8 tablespoons (113 grams) **unsalted butter**, melted
⅓ cup (76 grams) **whole milk**
¼ cup (59 grams) **dark rum**
1 tablespoon **vanilla extract**
3 large **eggs**, beaten

1 cup (113 grams) chopped **walnuts** (optional)
1 cup (170 grams) **chocolate chips** (optional)

1. MAKE THE TOPPING: In a small bowl, use your fingers to mix the butter, brown sugar, flour, and cinnamon into small, pea-size clumps and set aside.

2. Preheat the oven to 375°F. Butter a 10 × 5 × 3-inch (1½-pound) loaf pan (see Note) and dust with flour.

3. MAKE THE BATTER: In a large bowl, combine the flour, brown sugar, salt, baking powder, baking soda, and cinnamon.

4. In a medium bowl, mash the 3 bananas until smooth. Add the condensed milk and mix well with a wooden spoon to combine. Add the melted butter, whole milk, rum, vanilla, and eggs and stir to combine.

5. Pour the banana mixture into the flour mixture. Stir in the walnuts and/or chocolate chips, if using, being careful not to overmix. It's okay if there are some pockets of flour remaining in the batter.

6. Transfer the batter to the prepared loaf pan. Lay the sliced banana on top of the loaf (it's okay if it breaks into smaller pieces) and sprinkle the topping over everything. Cover the loaf pan loosely with aluminum foil and bake for 1 hour.

7. At this point, the sides of the bread will be cooked but the center will still be underbaked. Remove the foil and bake until a toothpick inserted into the center comes out clean and the top is browned, about 15 minutes longer. The banana bread can be wrapped in foil and stored at room temperature for up to 3 days.

Note: This recipe bakes in a 10 × 5 × 3-inch (1½-pound) loaf pan; if your pan is a standard 8½ × 4½-inch (1-pound) size, fill it about two-thirds full and bake the rest in a muffin tin (the muffins will need less time to bake, closer to 30 minutes).

PURPLE SWEET POTATO HAUPIA BARS

The striking purple center of this Hawaiian bar comes from Okinawan sweet potato—a dense, rich tuber originally from the Japanese island of Okinawa and grown locally in Hawaii. The top layer, made of thickened sweet coconut milk, is called haupia, and it's a popular dessert on its own. This three-layer bar isn't too sweet, so it can easily be enjoyed for breakfast or with an afternoon coffee. We made trays of them while responding to the 2018 eruption of Kilauea, on the Big Island of Hawaii. A farmer affected by the volcano's ash dug up his sweet potatoes and offered them to our team, so we bought his harvest and turned them into this treat.

MAKES SIXTEEN 1-INCH SQUARES

Softened butter for the pan

CRUST
1 cup (96 grams) **coarse almond meal**
1 tablespoon **light brown sugar**
1 teaspoon **ground cinnamon**
½ teaspoon **table salt**
8 tablespoons (113 grams) **unsalted butter**, melted

SWEET POTATO FILLING
¾ pound **purple sweet potatoes** (see Note), peeled and cut into 1-inch cubes
¼ cup (54 grams) packed **light brown sugar**
¼ cup (59 grams) **evaporated milk**
1 large **egg**, beaten
1 teaspoon **vanilla extract**
1 teaspoon **ground cinnamon**
½ teaspoon **ground ginger**
½ teaspoon **ground nutmeg**

HAUPIA
1 (13.5-ounce) can **full-fat coconut milk**
¼ cup (50 grams) **granulated sugar**
3 tablespoons **cornstarch**

1. Preheat the oven to 350°F. Butter an 8-inch square baking pan.

2. MAKE THE CRUST: In a small bowl, combine the almond meal, brown sugar, cinnamon, salt, and melted butter and mix with a fork until it's uniformly sandy. Press the crust firmly into the baking pan to form an even layer (the bottom of a measuring cup is great for compacting).

3. Bake until the crust is a deeper golden brown, about 15 minutes. Remove the pan from the oven and set aside to cool. Leave the oven on and increase the temperature to 400°F.

4. PREPARE THE SWEET POTATO FILLING: In a medium saucepan, bring 2 cups water to a boil. Add the sweet potato cubes and cook until the point of a knife can easily pierce them, 6 to 8 minutes. Drain the potatoes well and return them to the saucepan. Mash with a potato masher or wooden spoon until completely smooth. Let the potatoes cool at room temperature for 5 minutes, then add the rest of the filling ingredients and combine thoroughly with a wooden spoon or spatula.

5. Pour the filling onto the prepared crust and spread evenly. Bake for 10 minutes, then reduce the oven temperature to 325°F and bake until the center of the filling is set and doesn't jiggle, about 10 minutes longer. Remove from the oven and allow to cool completely.

6. MAKE THE HAUPIA: In a small, heavy-bottomed saucepan, combine the coconut milk, granulated sugar, cornstarch, and ¼ cup water, whisking to eliminate any lumps. Set over medium heat and cook, stirring constantly, until the mixture comes to a boil, then reduce to a simmer. Continue to cook, stirring until the mixture thickens enough to coat the back of a spoon, 6 to 8 minutes. Remove the haupia from the heat and let cool for 3 minutes before pouring over the sweet potato filling. Spread evenly over the filling, then refrigerate, uncovered, for 12 to 24 hours to set.

7. Cut into squares and serve. Store leftovers in an airtight container in the refrigerator for up to 3 days.

Note: Purple sweet potatoes, a specialty of Hawaii and the Japanese island of Okinawa, are fragrant, beautiful, and high in antioxidants. The most common variety available across the US is Stokes Purple.

TRES LECHES

Tres leches is an airy, light sponge cake that is soaked in—you guessed it—three milks. It's a go-to dessert to celebrate birthdays and other special moments when we're working in Latin America. One of the first times we made it was in Matamoros, Mexico, at a border-crossing camp for families coming north. A team member's daughter, Adriana, helped us in the dining hall. When she turned five, we asked what kind of cake she wanted. "Dos leches!" she said enthusiastically. Chef Elyssa Kaplan, not knowing which leche to leave out, made a traditional tres leches and served it to Adriana and her friends in the camp. This recipe actually has *four* leches in it but we imagine Adriana wouldn't mind. The cake is best after soaking in the fridge overnight.

MAKES ONE 9 × 13-INCH CAKE

Softened butter for the pan

CAKE
1½ cups (180 grams) **all-purpose flour**
1 tablespoon **baking powder**
½ teaspoon **table salt**
6 large **eggs**, separated
¾ cup (150 grams) **granulated sugar**
1 teaspoon **vanilla extract**
½ cup (113 grams) **whole milk**

SOAK
1 (12-ounce) can **evaporated milk**
1 cup **whole milk**
½ cup **sweetened condensed milk**
½ cup **heavy whipping cream**
½ teaspoon **ground cinnamon**

TOPPING
1 cup **heavy whipping cream**
1 tablespoon **granulated sugar**
½ teaspoon **ground cinnamon**
16 ounces **blueberries, raspberries,** or sliced **strawberries** (optional), for garnish

1. Preheat the oven to 350°F. Butter a 9 × 13-inch glass baking dish.

2. MAKE THE CAKE: Sift the flour, baking powder, and salt into a large bowl and set aside.

3. In a bowl (with an electric mixer if you have one), beat the egg whites until they're white and fluffy and hold their shape—the soft-peak stage. In a separate bowl, combine the egg yolks, granulated sugar, and vanilla and whisk to combine for a minute or so—the yolks should lighten in color and expand in volume.

4. Add the egg yolk mixture and the whole milk to the flour mixture and stir with a rubber spatula until no lumps remain. Carefully fold in the beaten egg whites, working gently so you don't deflate them.

5. Pour the batter into the prepared pan, gently level it with a rubber or offset spatula, and bake until a toothpick inserted in the center comes out clean, 30 to 35 minutes. Set on a wire rack to cool for 20 to 30 minutes.

6. MEANWHILE, MAKE THE SOAK: In a large measuring cup or glass jar, combine the evaporated milk, whole milk, condensed milk, and heavy cream. With a fork or a whisk, mix in the cinnamon.

7. After the cake has cooled, pierce the surface all over with a fork. Slowly pour the soak over the cake, making sure every part is covered. The milk will slowly seep into the cake. Cover the cake with plastic wrap and refrigerate overnight.

8. MAKE THE TOPPING: Place the bowl of a stand mixer (or a mixing bowl) in the freezer to chill. When you're ready to serve the cake, pour the heavy cream and sugar into the chilled mixer bowl and beat on high with the whisk attachment (or hand mixer) for 1 to 2 minutes, until the cream is sturdy enough to spread. (Alternatively, use a large bowl, a whisk, and your strong arm.)

9. Spread the whipped cream over the cake and sprinkle the cinnamon on top. If you'd like, decorate with fruit of your choice. Serve the cake immediately or refrigerate it for up to 8 hours.

SOFIA'S BUÑUELOS

The start of the Christmas season for many Guatemalans is December 7, known as Quema del Diablo: the burning of the devil. Throughout the historic center of Guatemala City, you can buy devil-shaped piñatas, known as Diablitos, and burn them to celebrate the holiday. Chef Sofia Deleon, owner of El Merkury in Philadelphia—and a member of WCK's Chef Corps—remembers celebrating Quema del Diablo with her grandparents: "When the clock hit 6 p.m., we burned the piñata with old newspapers and twigs to make a bonfire. Once the fire was gone, we proceeded to my favorite part: the food." Sofia's grandmother would make hundreds of buñuelos, fried dough balls served with a sweet citrusy honey that are traditionally made to celebrate the holiday. Here's Sofia's recipe, adapted from her abuela's.

MAKES ABOUT 20 BUÑUELOS

DOUGH
½ cup (118 grams) **warm water** (110° to 115°F)
2¼ teaspoons **active dry yeast**
½ cup (113 grams) **whole milk**
2 teaspoons grated **orange zest**
1½ cups plus 2 tablespoons (196 grams) **all-purpose flour**
½ cup (85 grams) **raisins**
2 tablespoons **canola oil**
1 tablespoon **granulated sugar**
½ teaspoon **kosher salt**

CITRUS SYRUP
1½ cups **granulated sugar**
½ cup **honey**
Strips of zest from 1 **orange**
Strips of zest from 1 **mandarin orange**
Strips of zest from 2 **lemons**
1 **cinnamon stick**

BUÑUELOS
Canola oil, for deep-frying
Powdered sugar (optional), for dusting

1. MAKE THE DOUGH: In a large bowl, mix the warm water and yeast with a fork. Let the mixture sit for about 10 minutes to dissolve the yeast.

2. In a small saucepan, combine the milk and orange zest and set over medium-high heat until the milk is 110° to 115°F. Add the warmed milk and zest to the large bowl with the yeast, then add the flour, raisins, canola oil, granulated sugar, and salt. Mix it with a rubber spatula until it's a sticky, thick batter. Cover the bowl with a kitchen towel and let rise in a warm place until it doubles in size, about 1 hour.

3. MAKE THE CITRUS SYRUP: In a small pot, combine all of the ingredients and 1½ cups water and stir briefly to combine. Bring the mixture to a gentle boil over medium heat until the sugar is melted and the mixture is fragrant, about 20 minutes. Remove the syrup from the heat and let the mixture steep and cool while you fry the buñuelos. Once it's cool, strain out the zest and cinnamon stick. (The zest strips are now candied, so reserve them to add to other treats.)

4. FRY THE BUÑUELOS: Line a large plate with paper towels. Pour at least 3 inches of canola oil into a Dutch oven, deep-fryer, or wide, heavy-bottomed pot and heat to 350° to 360°F.

5. Once the oil is hot, working in batches to not crowd the pan, coat a small (1½ tablespoon) ice cream scoop or a deep soup spoon in oil and drop small balls of dough into the hot oil. Depending on the size of your pot, you can make 3 or 4 at a time. Fry until golden brown, 1 to 2 minutes per side. It's a very fast process—you should be able to make about 20 buñuelos total, depending on their size. Use a slotted spoon to transfer them to the paper towels to drain.

6. To serve, put a few buñuelos in a bowl for each person and drizzle some of the citrus syrup on top: 1 or 2 tablespoons is nicely sweet, but if you like them extra sweet, add 2 to 3 tablespoons of syrup and an extra dusting of powdered sugar. (Sofia has a serious sweet tooth, so she loves the powdered sugar on top!)

THE DUCHESS'S LEMON OLIVE OIL CAKE

WCK found a simpatico partner in The Archewell Foundation, the nonprofit started by Prince Harry and Meghan, the Duke and Duchess of Sussex. To mark the two organizations' friendship, Meghan, an experienced baker and food lover, sent a cake to a group of female restaurateurs who partnered with WCK during the pandemic and community members for whom they provided meals. A letter was included: *"We hope you enjoy the offering we baked for you—a small token of thanks, from our home to yours. Our hope with this effort is to show that, when we all participate, even the smallest actions can have a ripple effect. Even individual actions can impact the whole of us."* Make this beautiful cake and share a slice with a neighbor to see that ripple effect in action.

SERVES 8 TO 12

CRYSTALLIZED ROSEMARY (OPTIONAL)

3 small **rosemary sprigs**, each no more than 1 inch long

1 large **egg white**, lightly beaten

2 teaspoons **granulated sugar** or **superfine sugar**

CAKE

Cooking spray

1⅓ cups (267 grams) **extra-virgin olive oil**

3 large **eggs**

1¼ cups (283 grams) **whole milk**

1½ tablespoons grated **lemon zest**

¼ cup (60 grams) **fresh lemon juice**

¼ cup (60 grams) **limoncello**

2 teaspoons **lemon extract** (optional)

1¾ cups (350 grams) **granulated sugar**

2 cups plus 2 tablespoons (255 grams) **all-purpose flour**

1½ teaspoons **fine sea salt**

½ teaspoon **baking powder**

½ teaspoon **baking soda**

Powdered sugar, for dusting

1. IF DESIRED, MAKE THE CRYSTALLIZED ROSEMARY: At least 6 hours before you plan to serve the cake, brush all sides of the rosemary, one sprig at a time, with a little of the egg white (you'll have egg white left over). Spread the sugar on a plate and press the rosemary into the sugar so the needles are lightly coated on all sides. Repeat with the remaining rosemary. Set aside on a wire rack to dry for at least 6 hours or up to overnight.

2. MAKE THE CAKE: Preheat the oven to 325°F. Line a 9-inch springform pan at least 3 inches deep (see Note) with a round of parchment paper and coat the parchment paper and the sides of the pan very well with cooking spray.

3. In a large bowl, whisk together the olive oil and eggs until emulsified. Add the milk, lemon zest, lemon juice, limoncello, and lemon extract (if using) and whisk to combine. Add the granulated sugar and whisk to combine. Add the flour, salt, baking powder, and baking soda and whisk until just incorporated; don't overmix. The batter will be on the thin side; this is normal.

4. Transfer the batter to the prepared springform pan. Place the pan on a baking sheet as insurance against leaks and bake until golden brown and domed in the center and a toothpick inserted in the center comes out clean or with just a few moist crumbs attached, 1 hour to 1 hour 15 minutes. (Begin checking at 1 hour.)

5. Remove the cake from the oven and let cool in the pan on a wire rack for about 1 hour. Then release the springform sides and carefully peel off the springform bottom. Set the cake on the rack to finish cooling.

6. Dust with powdered sugar prior to serving. If using, decorate the top with the sprigs of crystallized rosemary.

Note: Be sure to use a springform pan that's at least 3 inches deep for this cake. Most regular 9-inch round cake pans are no more than 2 inches deep and this cake will overflow.

SHARING JOY IN A BRUTAL WORLD

When Russia invaded Ukraine in early 2022, WCK arrived at the main border crossing between Poland and western Ukraine within twenty-four hours to see how we could offer support. The scope of the horror was beyond anything we'd ever seen, affecting tens of millions of Ukrainians. In the days following the invasion, we set up a kitchen just over the western border of Ukraine in Poland, cooking meals and partnering with local Polish restaurants and food trucks to serve the massive influx of refugees, many of whom left without much more than a bag of clothes. Most of the refugees were women and children; many men were required to stay and fight. The mood in the first months was bleak, especially in the bitter cold of winter.

You'll find misery, grief, and pain virtually everywhere you look in a war zone. But even in the midst of disaster, if you know to look for them, there are moments of humanity, dignity, hope, and yes, even joy.

You could stumble upon it while delivering meals to children's shelters and sharing a moment with the kids, telling a story or singing a song. Early in the war, José visited a kindergarten shelter for mothers and children in the western Ukrainian city of Lviv; as the father of three girls, he quickly found himself playing silly games with the kids. Or it could come when visiting communities close to the frontlines, some of which had been under occupation for weeks; families that had lived through unthinkable horrors would still meet our team with joy as we arrived with food.

Orthodox Easter, one of the biggest holidays in Ukraine, is usually celebrated with family, special meals, and sweet treats. In 2022, Easter fell two months after the beginning of the war, and the team knew just what we had to do: honor the traditions and culture of Великдень (Velykden, or "Great Day"). Our partners across the country made tens of thousands of pasky (or singular *paska*), traditional Easter cakes that are decorated either simply with a sugar glaze or with elaborate designs. "Paska for Ukrainians is a symbol of goodness, care, love, and family warmth," said Yuliya Stefanyuk, WCK's former Ukraine country director (her recipe is on page 274). We also distributed holiday meals and brightly colored eggs, a symbol of springtime and rebirth.

On June 1, in hope of making space for kids to just be kids, we celebrated Ukrainian Children's Day, a holiday of food, music, and dancing. In Dnipro, where many refugees from the embattled east were staying, we threw a pizza party with superheroes amid the threat of shelling. In Odesa, our partners served ice cream to kids at the zoo. "Children are our future, and what Ukraine will be like depends on what we invest in them," said Alisa Liptuga, our warehouse coordinator in Odesa.

"And the more we give them joy and make even small holidays for them, the happier they will be."

Ukraine was a test of everything WCK has learned over the years. In our kitchen in Przemyśl, Poland, just miles from the border with Ukraine, we cooked in volumes that we've mastered; 8,000 meals a day, seven days a week, to make sure the rapid flux of refugees would be fed. We also established partnerships with hundreds of restaurants and chefs in more than 1,000 cities and towns across the country, a practice we had tested throughout the pandemic, when we worked with 2,500 restaurants around the US.

To supply the nationwide operation, we needed to manage the logistics of getting ingredients and supplies to those restaurants, which required sending a train and a fleet of trucks crisscrossing the country's highways at all hours of the day—all while assessing risk and adapting to the day-to-day changes war brings. And finally, we tested all of the lessons we've learned about buying local; within a few months of the invasion, we were purchasing and distributing locally milled flour, sugar, canned meats and fish, baked goods, and more. The bread we distributed was made entirely with Ukrainian products—flour, salt, sunflower oil, and yeast—whose producers no longer had access to international markets due to the conflict.

It was also an opportunity to test new models that we'll continue working on. When José met with Samantha Power, the administrator for USAID, we learned that apple farmers in Moldova were having trouble selling their crops because Russia had previously been their largest buyer. So WCK bought 20 tons of apples to distribute in Ukraine, both supporting a national industry threatened by war and feeding people in need—a win-win, facilitated by a friendly partner.

The lessons we applied in Ukraine weren't just logistical. The values of WCK, the ones that form the outline of this book, were also confirmed. As the biggest operation we've ever undertaken—in terms of meal numbers, expenditures, volunteers, area covered, and nearly every other measure—we saw it all.

None of this work would have been possible without the resolute and constant work of our partners, both the ones who stayed in Ukraine to support families who remained in spite of the deadly circumstances and those in the neighboring countries who helped feed and nurture families who fled. WCK remains a small organization when compared to behemoths like USAID and the World Food Programme. The only way we can accomplish the projects we do and undertake an operation like Ukraine is through our boots on the ground, the thousands of cooks, bakers, drivers, logistics experts, and parents—the food fighters who, despite the situation, ensured their neighbors were fed, comforted, and sometimes even filled with joy.

PASKA
Ukrainian Easter Bread

Easter is one of the most important holidays in Ukraine—it's called Великдень (Velykden) in Ukrainian, which translates as "Great Day." Our work that began during the 2022 Russian invasion reached communities throughout Ukraine and in seven countries receiving refugees, mostly women and children (see more about the response in Sharing Joy in a Brutal World, page 270). During Orthodox Easter week, our restaurant partners prepared thousands of these traditional breads to distribute to families observing the holiday. The breads are often baked in tall cylindrical tins—28-ounce tomato cans work perfectly—though many families bake free-form round loaves, too. The beauty of pasky is their springtime decoration: golden braids, birds, or the Ukrainian trident are common adornments, as is a sweet white glaze. This recipe came from our Ukraine country director, Yuliya Stefanyuk, who learned it from her grandmother, who learned it from her grandmother. Serve the breads on their own or with softened butter and jam.

MAKES 2 MEDIUM ROUND BREADS OR 3 TALL CYLINDRICAL BREADS

BREAD
1¼ cups (284 grams) **milk**

1 cup (200 grams) plus 1 teaspoon **granulated sugar**

2 tablespoons **active dry yeast**

4½ cups (540 grams) plus 2 tablespoons sifted **all-purpose flour**, plus more for kneading and shaping

3 large **egg yolks**

16 tablespoons (226 grams) **unsalted butter**, at room temperature

1 tablespoon **kosher salt**

Oil for greasing the bowl

¾ cup (112 grams) **raisins**

¾ cup (112 grams) chopped **mixed candied fruit**

Egg wash: 1 **egg yolk**, whisked

GLAZE (OPTIONAL)
2 cups **powdered sugar**

1 teaspoon **vanilla extract**

2 tablespoons **whole milk**

1 teaspoon grated **lemon zest** (optional)

Food coloring (optional)

1. MAKE THE BREAD: In a small saucepan or in the microwave, warm 1 cup (226 grams) of the milk to lukewarm, about 110°F. Dissolve 1 teaspoon of the sugar in the milk and sprinkle the yeast on top, then mix in 1 cup (120 grams) of the flour. Let it sit, covered with a kitchen towel, in a warm place until it has doubled in size, 20 to 30 minutes—the time will depend on how warm your kitchen is.

2. In a stand mixer fitted with the whisk (or in a large bowl with a whisk), beat the egg yolks with the remaining 1 cup (200 grams) sugar until creamy and lightened in color, 3 to 5 minutes. Add all of the softened butter to the yolk-sugar mixture, mixing until the butter is well integrated, about 2 minutes. Add the remaining ¼ cup (58 grams) milk and beat for 3 more minutes, until the mixture is smooth and light.

3. Snap the dough hook onto the mixer (or use a rubber spatula) and add 3½ cups (420 grams) of the flour, the salt, the egg mixture, and the yeast mixture. Stir to combine all of the ingredients. The dough will be wet and sticky. Knead in the mixer (or transfer to a lightly floured counter and use your hands). As the bread is kneaded, moisture will be absorbed into the flour. If the dough still sticks to your hands, add more flour, 1 to 2 tablespoons at a time—the dough is ready when it doesn't stick to the mixer or your hands, about 10 minutes in a mixer (longer by hand).

4. Once kneaded, shape the dough into a ball and place it into a large oiled bowl. Cover with plastic or a damp kitchen towel and let the dough rise in a warm spot until it doubles in size, 1 to 1½ hours.

(recipe continues)

Coquito

MAKES ABOUT 7 CUPS (12 TO 14 SERVINGS)

1 cup **Puerto Rican white rum**, such as
   Don Q Cristal
2 **whole star anise pods**
2 **cinnamon sticks**
1 teaspoon **whole cloves**
1 teaspoon **anise seed**
1 (15-ounce) can **sweetened cream of coconut**,
   such as Coco López
7 ounces **sweetened condensed milk**
   (half of a 14-ounce can)
1 (12-ounce) can **evaporated milk**
1 (13.5-ounce) can **full-fat coconut milk**
Freshly grated nutmeg (optional), for garnish

1. In a small glass jar, combine the rum, star anise, cinnamon, cloves, and anise seed and let it sit for 3 to 4 hours to infuse the rum.

2. In a blender, combine the cream of coconut, sweetened condensed milk, evaporated milk, and coconut milk and blend on high for 1 minute to combine. Strain the infused rum into the blender (discard the spices) and blend for another 2 minutes. Strain the coquito into one large jar (at least 2 quarts) or multiple small jars to give away as gifts. Coquito can last chilled in your fridge for months—though you'll probably give away all your bottles before then.

3. When serving, you can garnish with a little freshly grated nutmeg.

VARIATIONS: There are as many coquito variations as there are families in Puerto Rico, so if we mentioned all the options, we'd have no space for anything else. Here are three we particularly like:

• Fisherman Alex Maldonado, a WCK Food Producer Network grantee, and his wife, Rosaly, make a **COFFEE-INFUSED COQUITO** by steeping the spices with coffee grounds in a moka pot.

• Make a **SPICE-DENSE INFUSION** by boiling whole cinnamon, cloves, star anise, and anise seed in 4 cups water, uncovered, for 30 minutes, then cooling it before adding it to the canned milks and rum.

• Some families make their own coconut milk and skip the Coco López. This gives you more control over the sweetness of your final coquito.

RUM SOUR

It's no secret that some of the more productive conversations on a WCK operation happen after a long day of work, over a meal and a drink. This was especially true in the early days after Hurricane María, when José and the Chefs For Puerto Rico team spent their days cooking for the island and their nights plotting how to expand their operations (turn the page for José's story about the cocktail). This recipe comes from Michael Norat, a former bartender at the restaurant Santaella (run by José Santaella, one of the original Chefs For Puerto Rico team members). José loved Michael's rum sours so much that he'd ask for them wherever they were—if Michael was available, he'd bring José some basil-infused simple syrup, the key ingredient for this complex, herbal take on the classic. Don Q Cristal, an inexpensive Puerto Rican white rum, will do just fine for this recipe—no need to spring for anything fancier.

MAKES 1 COCKTAIL

Ice
2 ounces **Puerto Rican white rum**, such as
    Don Q Cristal
1 ounce **fresh lime juice**
1 ounce **Basil Syrup** (recipe follows)
Pineapple juice, for topping
Ginger beer, for topping
Lime wheel, for garnish

In an ice-filled cocktail shaker, combine the rum, lime juice, and basil syrup and shake well for 30 to 40 seconds. Strain into a Collins glass filled with fresh ice. Top with a splash each of pineapple juice and ginger beer. Garnish with a lime wheel and serve.

Basil Syrup

MAKES A LITTLE OVER ½ CUP

½ cup **sugar**
½ cup **water**
½ cup tightly packed **fresh basil leaves**
    (about 1 ounce)

1. In a small saucepan, combine the sugar and water and bring to a boil over medium-high heat. Stir to dissolve the sugar and remove from the heat. Add the basil leaves, cover the saucepan, and let it steep for 30 minutes.

2. Strain out the leaves. Chill before using in a cocktail. The syrup can be stored in an airtight container in the refrigerator for up to 2 weeks.

IT ENDS IN THE BEGINNING . . .
WITH A RUM SOUR

José Andrés

Sometimes the day begins when you first wake up, you have a cup of coffee, some fresh orange juice maybe, you read the news and think about what the day will be bringing.

But sometimes it actually begins at the very end, after you've done everything you think you could possibly do in a day, served meals to thousands and met hundreds of people and visited a dozen towns. You're so tired you think you can't think anymore . . . your brain is like your phone, at 2 percent.

But then something miraculous happens: Someone hands you a rum sour.

It's a moment when your body says yes and your brain says yes and everything is working together. At that moment, late at night, you are at the hotel bar, you look around, and you see everyone else who is trying to get the same difficult work done in a disaster zone. They are all there, all drinking a rum sour, too. It's in that instant you realize: We are all in this together. You start a conversation here, there, make some connections, and all of a sudden you understand what your next day should look like, a new path forward for how to do the best job possible, get the most meals delivered to the most communities.

To me, rum sour is the taste of the Caribbean. It was when I was first in Haiti, even before World Central Kitchen had a name, that I started to drink them. There, they are very delicious and straightforward: You have the rum (agricole style, made from sugarcane, not molasses), the lime, and the sugar . . . that's it. Later, in Puerto Rico, I had the frothy version with egg whites, and then an incredible modern version from the restaurant Santaella in San Juan, with a beautiful basil syrup.

If you're in the Caribbean, drinking a rum sour is supporting local agriculture. There are amazing rums everywhere, from Barbancourt and the clairins of Haiti to the Bacardí, Don Q, and Barrilito of Puerto Rico. Who is growing the sugarcane? A farmer! Who is growing the limes? A farmer! This is just common sense, people!

Let me tell you a short story about my first rum sour in Puerto Rico after Hurricane María. The day I arrived on the island, just a couple of days after the storm, the island was still mostly without power. It was crazy. As we drove around San Juan, we saw trees in the middle of the highway, and we had to navigate around downed lampposts and power lines. Our phones weren't working, though we found one place on the highway where you could get a signal. (We knew the spot because there were probably a hundred people standing on the edge of the road to connect, letting their relatives know they were okay.) There were no police, no military, no official presence—just destruction as far as the eye could see.

At the end of the day, I went to visit my friend Jose Enrique, who runs one of the best restaurants in Puerto Rico. Since the hurricane, he had been cooking for the neighborhood of Santurce out of his beautiful bright pink restaurant. I needed to sit and think, meet with a few friends and chefs on the island to understand what we should do. As the sun was setting, we carefully drove through the dark to his restaurant. When we got there, we used our dying iPhone flashlights to make rum sours with the last cubes in the ice machine. It was almost pitch black as we sat at the bar, sipping on maybe the last cold drinks on the island.

This was the moment of transformation. For me, for WCK, maybe even for the future of the island. Over those rum sours we figured out what we had to do . . .

We had to start cooking.

BUILDING BLOCKS

—

ACCOMPANIMENTS, SAUCES, AND BASES

Anpil ti patat fè chaj
(A lot of small potatoes
makes a whole load)

—HAITIAN SAYING

THESE BUILDING-BLOCK RECIPES ARE USED THROUGHOUT THE BOOK TO BUILD FOUNDATIONS FOR DISHES OR COMPLEMENT OTHERS. Two of them—Haitian Épis (page 290) and Puerto Rican Sofrito (page 294)—act as "mother sauces" for many dishes in their respective cuisines, so it's not a bad idea to double or triple the batch and store them properly if you're planning to cook a lot from the book. The hot sauces come from their own corners of the world, but who are we to say that a Puerto Rican Pique (page 293) doesn't go with Lamb Massaman Curry (page 182) or that Indonesian Sambal (page 289) isn't a perfect complement for Braised Pork al Pastor (page 60)—your taste is your taste. Finally, a few of these dishes—the Refried Beans (page 296), Pikliz (page 290), and Bannann Peze (page 288)—are tasty in their own right if you want to try them solo, though they are also perfect complements to their companion dishes throughout the book.

PIKLIZ

While every household has their own spin on pikliz (pronounced PEEK-leez), a pickled slaw-like condiment popular in Haiti, the base of the recipe is cabbage and carrots, hot chiles (usually Scotch bonnets), and acid—sour orange is common on the island, while vinegar and lime are used abroad. Pikliz can marinate for hours, days, or weeks, depending on the taste and texture you're going for—a shorter spell will leave the cabbage crunchier and the pikliz fresher tasting, while a longer pickle may introduce some deliciously fermented flavors. No matter how long you let your pikliz go, its zippy acidity is perfect for cutting through fat and richness, which makes it an ideal tablemate for Griot (page 52) and Bannann Peze (page 288).

MAKES ABOUT 2 CUPS

¼ large head **red cabbage**, thinly sliced
2 small **carrots**, shredded
1 **yellow bell pepper**, thinly sliced
½ small **red onion**, thinly sliced
½ **Scotch bonnet pepper**, cut into thirds, with seeds
½ cup **distilled white vinegar**
3 tablespoons **extra-virgin olive oil**
5 **fresh thyme sprigs**, leaves only
Juice of ½ **lime**
2 tablespoons **sugar**
2 teaspoons **kosher salt**
¼ teaspoon **freshly ground black pepper**

In a medium bowl, combine the cabbage, carrots, bell pepper, onion, and Scotch bonnet. In a small bowl, whisk together the vinegar, olive oil, thyme leaves, lime juice, sugar, salt, and pepper. Pour the dressing over the vegetables and mix well to combine. Let it sit for at least 15 minutes before serving, though it tastes even better after sitting for 24 hours. It can be refrigerated in an airtight container for a few weeks.

ÉPIS

Épis, the Kreyòl word for "spice," is the backbone of most savory Haitian dishes. It's another recipe with infinite variations, but almost all épis recipes have a base of some variety of alliums (garlic, onions, scallions) blended with oil. Our épis is stripped down: just scallions, garlic, and olive oil. Other recipes for épis include bell peppers and chiles, fresh and dried herbs (such as parsley and thyme), warm spices (such as cloves), vinegar, water, or bouillon—it can be as simple or complex as you like. This one has a vibrant neon green brightness that gives dishes a depth of flavor that's distinctly Haitian.

MAKES ABOUT 1 CUP

1 bunch **scallions**, roughly chopped
1 head **garlic** (8 to 10 cloves), separated into cloves and peeled
¼ to ½ cup **extra-virgin olive oil**, as needed

In a blender, combine the scallions, garlic, and just enough olive oil to get the blades moving and blend until you have a smooth, loose, bright green paste. Use immediately or refrigerate in a glass jar or other airtight container for up to 4 days, or in the freezer for up to 3 months.

PIQUE

This recipe comes from one of WCK's Puerto Rican grantees in the Food Producer Network, La Placita 21. The organization, which is connected to the Puerto Rican Down Syndrome Foundation, trains adults with developmental disabilities in horticulture and food manufacturing. The process occurs through, as coordinator Mayra Gonzalez Becerra puts it, *aprendo haciendo*, or "learning-doing." "Each of the people contributes work and produces fruit both in horticulture and in the making of products. We recognize their contribution to society and society should recognize them as productive, creative beings." The major products from Placita 21 are sofrito, alcoholado (menthol- and eucalyptus-infused rubbing alcohol used as a home remedy for fevers and aches), and pique, the island's famously hot chile-infused vinegar. Get a bottle going now and in two weeks you'll have a perfect accompaniment for Sancocho (page 181), Arroz con Pollo (page 147), or anything else you can dream up. Tiny, spicy *ajíes caballeros* ("gentleman's pepper") are classic for pique, but Thai bird chiles will do in a pinch.

MAKES 1½ CUPS

1 cup (about 4 ounces) **ajíes caballeros** or **Thai bird's eye chiles**
2 **culantro leaves** or 2 sprigs **cilantro**, chopped
2 **garlic cloves**, peeled
1 **bay leaf**
½ teaspoon **coriander seeds**
½ teaspoon **black peppercorns**
1½ cups **distilled white vinegar** (or a combination of **distilled white** and **apple cider vinegars**)

Wash and dry the chiles and culantro or cilantro—there should be no residual moisture. Sterilize a jar big enough to hold about 20 ounces, or a few smaller ones. To your jar(s), add the chiles, culantro or cilantro, garlic, bay leaf (break it up if using more than one jar), coriander, and peppercorns. Fill it (them) with vinegar, then cap tightly and rinse the bottle(s). Let the pique sit in a dark place for at least 2 weeks before serving—the longer you let it sit, the hotter it will get. It will keep for months. Splash the spicy infused vinegar onto anything and everything, leaving behind the solids.

ADOBO BORICUA

While most adobos are wet marinades, as is used in the famous Filipino dish, Puerto Ricans usually use adobo seco, an all-purpose dried spice blend that makes its way into meat dishes, rice dishes, and stews (and our Sierra en Escabeche, page 70). There are commercial adobos on the market that will give your dish some Puerto Rican flavor, but this recipe, from WCK's chef Alejandro Perez, gives a certain "un no sé qué." The word *Boricua*, used to describe people or food or music from Puerto Rico, comes from the word *Borinquen* (or *Borikén*), the island's name when it was inhabited by Indigenous Taínos before Spanish colonization.

MAKES 1¼ CUPS

¼ cup **onion powder**

¼ cup **garlic powder**

2½ tablespoons **fine sea salt**

2 tablespoons **dried oregano**

1½ tablespoons **ground coriander**

1 tablespoon **achiote powder**

1 tablespoon **dried culantro** (or a 50/50 blend of **dried cilantro** and **dried parsley**)

1 tablespoon **freshly ground black pepper**

1 tablespoon **ground cumin**

1 tablespoon **pimentón** (smoked paprika)

½ tablespoon **sweet paprika**

½ tablespoon **dried cilantro**

In a jar, combine the onion powder, garlic powder, salt, oregano, coriander, achiote, culantro, black pepper, cumin, pimentón, sweet paprika, and cilantro. Seal the jar and shake to combine. Store in a cool spot away from moisture for up to 3 months.

SOFRITO

Sofrito, like adobo, means different things to different people across the Spanish-speaking world (see Adobo Boricua, left). The key ingredients for Puerto Rican sofrito, the foundation of many of the island's dishes, including Arroz con Pollo a la Manolo (page 147), are ají dulce peppers and culantro. Ajíes dulces, small bright pods, resemble habaneros but are mild—*ají dulce* means "sweet pepper" in Spanish. Culantro, known as *recao* in Puerto Rico, is a dark green, robust, and earthy herb in the cilantro family. Since both of those ingredients can be difficult to find if you don't have a Latin market nearby, feel free to substitute red bell pepper for the ají dulce and cilantro for the culantro; the flavor of the final sofrito will be a bit different, but the layers of flavor will still have that *sabor boricua*—the "taste of Puerto Rico."

MAKES ABOUT 2½ CUPS

1 large **yellow onion**, roughly chopped

10 **garlic cloves**, roughly chopped

15 **ají dulce peppers** or 1 large **red bell pepper**, roughly chopped

3 **cubanelle peppers** (also called Italian frying peppers), roughly chopped

1 bunch **culantro** and/or **cilantro**, roughly chopped

In a food processor, combine the onion, garlic, peppers, and culantro and blend until you get a loose, smooth puree. Sofrito can be kept in an airtight container in the fridge for up to 1 week, or freeze it in small portions for up to 3 months.

Kristin Teig, David Koung, Judi Orlick, Giulietta Pinna, and Victoria Granof: The dream team of our photo shoot, the ones who are able to capture the beauty in comfort cooking . . . even if Victoria couldn't stay the week, you left us in Judi's very capable hands! And Julian Nguyen, Katie Scally, and Eddy Rye Sexton . . . without your hands, this book would not be the same (literally!).

To the people of What Took You So Long, my friends Alicia Sully, Sebastian Lindström, and Clara Wetzel, plus the incredible work of Nilaya Sabnis and Natassja Ebert.

Kim Witherspoon, my old and dear friend, who is always sitting on my side of the table. And Richard Wolffe, who is a champion of every project with my name on it.

Stephen Colbert, my brother who has done so much for World Central Kitchen, who is selfless and supportive . . . with you on our side, we are not alone.

The many friends of WCK who shared your recipes: Michelle Obama, who is one of the most gracious people I have ever met and ever hope to meet. Meghan, The Duchess of Sussex, is an inspiration to us all and a dedicated WCK supporter. Aline Kamakian, who showed me and so many the meaning of bravery. Eric Adjepong, who makes the world a more thoughtful place. Reem Assil, a strong believer in the power of community. Sanjeev Kapoor, who has for years taught me lessons in the kitchen and in life. Tyler Florence, whose family has been there for WCK and the community in California whenever there is a need. Brian Yazzie, who was already feeding the most vulnerable residents when we first started working together. Marcus Samuelsson, who I am lucky enough to call a friend and committed advocate for food access. Ayesha Curry, someone I look up to for so many reasons, including the work you do for the people of Oakland. Emeril Lagasse, who is both a legend and a friend of mine after all these years. Guy Fieri, a man of the people in every sense. Brooke Williamson, one of the most talented people I have ever met. And everyone else who thoughtfully gave recipes to this book . . . Rima Aritonang, Gaby Maria Chirinos, Elsa Corrigan, Sofia Deleon, Kelly Eastman, Nadia Ghulam, Yaritza García Ortiz, Kamal Mouzawak, Michael Norat, Teresa Picos, Carmen Rivera, Yuliya Stefanyuk . . . you will forever be part of World Central Kitchen!

To Carlota, Inés, Lucía: you have always put up with your dad who leaves for weeks on end, to Haiti or Puerto Rico or Ukraine, and even if you worry you still believe in me . . . and sometimes you even come along for the journey. I have told you before and I'll tell you again . . . you are our future.

To Tichi . . . from the very first moment I dreamed up World Central Kitchen, you were dreaming of it right next to me.

To WCK past, present, and future: you are the ones who make this all happen, who fight with empathy and bring hope wherever you go. Wherever there's a fight . . . you know the rest!

THANK YOU TO THE FOLLOWING PHOTOGRAPHERS WHO DOCUMENT OUR WORK:

David Andrade
James Buck
Emily Caldwell
Augustin Campos
Paty Carmona
Anjali Daryanani
Kelly Galleguillos
Oleksandr Golub
Jay Hanna
Scott Hoag
Chris Kousouros
Tina Krüger
Mykola Kulina
Zaina Mahmoud

Dan Martensen
Eduardo Montepeque
Jonathan Olinger
Mikel Ponce
Augustinus Priyomulyono
Gabriel Rodriguez
Sofie Rordam
Rafael Ruiz
Nadir Siddiqui
Nessim Stevenson
Kevin Szmir
Cris Toala Olivares
Enzo Tomasiello

INDEX

This book is dedicated to everyone who understands the power of a hot meal in a time of need.

Library of Congress
Cataloging-in-Publication Data
is available upon request

ISBN 978-0-593-57907-7
eISBN 978-0-593-57908-4

Printed in China

Photographer: Kristin Teig
Photography Assistant: David Peng
Production Assistant: Samantha Higgins
Recipe Developer: Elyssa Kaplan
Food Stylists: Judi Orlick and
Victoria Granof
Prop Stylist: Giulietta Pinna
Editor: Raquel Pelzel
Editorial Assistant: Bianca Cruz
Book and cover design by:
Stephanie Huntwork
Production Editor: Serena Wang
Production Manager: Kelli Tokos
Compositor: Merri Ann Morrell
Copy Editor: Kate Slate
Indexer: Stephen Callahan
Marketer: Joey Lozada
Publicist: David Hawk
Front cover photograph by: Kristin Teig
Back cover photographs by:
Natassja Ebert and Nilaya Sabnis

10 9 8 7 6 5 4 3 2 1

First Edition